The Dilemma of Sustainability in the Age of Globalization

Globalization and Its Costs

Series Editor: Dhirendra K. Vajpeyi

The last two decades of the twentieth century witnessed drastic political and economic changes of tremendous importance. As the sole superpower in world affairs, the United States has used its economic and military power to shape the rest of the world in its own image. Hence the need to develop a balanced, just, and holistic approach not only to meet the narrow trade and finance interests of developed democracies but also to encompass other crucial global concerns such as environmental degradation, human rights, immigration, private and public governance, poverty, income inequality, and political instability—issues and challenges directly or indirectly connected to human security.

Failure to manage the process and strike a balance between its political and economic facets will create more Talibans, Al-Baghdadis of Islamic State in Iraq, and other global disorders. Though globalization has elevated hundreds of millions of people around the world from dire poverty, it has posed new challenges to humanity. Globalization and Its Costs will include analytical and empirical work from scholars in a comparative context. Topics should be of current interest, interdisciplinary and policy-oriented, and broadly related to human security and sustainable development paradigms.

Titles in the Series

Corporate Social Responsibility and Sustainable Development in Emerging Economies, edited by Dhirendra K. Vajpeyi

Politics, Poverty, and Microfinance: How Governments Get in the Way of Helping the Poor, by Brian Warby

The Dilemma of Sustainability in the Age of Globalization: A Quest for a Paradigm of Development, by Mohamed El-Kamel Bakari

The Dilemma of Sustainability in the Age of Globalization

A Quest for a Paradigm of Development

Mohamed El-Kamel Bakari

LEXINGTON BOOKS
Lanham • Boulder • New York • London

Published by Lexington Books
An imprint of The Rowman & Littlefield Publishing Group, Inc.
4501 Forbes Boulevard, Suite 200, Lanham, Maryland 20706
www.rowman.com

Unit A, Whitacre Mews, 26-34 Stannary Street, London SE11 4AB

British Library Cataloguing in Publication Information Available

Library of Congress Cataloging-in-Publication Data

Names: Bakari, Mohamed El-Kamel, 1972- author.
Title: The dilemma of sustainability in the age of globalization : a quest for a paradigm of development / Mohamed El-Kamel Bakari.
Description: Lanham : Lexington Books, 2017. | Series: Globalization and its costs | Includes bibliographical references and index.
Identifiers: LCCN 2017028567 (print) | LCCN 2017034480 (ebook) | ISBN 9781498551403 (Electronic) | ISBN 9781498551397 (cloth : alk. paper)
Subjects: LCSH: Sustainable development.
Classification: LCC HC79.E5 (ebook) | LCC HC79.E5 B3468 2017 (print) | DDC 338.9/27—dc23
LC record available at http://lccn.loc.gov/2017028567

∞™ The paper used in this publication meets the minimum requirements of American National Standard for Information Sciences Permanence of Paper for Printed Library Materials, ANSI/NISO Z39.48-1992.

Printed in the United States of America

In the memory of my father. To my cherished mother, my dear wife, and my precious children: Maram, Mourad, and Mariem

Contents

Acknowledgments

In writing this book that has been in gestation for almost a decade, I have definitely accrued many debts. I would like to express my deep gratitude to Professors Mounir Triki and Mohamed Mansouri for their invaluable guidance and discerning observations. I am so grateful to them for having been such an unfailing source of intellectual support throughout the arduous process of writing this book. I also want to thank all my friends and colleagues who reviewed and commented on the various drafts of this work. Very special thanks go to Professor Kenneth Weisbrode for his very constructive review and obliging comments that helped me fine-tune many parts of this book. In addition, I am indebted to all my family for their unflagging support and patience during a long period of exacting research before this book took shape.

Finally, I would like to acknowledge the kind support, noticeable professionalism, and outstanding editorial skills of a whole team of very dedicated and supportive editors working for the publisher of this book, namely Lexington Books.

Abbreviations

AL	Arab League
AfDB	African Development Bank
APEC	Asia-Pacific Economic Cooperation
CBD	Convention on Biological Diversity
CITES	Convention on International Trade in Endangered Species of Wild Fauna and Flora
CFCs	Chlorofluorocarbons
ECOWAS	Economic Community of West African States
ELC	Environment Liaison Centre
ELCI	Environment Liaison Centre International
ECLA	Economic Commission for Latin America
ECLAC	Economic Commission for Latin America and the Caribbean
ECOSOC	UN Economic and Social Council
EEC	European Economic Community
EPA	Environmental Protection Agency (U.S.)
ESI	Environmental Sustainability Index
ETMs	Environmental Trade Measures
EU	European Union
FAO	Food and Agriculture Organization
FOEI	Friends of the Earth International
GATS	General Agreement on Trade in Services

GCS	Global Civil Society
GDP	Gross Domestic Product
GEF	Global Environmental Facility
GNP	Gross National Product
HPI	Happy Planet Index
LDCs	Least Developed Countries
LRTAP	Convention on Long-Range Transboundary Air Pollution
IBRD	International Bank for Reconstruction and Development
IUCN	International Union for the Conservation of Nature and Natural Resources
IEEP	International Environmental Educational Program
IGOs	Inter-Governmental Organizations
IMF	International Monetary Fund
IMO	International Maritime Organization
ISEW	Index of Sustainable Economic Welfare
NAFTA	North American Free Trade Agreement
NIEO	New International Economic Order
NGOs	Non-Governmental Organizations
NSMs	New Social Movements
OAU	Organization of African Unity
ODS	Ozone Depleting Substances
OECD	Organization for Economic Co-operation and Development
OPEC	Organization of Petroleum Exporting Countries
PCSD	President's Council on Sustainable Development (U.S.)
SAARC	South Asia Association for Regional Cooperation

TNCs	Trans-National Corporations
TRIPS	Agreement on Trade-Related Aspects of Intellectual Property Rights
TRIMS	Agreement on Trade-Related Investment Measures
UNCED	United Nations Conference on the Environment and Development
UNCLOS	United Nations Convention on the Law of the Sea
UNDP	United Nations Development Programme
UNEP	United Nations Environmental Programme
UNESCO	United Nations Education, Scientific and Cultural Organization.
UNICEF	United Nations Children's Fund
WCED	World Commission on Environment and Development
WHO	World Health Organization
WSSD	UN World Summit for Sustainable Development
WTO	World Trade Organization
WWF	World Wide Fund for Nature

Introduction

An Overview of the Contemporary Sustainability Challenges

The Industrial Revolution brought about revolutionary changes in patterns of production and consumption, in energy uses and transportation, in industry, agriculture, and services, transforming living conditions, and with them the whole environment, in ways that had not been known before. By and large, modern industrial societies have been increasingly dependent on economies that are based on fossil energy, use huge quantities of non-renewable resources, and cause considerable environmental damage. This unrelenting drive for continuous economic growth commits such societies to increasing levels of production and consumption, which comes usually at the expense of the environment, society, and culture. Although significant social and economic changes in the last few decades have introduced new types of information-based technologies and services-oriented economies, environmentalists still pointedly argue that some of the damage done to the environment might very well be irreversible.

Current global ecological problems (e.g., ozone layer depletion, climate change, and global warming) along with increasing poverty, especially in the southern hemisphere, have led many critics to question the predominant socio-economic paradigm of development that manifests itself in the neo-liberal capitalist economic policies mainly in the developed countries. In fact, one of the most significant current discussions in development and environmental studies today revolves around the question of whether this current paradigm has the potential to handle a whole range of new environmental, social, and developmental challenges that our world is facing. Hence, concern about the environment has taken on a new meaning at the beginning of the twenty-first century with the realization that this is the first generation to have had such a significant impact on the whole planet at a global level.

Academically, it is becoming increasingly difficult to ignore the different attempts in recent years to establish new approaches to development that reverse environmental degradation and cater to the social and cultural needs of people in both developed and developing countries. The 1960s and 1970s, in particular, witnessed a surge in public awareness of the negative environmental consequences of continuous economic growth and the high rates of consumption associated with the prevailing lifestyles in industrial countries. The last few decades of the twentieth and the early twenty-first century have also witnessed a steadily growing presence of the environmental issue on the global agenda following important post-WWII geo-political changes such as alleged end—or ebbing—of the Cold War and the collapse of the communist bloc, which seemingly meant more room for cooperation between the two superpowers and set the stage for the inception and evolution of global environmental politics based. Notwithstanding, these transformations have also meant some hard choices for the modern nation-state, struggling to keep its sovereignty intact in the face of new global phenomena such as globalization and sustainability.

The post-WWII period also witnessed the prominence of environmentally informed writings that criticized the abuse of the environment in America. These texts include Rachel Carson's *Silent Spring* (1962), Charles A. Reich's *The Greening of America* (1970), Theodore Roszak's *Making of a Counter Culture* (1969) and *Where the Wasteland Ends* (1972), and E.F. Schumacher's *Small is Beautiful* (1973), among others. A few years later, the publication of *The Limits to Growth* by Meadows et al., who had formed an environmental think-tank known as the Club of Rome in 1972, sparked off a worldwide backlash against the prevalent patterns of using the natural resources to fuel the economic boom. In 1983, the World Commission on Environment and Development (WCED) embarked on a major study that would firmly establish the concept of "sustainable development" in the literature of environmental and development studies. Four years later, the outcome was a document entitled *Our Common Future,* which is popularly referred to as the *Brundtland Report* in many documents. This document sets forth what has come to be the most popular definition of sustainable development as "development that meets the needs of the present without compromising the ability of future generations to meet their own needs" (1987, p. 43). Although it has gained authoritative status in UN global forums and conferences such as the 1992 Rio Conference, this definition has attracted serious criticism for setting out economic growth, industrial modernization, and free market imperatives as key tools in the sustainability approach it defines. These criticisms revolve mainly around an accusation that the report implies a double-standard approach to peoples' needs in the North and the South, being suspiciously open-ended and ambiguous as it is.

The rise of environmental politics was also sparked by global factors such as the widespread global public awareness of environmental degradation in the 1980s and 1990s, the vital role of Inter-Governmental Organizations (IGOs) and Non-Governmental Organizations (NGOs), and the activism of green protest movements especially in North America and Western Europe. Some shocking, large-scale environmental accidents that occurred in the closing decades of the twentieth century such as those accidents associated with nuclear power in 1979 in Harrisburg, Pennsylvania, in the U.S.A. and in 1986 in Chernobyl, in the former Soviet Union, also galvanized mainstream activists into taking action. Environmental activism has been significantly stirred by different local, national, and global NGOs which have come of age and become better organized and financially more resourceful over the past few decades. In fact, this proliferation of NGOs, IGOs, and other international bodies has had an important role in spreading the environmental cause and exposing many of what environmentalists see as the social and ecological excesses of the prevailing neoliberal capitalist model of growth, especially in the Western industrialized countries.

At the social level, the spreading frustration and dissatisfaction with the whole socio-economic paradigm of development in the industrialized countries during the last few decades has grown into mainstream distrust of the viability of the current political, economic, and social systems in the face of growing developmental and ecological challenges. The social vacuum that seems to have been created by the erosion of states' sovereignty and the shortcomings of the global governance system paved the way for the rise of a whole set of new post-materialist values related to development. Thus, while some views highlight the importance of an array of new, post-materialist values that came to the fore as a reaction to the excesses of the current paradigm of development, others dwell on the need to establish a new model of development that both counterbalances the effects of globalization on the state's sovereignty and fulfills the waning state's social obligations.

In the literature of developmental and environmental studies, however, there has been little agreement on what sustainable development stands for, and the controversy over its definition has raged unabated since this concept was first presented in the 1987 *Brundtland Report*. As a matter of fact, a considerable amount of writing has been published on the inception of sustainability and the different definitions given to this concept. Though regarded by some scholars as a sign of the richness of the literature on sustainable development, the proliferation of different, sometimes conflicting, definitions of such a recent concept is considered by other critics as an indication of the prevailing vagueness of this project. Some other scholars also voice their suspicion that while sustainable development appears to be imposing constraints on business and the industrial sector, it, in fact, covers for, and even supports, intensifying industrial growth. Other views still see sustainable development as a radical project because it challenges the current paradigm of development.

By and large, the first serious discussion of the concept of sustainability emerged during the 1970s following the United Nations Conference on the Human Environment in 1972. As most nations became increasingly aware of the global nature of the new ecological threats, environmental issues have become firmly established on the political global agenda. Both the UN Stockholm Conference in 1972 and the Rio Conference in 1992 have been important milestones in the evolution and maturing of environmental politics, moving the issue of the environment center stage in global politics. In the light of these conferences and other major environmental events, the essence of human development started to be conceived as broader than economic growth, thus encompassing other social, cultural, and environmental aspects of human progress.

Historically, the rise of neo-liberal capitalism, based largely on free market policies and the primacy of economic growth, has usually been considered as the starting point of environmental degradation. This belief has been considerably boosted by the emergence of "the limits to growth" thesis in the early 1970s. The popularization of this thesis has also caused a heated debate between neoliberal economists, who still insist that the solutions for environmental problems necessitate more economic growth, and others who argue that unfettered economic growth and sustainable development have mutually exclusive goals. More recently, literature has emerged that offers contradictory findings about the feasibility of implementing this project in the contemporary context of neoliberal capitalism and intensifying trade liberalization. While many economists and thinkers assert that, in most cases, free trade can actually lead to environmental improvement if environmental considerations are taken seriously in global trade policies, other critics believe that the process of trade liberalization has had dire ecological consequences. Amid this heated discussion, more and more criticisms have also been aimed at the current socio-economic paradigm of growth, especially in the industrialized countries, for its destruction of the environment and for its instrumental use of nature. Critics argue that the capitalist commitment to economic growth and material advancement is no longer an asset in the sought-after new paradigm. On the contrary, making economic growth a nation's paramount priority is, in the view of many critics, a serious flaw, and even more so if this priority is maintained at the expense of social equity and environmental protection.

Theoretically, the concept of sustainability is discussed in this book within a frame of reference comprising the classical development theories of Adam Smith, Karl Marx, Friedrich Engels, and Max Weber as well as of the modernization theories of Walt W. Rostow, Samuel Huntington, and their colleagues. The discussion also entails criticisms from some Dependency Theory thinkers such as sociologists Andre Gunder Frank and Fernando Henrique Cardoso, who developed this theory as a response to the predominant discourse of Modernization. In response to critiques of the Dependency Theory, however, some theorists, including most notably Immanuel Wallerstein, have taken their ideas in a new direction and came up with their own vision of development that they refer to as "World Systems Theory." This discussion also entails notable criticisms of the modernization project for being exported to the developing countries after the period of decolonization as an ostensibly flawless recipe for modernization.

For the most part, this book is based on the current discussion of sustainable development in a context of globalization. On the one hand, some neo-liberal theorists and economists such as Jagdish Bhagwati (2007), Johan Norberg (2003/2007), Paul Krugman and Anthony J. Venables (1995) defend globalization as the "engine of wealth creation" that will ultimately benefit all segments of society in both developed and developing countries thanks to what is commonly referred to as "trickle-down theory." On the other hand, other critics including Philip McMichael (2017, 2007), Leslie Sklair (2007), James G. Speth (2003, 2005, 2008), Robert H. Wade (2007), and Vandana Shiva (2003, 2005, 2008), among many others, have over the past decades contributed significantly to the creation and development of an anti-globalization discourse that aims mainly at exposing what they see as the excesses of this phenomenon and the resulting uneven distribution of wealth. The discussion of sustainability in a context of globalization also entails the different viewpoints of many critics who defend two conflicting claims. Some views point out that the overwhelming process of globalization insidiously implies a negative bearing on the indigenous cultural landscapes in the developing countries, and condemn the popularization of what scholars Jerry Mander (2003) and Stuart Hart (2009) refer to as "global monoculture." Other viewpoints confirm, on the other hand, that globalization forces can actually be harnessed to serve social and ecological ends and boost sustainability.

In most of the literature, however, little attention has been given to the affinity between the anti-globalization discourse and the sustainability discourse in many areas related to development options and issues of economic dependency. Despite the richness of the literature on both sustainability and globalization, little research has been carried out on the aspects of affinity between these two phenomena, and not enough studies have been pursued on the potential to make them compatible. In a similar vein, there has also been little analysis and discussion in the literature about the different types of obstacles facing sustainable development today. As a matter of fact, much uncertainty still exists among researchers about whether this emerging project can be effectively implemented today, and it is not clear what factors can help in changing today's paradigm of growth from unfavorable to favorable for the implementation of sustainability. Against such a backdrop, very few scholars have been able to draw on any structured research into whether the consensus on sustainability declared at different global summits is still valid today given the proliferation of different "weak" and "strong" versions of sustainable development. Indeed, much of the existing literature on sustainable development fails to pinpoint the root causes of the impasse that the project of sustainable development has reached thus far. Likewise, little attention has been given to the potential of the new, holistic approaches to sustainability that offer promising views of harmonizing industry, trade, and environmental policies to ease the transition from an unsustainable to a sustainable model of development.

These gaps in the literature have heightened the need for an in-depth research on the viability of implementing the project of sustainable development in a context of neoliberal capitalism with a clear diagnosis of the type of impediments it faces today. The main objectives of this book, therefore, are manifold: First, it investigates to what extent the project of sustainable development is a challenge to the prevailing socio-economic paradigm of development and whether globalization has supported or hampered the efforts to implement sustainability. Secondly, it aims at pinpointing and discussing the aspects of affinity and incompatibility between these two paradigms of development. Thirdly, it is also my aim to determine and analyze the root causes of the current impasse that sustainable development has reached with special focus on the potential of some new initiatives to revive this project.

The overall structure of this book takes the form of four themed chapters. Chapter 1 begins by laying out the theoretical dimensions of sustainability. In trying to find an answer to the above-mentioned research inquiries, this chapter sheds new light on the inception and evolution of the project of sustainable development through an examination of the political, intellectual, social, and ecological changes that paved the way for its emergence. In addition to spelling out a theoretical and conceptual exploration of this emerging project, the first chapter closes with a critique of the most widely used definition that has gained authoritative status in the literature on sustainable development, namely the WCED's definition. The second chapter of this book is essentially concerned with examining the seeds of the incompatibility between the current socio-economic paradigm of growth and sustainable development in the light of a brief survey of major development theories. Precisely, this chapter will examine the way in which the classical theories of development that have guided human growth for centuries deal with the environmental issue, and whether they are capable of accommodating the global ecological challenges of the twenty-first century. This chapter also investigates the effects of globalization on the evolution of sustainable development and efforts to implement it. Although I highlight a few similarities between globalization and sustainable development in the second part of this chapter, my main focus is basically going to be on the mismatch between these two projects and the repercussions of this incompatibility on the implementation of sustainable development. To meet this research aim, I launch a thorough juxtaposition of the two projects' theoretical underpinnings.

Chapter 3 of this book discusses in more depth how sustainable development has constituted a challenge to the neo-liberal capitalist paradigm of growth and sheds light on the different economic, ecological, and cultural areas over which these two paradigms clash. Basically, this chapter provides an in-depth discussion of the fundamental contradictions between the current paradigm of growth and the project of sustainable development. The whole chapter is based therefore on a fundamental distinction between two categories of obstacles to the implementation of sustainable development, that is, extrinsic and intrinsic obstacles. The first part of this chapter deals with the extrinsic obstacles while the second part tackles the intrinsic ones. The final chapter draws upon the entire argument of this book, tying up the various aspects of the sustainability impasse and the factors that perpetuate this gridlock. The root causes behind the sustainability impasse will be the focus of the first part of this chapter. In the second part, however, I will discuss the main propositions of this book in the light of some new initiatives aimed toward a more effective implementation of sustainable development. I sort the propositions of this book into different categories according to three levels, namely the political and institutional level, the economic level, and the social level. Finally, the conclusion gives a brief summary and a critique of these propositions, and includes a discussion of the limitations and the implications of these findings for future research into this area.

Given the highly interdisciplinary nature of sustainability, a holistic approach is utilized throughout this book, integrating literary, economic, political, and scientific material to conduct a thorough analysis of the inception and evolution of sustainable development as an alternative paradigm of growth. In employing such interdisciplinary modes of enquiry, I attempt to illuminate the different, far-reaching aspects of incompatibility between sustainable development and today's model of growth, and explore the potential for a harmonization between these two paradigms so that they become mutually inclusive instead of exclusive. To achieve this aim, I employ a critical comparative analysis of the two vying paradigms of development, based on a thorough juxtaposition of their theoretical and ideological underpinnings and backed up by lucid examples, statistics, and case studies. Thus, comparing and contrasting the approaches to growth, nature, and society, among other elements, in each one of these paradigms constitute the backbone of the methodology undertaken in this book.

This book draws upon diverse primary as well as secondary sources tackling the inception, evolution, and implementation of the project of sustainable development as well as other political, economic, and social issues closely related to it. My work is essentially based on analyses and critique of primary sources including some seminal writings that first defined the concept of sustainable development such as the WCED's document, *Our Common Future* (popularly known as the *Brundtland Report*);

global summits declarations such as the 1992 United Nations Conference on Environment and Development's *Agenda 21* and *Rio Declaration on Environment and Development*; United Nations' reports such as *The United Nations Global Impact,* and Earth Charter Commission's *The Earth Charter*; in addition to some NGOs' and IGOs' reports such as World Wide Fund for Nature (WWF, 2012)'s document, *Living Planet Report 2012,* and the World Trade Organization's declarations such as *Doha Declarations.*

This book draws also upon the views of many politicians such as former U.S. presidents George W. Bush and Bill Clinton, former Vice President Al Gore, former British Prime Minister Tony Blair, former French Prime Minister Lionel Jospin, and the Secretary-General of the Rio Conference, Maurice Strong, among others. Theoretically, this work touches upon classical writings of Adam Smith (1723—90), Karl Marx (1818—83), Friedrich Engels (1820—95), Max Weber (1864—1920), and Walt W. Rostow (1916–2003). In addition, it incorporates readings and discussions of the writings of contemporary thinkers such as the sociologist Andre Gunder Frank (1929—2004), Brazilian sociologist Fernando Henrique Cardoso, Immanuel Wallerstein, the American author Thomas Friedman as well as some benchmark studies such as *The Limits to Growth* by Donella H. Meadows, Dennis L. Meadows, Jørgen Randers, and William W. Behrens III. Moreover, this work makes use of a wide array of statistics and scientific studies conducted by the United Nations, the World Bank, and different other IGOs and NGOs. It also draws eclectically on a wide array of secondary sources in American studies, development and environmental studies, international relations, political science, economics, ecology, among other disciplines.

Due to practical constraints, this book cannot provide a comprehensive review of all the seminal writings about the inception and evolution of the project of sustainable development. In addition, the scientific uncertainty that shrouds the environmental issues today and the difficulty of predicting what many global ecological changes will entail constitutes another constraint on research in the field of environmental and development studies. Finally, the persistent ambiguity that characterizes most of the approaches and interpretations of sustainable development has also had a bearing on the clarity of this concept. All these types of constraints may very well affect the coherence of the approaches undertaken by researchers and impact the consistency of their analyses, which makes probing the area of sustainability all the more challenging.

ONE

The Late Twentieth-Century Developmental Challenges and the Inception of Sustainable Development

Over the last half of the past century and the beginning of the twenty-first century, the capitalist model of development has progressively become the predominant paradigm of growth and has been presented as a successful model for the developing countries to follow. By the closing decades of the twentieth century, however, this model has been called into question by many critics (e.g., environmentalists and anti-globalization activists) who argue that some ethical, developmental, and environmental challenges expose the increasingly obtrusive shortcomings of this paradigm. Because of this model's alleged defects and the exigencies of modern times, seeking another alternative became a compelling necessity. Environmentalists, theorists, and mainstream activists today argue that the current conventional paradigm of development is no longer responsive to the needs of the post-industrial society and incapable of dealing effectively with the twenty-first century challenges such as global environmental threats and the overwhelming process of globalization. Though its early modes of activism revolved simply around forging single-issue ecological agreements and conventions, the American environmental movement adopted the concept of "sustainability" by the closing decades of the twentieth century as its principal raison d'être in the face of these different types of challenges. Theoretically, this new project is the fruit of the marriage between two wide realms of studies—environmental studies and development studies.

Although it has been widely heralded by environmentalists and NGOs as a comprehensive paradigm of development, the project of sustainable development has engendered a lot of suspicions and apprehensions especially among the developing countries which, by and large, are still willing to replicate the Western capitalist model of growth. As a result, the project of sustainable development has also been called into question not only by advocates of the current capitalist model of development but also by many environmentalists themselves. It is my aim, therefore, in this chapter, to shed light on the different circumstances and factors which favored the appearance of sustainable development as an alternative model of growth. I also intend to launch a theoretical and conceptual exploration of this new project, focusing duly on the challenges that this new project poses to the predominant capitalist model of development. In portraying the socio-economic context that this new project evolved in, it is my aim to throw more light on the early seeds of an inevitable clash between the two models of development, much of which will be dealt with in chapters 2 and 3.

THE RISE OF ENVIRONMENTAL POLITICS

One of the most important factors that paved the way for the inception and evolution of the project of sustainable development is the rise of environmental politics[1] at the global level in the last few decades of the twentieth and the early twenty-first centuries. Clearly, post-WWII geopolitical changes such as the end, or ebbing, of the Cold War and the collapse of the communist bloc meant more room for cooperation between the two superpowers and relatively eased the cutthroat rivalry between them. The increase in public awareness of global environmental threats and the widespread dissatisfaction with the current model of development in Western countries during the 1960s and 1970s also contributed greatly to the ascendancy of environmental politics in the global political agenda. This preeminence of the environmental politics became all the more manifest as concerns with single ecological issues like desertification, marine and soil pollution, and high rates of extinction of some species gradually metamorphosed into a concern with the increasingly unsustainable model of development and style of living in both the developed and developing countries. Amid these intensifying economic, social, and intellectual changes, the project of sustainable development came as a culmination of decades of global activism and worldwide discussions, especially in UN global conferences from the early 1970s onwards, which ultimately crystallized into what is now referred to as environmental politics. It is my aim, therefore, to pinpoint the far-reaching dimensions that the new paradigm of sustainable development has given to contemporary environmental politics, now touching upon a wide variety of issues such as trade liberalization, the North-South divide, and globalization.

The Environmental Issue from Periphery to Center Stage

Ever since the early 1970s, there has been a growing recognition among decision-makers at the global level that many trans-boundary environmental problems could not be single-handedly tackled by one state at the national level. As a consequence, modern states have had no other choice but to devise a new kind of international agreement, dubbed "regimes,"[2] to tackle these global issues such as the ozone layer depletion, global warming, biodiversity loss, and toxic waste export, among many others. In the last few decades, creating regimes and signing treaties[3] was the main aim in different types of conferences attended by politicians, scientists, economists, investors, researchers, and environmentalists who were all concerned about the high rates of environmental degradation worldwide. Together, these participants tried to establish a common understanding of one specific issue (e.g., deforestation, marine and soil pollution, biodiversity loss, desertification, etc.) and discuss possible solutions and strategies for implementing the different types of treaties they agreed upon.

By and large, environmental politics evolved primarily around single issues and regimes that required cooperation among two or more countries. As such, environmental politics differs from politics in general in many respects: For example, this emerging type of politics places a huge emphasis on cooperation, consensus-building, and bottom-up policies of decision making, which is not always the case with politics. Spotlighting the main features of this new type of global environmental politics, James Connelly and Graham Smith put it in the following terms:

> Environmental concern spans a range of interlocking issues from the local to the global. It challenges our thinking on fundamental questions concerning human beings and the natural world. It challenges us to engage in acts of collective sacrifice and to cooperate in ways which have never previously been achieved. It challenges us to adopt new technologies, new methods of working together and new ideas of international relations. (Connelly and Smith 1999, p. 1)

According to many observers (e.g., Caradonna, 2016; Dresner, 2002; Chasek, Downie, & Brown, 2010), the 1972 United Nations Conference on Human Environment (also known as the Stockholm Conference) represented a landmark in the recognition of environmental issues in global politics. In fact, during the decades following this conference, many governments took concrete action to solve ever-rising and intensifying local, regional, and global environmental problems. This inter-governmental conference is particularly important because of the legitimacy it lent to environmental concerns in international politics and the clear link it established between environmental and developmental concerns. It also helped to launch a set of specialized bodies targeting environmental and developmental issues such as the United Nations Environment Programme (UNEP) and the Environment Liaison Centre (ELC). Concurrently, other international organizations and pressure groups concerned with environmental issues have grown enormously in number and in political significance from the 1970s onwards.[4]

As the number and scale of ecological problems increased considerably in the last few decades, the environmental issues moved firmly to the center stage of international politics. The rise of environmental politics was sparked off mainly by global factors such as widespread global public awareness, the vital role of Inter-Governmental Organizations (IGOs) and Non-Governmental Organizations (NGOs), platforms of Green parties, activism of green protest movements mainly in the United States and Western Europe[5] as well as some shocking large-scale environmental accidents that occurred in the closing decades of the twentieth century. The most notorious accidents were those associated with nuclear power in 1979 in Harrisburg, Pennsylvania, in the United States, and in 1986 in Chernobyl, in the former Soviet Union as well as the accident of the oily surface of the Cuyahoga River in downtown Cleveland which caught fire, and that of the tanker Exxon Valdez, which hit reef off Alaska, dumping 76,000 tons of oil into the sea, causing North America's largest oil spill in 1989. Above all, the role of active NGOs was vital in raising public awareness "reacting against the environmental impact of industrial development, especially contamination of land, air and water from industrial and agricultural chemicals" (Thomas, 1992, p. 23). Referring to the inception of the environmental movement, Janett Marinelli points out that "all elements—history, recent events, and a growing awareness of common values—were praised to coalesce in a fusion of these concerns and the birth of America's environmental revolution" (1991, p. 2).

Although the 1972 UN Stockholm Conference has always been considered as a watershed in the history of the environmental politics, environmental activism in America dates back much further.[6] Conventions on maritime pollution control, for example, were already drafted twenty years earlier than the 1972 Stockholm Conference by the International Maritime Organization (IMO) and the constitutional mandate of the UN Food and Agriculture Organization (FAO) for the conservation of natural resources was formulated in 1945. The initiative of President Theodore Roosevelt in 1909 to convene a world conference for natural resource conservation[7] is often cited as the first serious, though unsuccessful, attempt to establish a sound global environmental management. Jessica Sheffield asserts, for instance, that "the modern environmental movement draws inspiration from the themes Roosevelt introduced in his many conservation speeches" (2010, p. 103).

Throughout the 1970s, however, the environmental issues came to the fore in many UN agencies and NGOs, which helped consolidate the rising public awareness of these ecological concerns through global forums and debates following the UN Stockholm Conference in 1972. Observers (e.g., Zurn, 1998; Thomas, 1992) note that most of these agencies were particularly effective in mobilizing public opinion on different environmental issues, thus pushing them to become high profile issues on both the national and international political agendas. Besides, the NGOs' and IGOs' activism helped also spark off an intensifying scholarly attention and scientific concern with the environment, pushing it further up on the global political agenda. Rodney G. Peffer argues, for instance, that "many, if not most environmental issues, and certainly the most vexing and important ones, entail major global consequences and thus cannot be restricted to local issues of sovereignty" (1998, p. 142), a view equally shared by Bernard Rollin, who asserts that "even a cursory examination of some major environmental issues affecting the non-sentient environment indicates that those problems are insoluble outside the context of international justice" (1988, p. 136).

Increasing public awareness, growing scholarly interest, and rising activism of IGOs and NGOs in the last few decades have all impacted positively on the evolution of environmental politics, thus pushing the environmental issue from periphery to center stage on the global political agenda. Recent as it is, environmental politics has been informed by many other phenomena such as trade liberalization, North-South divide, and globalization. In addition, the nature of the new ecological threats, being global and imminent, has considerably shaped the features of environmental politics. According to many observers (e.g., Dobson, 2016; Rosenbaum, 2017; Boster, Kempton, & Hartley, 1996), the 1970s and 1980s witnessed a worldwide spread of environmental public awareness at the level of citizenship, as NGOs' membership rose enormously.[8] Green movements witnessed a remarkable surge in the number of people who joined them in order to express their dissatisfaction with the way governments were dealing with environmental issues in their countries (Rosenbaum, 2017; Silverstein, 1993). "Like a patriotic surge," argues Victor Scheffer, "the [environmental] movement swept across boundaries of age, sex, intellect and social class"(1991, p. 9). The same period also witnessed a development of a vast worldwide network of NGOs[9] which were concerned either wholly or in part with environmental issues. Gradually, these NGOs developed from some consciousness-raising groups into well-established organizations with scientific research, assessment, and management capability.

NGOs have also expanded their interests from specific areas or issues (e.g., pollution, desertification, loss of biodiversity) to encompass a deeper concern with the necessity of seeking a balanced, environment-friendly model of development. Some of the green movements have indeed developed into green political parties, mainly in West European democracies, where they consolidated their grass-roots basis and partook in political life.[10] Observers point out that the German and the Belgian green parties have proved the most successful, citing the example of the German green party, that is, Die Grünen, which has become the third strongest German political party at the 1994 federal election. Other successful popular green parties in Western Europe include Groen and Ecolo in Belgium, the Swiss Green Party and the Swedish Miljopartiet in Switzerland, the Finnish Green League in Finland, Les Verts in France, the Austrian Alternative Grüne österreich in Austria, and De Groenen in the Netherlands (Carter, 2007, pp. 89–90). In Eastern Europe, some environmental movements have even played a role in pushing for domestic political change: in Bulgaria, for example, the "Ecoglasnost environmental movement" coalesced with the Union of Democratic Forces to call for political pluralism to be adopted in the country (Thomas, 1992, p. 31).

Globally, the decade of the 1980s saw a series of environmental disasters with devastating and far-reaching consequences. The most notorious and ominous ecological accidents were those associated with the nuclear power in 1979 in Harrisburg, Pennsylvania in the US, and in 1986 in Chernobyl, in the former Soviet Union, which provided the anti-nuclear power groups and the environmentalists throughout the world with a powerful cause. These catastrophes heightened public awareness of the pressing environmental issues both locally and globally. More importantly, public confidence in governments and business elites was severely eroded because of these catastrophes and the reported serious abuses of the environment.[11] Observers (e.g., Peterson, 2002) point out that more and more citizens in the United States would no longer accept a decaying environment for the sake of industrial and economic growth. At this particular juncture, voices started to decry the incapacity of single countries to solve global environmental problems, and seriously questioned the responsiveness of the modern state system to the compelling environmental issues. Critics, thus, pointedly inquired how "states with apparently divergent interests [were] expected to cooperate in a manner that is effective in responding to international environmental problems" (Connelly & Smith, 1999, p. 187).

As the states of Eastern Europe opened up politically, radioactive experts discovered that the likelihood of further nuclear incidents was very high because of many design flaws and poor maintenance of nuclear power stations in those countries. According to Caroline Thomas (1992), this situation galvanized public opinion in many Western and Eastern European countries (e.g., the United States, the United Kingdom, Germany, Bulgaria, Ukraine, and Russia) into calling for more attention on the safety standards at chemical plants and nuclear reactors. Thomas (1992) also decried the way many governments dealt with those environmental disasters, pointing out that instead of dealing with those global threats within a whole developmental strategy that protects the environment, these countries opted for rather limited, short-term solutions such as massive clean-ups and shutting down some sites. This limited vision caused the whole political and institutional system of the nation-state to be seriously called into question by some critics who started to inquire "whether the administrative state is institutionally capable of providing a flexible and coordinated response to the complex, systematic and increasingly trans-boundary nature of many ecological problems" (Eckersley, 1998, p. 356).

The mounting pressure exerted by IGOs and NGOs nationally and internationally together with the growing public awareness of the new ecological exigencies resulted in an important boost to the environmental issues on the global political agenda. Hence, the superpowers were faced with such growing concerns over environmental issues and found themselves in a new context that necessitated more collaboration to stop environmental degradation. As a consequence, for the first time in global politics, the environmental issues were placed alongside high profile global issues such as disarmament, nuclear threats, economic crises and other developmental and security issues. By the turn of the century, however, the environmental issue seemed to have lost ground in the light of an intensifying process of globalization that started to catch the attention of politicians, economists, and activists alike. This process of globalization, in my view, has brought in new dimensions to the area of environmental politics.

Changes in Global Politics and the Weakening of the Nation-State

In the wake of an accelerating process of globalization and the rise of global politics, the role of the nation-state is believed to have waned and its sovereignty weakened. There is a growing conviction among scholars[12] that the nation-state has lost control over important key political, economic, and social issues that were previously considered internal state affairs to global institutions. While there is controversy about the exact effect of globalization on the nation-state system, most of these observers agree that the process of globalization has had a strong bearing on the sovereignty of states, as legislation and decision-making regarding global issues such as trade, capital flow, financial regulation, and environmental degradation transcend the jurisdiction of any single state. Against such a backdrop, my aim throughout this section is to examine the implications of the weakening of the state's power on environmental politics.

The weakening of the nation-state is a result of many historical, political, and economic changes, the most influential of which being the post-Cold War political changes and the intensification of the process of globalization at the turn of the century. Many views argue that the demise of the former Soviet Union changed the world political system from a bipolar to a rather "unipolar" system (Krauthammer 2002; Sakamoto, 1994; Altvater, 1998), or to a "uni-multipolar" system (Huntington, 1999), with the United States holding an unrivalled military hegemony among other strong nations. This new room for global cooperation was particularly propitious for the development of environmental politics through global summits and conferences that helped merge environmental and developmental concerns into one global agenda.

On the whole, the Cold War period was mainly an era of ideological conflict between the two vying blocs: while the United States advocated liberal democracy, capitalism, and the American way of life, the former USSR presented communism as the final, highest stage of historical development that humankind can reach. During the Cold War years, each bloc held the position that the challenge to its ideology stemmed mainly from outside, overlooking a few attempts of self-criticism and reform from within.[13] The outside threat, therefore, seems to have prevented any introspective rethinking of the development paradigm these two blocs adopted. To my mind, the waning of self-criticism at that particular juncture in history provides important insight into why the prospects for the project of sustainable development were not favorable yet at that time. The Swedish diplomat and scholar Bo Kjellén (2008) points out, for example, that there was some kind of "semi-globalization" evolving inside each bloc, which helped create two different worlds with different ideologies, different economies, and different lifestyles. Kjellén explains that "the Cold War enabled this semi-globalization to proceed within the two worlds; the break-down of communism in the Soviet Union meant that their socialist model had proved unworkable, and that globalization from that moment would proceed in line with the principles of the market economy" (2008, p. 22).

Even the issue of the state's national security was until recently shaped mainly by the contest between these two superpowers and the subsequent arms race. The scope for single states to initiate independent foreign and defense policy was considerably limited in a system that was dominated by the two superpowers and the corresponding rival blocs. Within this context, one major obstacle to initiating a new paradigm of development, in my view, was the unwillingness of politicians in the two vying superpowers to admit any fundamental flaws in their ideologies and modes of growth. After the end of the Cold War, however, the political climate changed from unfavorable to favorable toward environmental politics, as new room for global cooperation was created. In the wake of the late 1980s geo-political developments, it was clear that a global change was under way. Yet, given the diverse factors affecting global politics at that time, predicting the nature of the new global changes was difficult for most observers. As a matter of fact, the features of the "New World Order" following the end of the Cold War and the diminishing of the bipolar global system were far from clear. The post-Cold War economic changes have also had several political, cultural, and even ecological repercussions as the capitalist economic system has become the backbone of the Western paradigm of development. Elaborating on this issue, Valentine M. Moghadam argues that "integration into the global economy is being touted as the only solution to economic crisis and as the only path to economic growth open to developing countries, given the end of the communist bloc and its alternative socialist economic system" (2007, p. 138).

The breakdown of the communist bloc coincided also with unprecedented scientific and technological development, especially in the fields of communication and transportation. This boom in telecommunication technologies introduced additional factors into the post-WWII geopolitical changes. Thanks to breakthroughs in communication technologies, the environmental movement reached new heights with millions of mainstream activists partaking in worldwide campaigns to draw public attention to the environmental issue and raise awareness of it. Shedding more light on these campaigns and demonstrations, observers noted that "their [i.e., environmentalists'] demonstration was as zany as it was serious—a dramatic counterpoint that caught the attention of the [American] nation. New Yorkers paraded down fashionable Fifth Avenue wearing gas masks. In Florida, students staged a mock trial and convicted Chevrolet of air pollution" (Marinelli, 1991, p. 1). As a consequence, the political and intellectual climate, especially in the United States, grew more receptive to calls for rethinking and examining the conventional model of growth that had been predominant in most parts of the world ever since the Industrial Revolution. James G. Speth, for example, contends that "the end of the Cold War and the West's long struggle against communism opens the door—creates the political space—for the questioning of today's capitalism" (2008, p. 195). This openness to change was further encouraged by a surge of public awareness following a series of several alarming environmental incidents during the 1970s and 1980s and the new types of global ecological threats that started to menace the whole planet.

As the trans-boundary nature of global environmental threats like global warming, ozone layer depletion, and biodiversity loss grew all the more ominous, the ability and readiness of the current international political system started to be called into question. Deep concerns about whether the system is sensitive enough to the environmental challenges and capable of finding the appropriate solutions to ecological problems were voiced by many activists and environmentalists.[14] "The international political system, based on the pursuit of state interest tempered by a very limited recognition of global interdependence," contends Thomas, "is ill-equipped to deal with such global problems" (1992, p. 2). This questioning of the ability of the international political system to deal with the new type of global environmental threats led many environmentalists and thinkers to start theorizing about an alternative model of development that could reconcile both economic growth and environmental exigencies. These interests to rethink the current paradigm of growth have found favorable space for introspective self-criticism and reconsideration of some conventional and deeply entrenched developmental options in the post-Cold War political scene.

With the tension between the two blocs easing off in the post-Cold War era, the last two decades of the twentieth century witnessed an ascendancy of the environmental issues on the political agenda of the two superpowers. In a speech before the UN General Assembly in 1988, Soviet Foreign minister Edward Shevardnadze, for instance, put it as follows: "the biosphere recognizes no division into blocs, alliances, or systems. We all share the same climatic system and no one is in a position to build his own isolated and independent line of environmental defense" (as cited in Renner, 1989, p. 44). President Clinton, in turn, declared in his speech at U.S. Botanical Gardens in 1993 that "after the Cold War, we face the challenge of helping Russia achieve a healthy democracy, a healthy economy and a healthy environment" (1993). On another occasion, he also confirmed that Americans must "make environment a core foreign policy objective and provide the leadership needed to put all nations on a cleaner, more sustainable path to prosperity" (2000, p. 25). With this new space for international cooperation following the end of the Cold War, environmental politics started to grow out of its limited national scope and become part of global politics. During this process, however, many new actors entered the realm of global environmental politics, bringing in numerous complicated issues that have become inextricably intertwined with the issue of the environment.

The transformations in the landscapes of global politics, and in global environmental politics in particular, played an essential role in highlighting the magnitude of the new ecological exigencies and concomitant developmental challenges (Rosenbaum, 2017; Dobson, 2016). Empowered by the unrelenting process of the economic, social, and political interdependence that globalization has brought about, many IGOs and NGOs have assumed due responsibility for taking decisions that directly affect the citizens' livelihoods worldwide. Organizations such as Greenpeace, the World Wide Fund for Nature (WWF, 2012), Friends of the Earth International (FOEI), Earth First!, the United Nations Environment Programme (UNEP), and the United Nations Development Programme (UNDP), among a few others, have noticeably become a very important element in global politics. Many of these organizations helped popularize the environmental cause and set the stage for an alternative model of growth. It is my aim, therefore, to spotlight the vital role these IGOs and NGOs had in highlighting the need for a new paradigm of development.

In the closing decades of the twentieth century, many NGOs witnessed important transformations in their structures and methods of activism. Thanks mainly to breakthroughs in communication technologies, NGOs have come of age: they are now better organized and financially more resourceful than before, and employing highly trained experts in economics, sociology, environmental sciences, and many other fields pertinent to the issues these NGOs are promoting (Rosenbaum, 2017; Baker, 2006; Raustiala, 1997). Contemporary NGOs have also developed strong strategies to cooperate among themselves and make good use of new technology. More importantly, observers note that "through coordinated activities, INGOs [International Non-Governmental Organizations] influence internal political relations between states . . . [and] are able to bypass national governments and operate directly in world politics" (Choudhary, 2004, p. 15). These new abilities in the hands of NGOs and other international organizations have facilitated the ascendancy of global environmental politics and promoted the environmental issue worldwide.

Given the important role of NGOs as a new actor in global politics, it is essential, in my view, to discuss the notion that there has been a significant "transference of authority of the state to these global institutions" (Jegede, 2001). In fact, many researchers (e.g., Chasek, Downie, & Brown, 2010; Thomas, 1992) have already pointed out the growing role of these institutions and organizations in the lives of citizens of the developed and developing countries alike. International organizations such as World Health Organization (WHO), World Commission on Environment and Development (WCED), World Trade Organization (WTO), the International Bank for Reconstruction and Development (IBRD), along with international NGOs engaged in large scale campaigns to improve the social and working conditions of tens of millions of poor people. Some of them also work to achieve better protection for the environment, ethnic minorities, women, and indigenous communities. Dubbed by Lester M. Salamon (1999), "global associational revolution," this upsurge of these IGOs and NGOs has dramatically blurred the spheres of influence of the nation-states and caused global politics to encroach on national politics and sovereignty. For some other critics, this "global associational revolution" can be understood better when placed "in the contemporary context of the widespread crisis/retreat of the state, collapse of state socialism, questioning of the "neoliberal consensus" referred to as "Washington consensus," and continuing/aggravating environmental degradation and social deprivation/exclusion" (Choudhary, 2004, p. 2). Thus, the retreat of the state's sovereignty has had serious implications for the evolution of environmentalism as ecological issues required high levels of international cooperation.

At the regional level, the world has witnessed a steady increase in the number of organizations during the closing decades of the twentieth century. Regional organizations such as the European Union (EU), Economic Community of West African States (ECOWAS), South Asia Association for Regional Cooperation (SAARC), Arab League (AL), African Development Bank (AfDB), and the Organization of African Unity (OAU), among others, have also taken, to different degrees, control of some important economic, social, and political issues within their member states. Issues such as trade barriers, security measures, immigration control, and even educational reforms and regulations are gradually slipping out of the state's hands to become common issues that these regional organizations are entitled to deal with. As a result, it has become one important feature of today's global politics that "the sphere of influence of the state is shrinking with the growing number of regional and international organizations" (Jegede, 2001).

The proliferation of NGOs and their remarkable success in rallying mainstream support for important issues such as opposing nuclear arms and protecting the environment has given rise to an international system in which the nation-state's power and influence have been overshadowed and weakened over the years (Gruber, 2004). David Held and Anthony McGrew further argue that the whole system of governance based on sovereign nation-states has to be rethought given the "the way processes of economic, legal, political, and military interconnectedness are altering the nature, scope, and capacity of the sovereign state from above" (1994, p. 79). Other views (e.g., Jegede, 2001), however, contend that the nation-state has deliberately handed over some of its roles especially in common issues such as immigration and economic policies to these regional and global organizations. This proliferation of Transnational Corporations (TNCs) constitutes yet another element that has considerably contributed to the weakening of the sovereignty of nation-states at the turn of the twentieth century. Due to the unrelenting process of the globalization of the market economy, observers argue that "the centers of gravity of the economic forces commanding capital growth have shifted outside the frontiers of individual states" (Jegede, 2001). In their book, *The Global Trap: Globalization and the Assault on Property and Democracy*, Hans-Peter Martin and Harald Schumann claim that what came to be known as the world market is in essence built upon as many as 40,000 TNCs of varying shapes and sizes and with such huge capital and resources that their influence and power exceed that of many nation-states (1997, p. 7). Thus, in a context of economic globalization, TNCs have gained economic and even political power that has enabled them to encroach on the sovereignty of nation-states and especially those that are disadvantaged by this global economic system.

By and large, the very concept of state's sovereignty still carries within it the marks of its earliest formulation during the earlier epoch when the nation-state system was being forged. Throughout long decades of national governance, the sovereignty of the nation-state was rarely, if at all, questioned mainly because "it was generally assumed that the state had control over its own fate, subject only to compromises it must make and limits imposed upon it by groups and forces operating within its territorial boundaries, and by agencies and representatives of other nation-states" (Held & McGrew, 1994, p. 71). In the closing decade of the twentieth century, however, several profound transformations have re-shaped the concept of sovereignty once and for all. These transformations include a global and expansive system of trading and financial exchange that goes beyond the control of any single nation-state as well as the extensive network of telecommunication that transcends national borders and evades most forms of national regulations. In addition, the power and activities of a vast array of international organizations became a determining factor in global politics (Salih, 2001). The internationalization of security structures has also significantly limited the scope for the unilateral use of military force by a single nation-state and limited its sovereignty.

The recent weakening of the nation-state's sovereignty has been manifest both internally and internationally. Domestically, the erosion of this sovereignty has engendered a dwindling capacity to provide welfare services for the citizens and weaker concerns with the protection of the environment (Sydee & Beder, 2009; Dale, 2001). The rapid, unprecedented breakthroughs in communication technology and transportation are also relentlessly eroding the boundaries between what used to be separate national markets, thus transforming the whole structure of national economies and imposing deeper degrees of interconnectedness on the world economy. Many studies (e.g., Kütting 2003; Sydee & Beder, 2009; Robbins, 2009) have come to the conclusion that with the globalization of the neoliberal capitalist economic system and the concomitant waves of deregulation and privatization, maintaining a reliable welfare system has been relegated to a peripheral position in most governmental policies of development.

The sovereignty of the nation-state has also been eroded even more deeply by the development of international law which has subjected governments, IGOs, and NGOs to new systems of legal regulations. As a consequence, "the 'impermeability' that characterized the classical model of the sovereign state for centuries is being widely challenged" (Sakamoto, 1994, p. 2). In essence, the very nature of this law transcends the will of nation-states, and sometimes poses significant constraints on their sovereignty or interferes in what are usually considered a state's domestic affairs. However, in modern times, the question has arisen why interference in domestic affairs should be considered intrinsically impermissible at a time when no major development in one country can be immune from external interactions. Hence, the structure of the "classical" sovereign state system and its compatibility with a changing global governance system are now being questioned. James Connelly and Graham Smith argue, for instance, that "environmental problems can [also] be seen as a challenge to this principle of [state] sovereignty, particularly as it embodies the idea of complete dominion over the resources within a state's territory rather than the idea of stewardship so central to green thinking" (1999, p. 186).

On the whole, the post-Cold War period witnessed many transformations that heavily impacted the evolution of environmental politics and the state's sovereignty. On the one hand, the important geopolitical changes that followed the end, or ebbing, of the Cold War helped establish a solid ground for international cooperation between former rivals, thus pushing environmental politics to new heights by the turn of the century. This ascendancy was no doubt consolidated by the breakthroughs in communication technologies that ushered in the environmental issue in global politics. On the other hand, some of these post-Cold War changes, the advent of globalization, and transformations in global politics have had a noticeable impact on the sovereignty of the nation-state which seems to have lost some of its prerogatives to these new global forces. This weakening of the state's sovereignty in the light of an intensifying globalization has, in my view, cast a pall on the soundness of the existing global governance system and whether it is still able to accommodate all these new changes.

Inadequate Global Governance and the Need for a New Alternative

The prominence of the United Nations' role in the second half of the twentieth century and the post-Cold War changes in the global governance system have had an important impact on the sovereignty of nation-states and their roles. Issues such as environmental degradation, rocketing population growth, and barriers to trade, among many others, have ceased being the internal affairs of the nation-state only and grown into global issues that no state can single-handedly manage without resorting to the global governance system for help. My aim in this section is twofold: First, I want to shed light on the importance of the UN's role in the post-Cold War period and its implications for the emerging project of sustainable development. Secondly, it is my aim to examine and discuss how this new global governance system took some conventional roles over from the state and how successful it has been in fulfilling the concomitant obligations such as maintaining the welfare system or protecting the environment.

After having been marginalized in the two superpowers' foreign policies during the Cold War years, the United Nations regained some of its influence and became an important player in global diplomacy in the closing decades of the twentieth century.[15] This ascendancy coincided with the ever-increasing power of international financial organizations and TNCs that have had a strong influence on developmental options of many countries. These transformations have also brought a strong process of economic globalization that cuts across borders between states, societies, and regions. It has become evident that no sovereign country can now act in isolation from other states and singlehandedly deal with the rising global issues without inflicting potential economic or political damage on itself.

By and large, the whole structure of the global governance[16] has undergone profound transformations in the last few decades of the twentieth century. The weakening of the state's sovereignty, the emergence of new global threats such as terrorism and ecological problems, and the ascendancy of global politics made this global system exhibit the characteristics of a "multi-polar" distribution of political and economic power. In fact, states have increasingly been engaged in multilateral forms of governance (e.g., EU, Arab League, SAARC, and OAU) and most countries are parts of different international agreements and organizations (e.g., WTO, NAFTA, NATO, and OECD) that manage specific global issue areas such as trade liberalization, the environmental challenges, security, and so on. Japanese theorist Yoshikazu Sakamoto highlights the nature of the hard choices that the new global changes put the nation-state in front of:

> It was clear that, under the technological and industrial conditions of Fordist mass production and mass consumption [. . .] the days of the classical sovereign state system were numbered. It is probably no accident that, while states with ethnocentric particularist ideologies failed to retain their hegemonic empires, only states with international/universalist ideologies demonstrated their compatibility with the scale of political economy and military technology that transcends classical national boundaries. (1994, p. 28)

As a result of these new transformations, the global governance system has expanded, including new styles of collective decision-making that draws upon Inter-governmental Organizations (IGOs) and an increasing number of Non-Governmental Organizations (NGOs). Miles Kahler points out that what really distinguishes this era of global governance from the previous ones is that this is the first time that those IGOs, NGOs, and pressure groups are at the center of a fierce conflict over the control and direction of global policy (2003, pp. 1–3). The prominence of many new actors in global politics has led critics to question the complete sovereignty of nation-states with regard to their internal affairs, accentuating how "state autonomy is threatened with the international regime imposing tighter constraints over the nation-state to pursue independent policies within its domestic affairs" (Choudhary, 2004, p. 14). Observers (e.g., Hart, 2009, p. 19) also note that through their unique way of forging consensual decision-making, these organizations have even penetrated the different channels and modes of global governance and gained control over many effective tools that used to be deployed by the nation states.

Over the past few years, academic studies and statistics[17] have increasingly pointed to the decline in the government's ability to maintain a reliable welfare system for its citizens mainly as a result of the effects of globalization on the national economies of many countries. Franz Hartmann contends, for instance, that "the entrenchment of international free trade via GATT and NAFTA-type agreements, the instantaneous transfer of capital to anywhere in the world, the dismantling of government regulations and welfare programmes have created a global economy that favours the wealthy" (1998, p. 342). Even the traditional model of the welfare state in Europe is now believed to be under pressure of the forces of a globalized economy. In fact, statistics show that there has been a steady decline in public expenditure in many European countries because of these global economic trends (Thomas, 1992, p. 6). As a result, the power of the nation-state to maintain its full sovereignty and influence over its citizens is receiving another blow from these forces of globalization. "As the economies of nations become increasingly joined up and interdependent," explain some observers, "individual nation seems to be losing the political clout and economic power to stop this trend" (Jegede, 2001).

Although it has weakened the nation-state's established political and economic structures that safeguarded its sovereignty for so long, globalization is widely criticized for failing to generate a viable alternative that meets the state's obligations toward its citizen and the environment. Shedding light on this discrepancy, Professor Ann Dale contends that "as the forces for globalization continue to accelerate, and corporate activity is no longer tied to a sense of place, there are few or no social obligations for communities and nations to create work for people or even to maintain a regional resource base" (2001, p. 84). Pointing to the "misconception" that globalization is going to benefit the poor and disadvantaged, Dale confirms that "although this intense globalization of the economic system appears to be creating space for new avenues of economic growth, this is merely an illusion" (2001, p. 84).

In a context of a weakening welfare system and intensifying economic globalization, calls for adopting an alternative model of growth intensified. Theorists, economists, politicians, and mainstream activists voiced their desire to seek an alternative paradigm of development that would heal the excesses of the contemporary capitalist mode of growth before it is too late. A paradigm that is able to balance between sound development and the protection of the environment has been the demand of a big number of NGOs, thinkers, and activists in both the developed and developing countries. Preserving the necessary roles of the state as based on the principle of partnership between states rather than on the notion of dominance or power hierarchy has also been voiced as a prerequisite of this desired alternative. Ultimately, the skepticism about the viability of the current governance system and all expectations of the researchers dissatisfied with the predominant model of growth were actually paving the way for the project of sustainable development to gain momentum in global politics.

Socially, the erosion of the state's sovereignty in a context of a changing global governance system and intensifying process of globalization brought about new forms of social unrest that has characterized the post-industrial nations (Pichardo, 1997). The inadequacy of the current system of global governance and the dissatisfaction with the current paradigm of growth has constituted an incentive for considering viable alternatives. More to the point, the vacuum created by the erosion of state sovereignty and the shortcomings of the new systems of governance underpins the rise of a whole set of new ethics related to development. Adrian Martin and John Huckle argue that this vacuum can have dire consequences given that "the modern state [. . .] has collapsed in much of the world and a lack of effective governance offers little prospect of reconciling the imperatives of global markets with the needs of social cohesion and environmental conservation" (2001, p. 231).

This waning state's social role led many thinkers, economists, different social movements, and NGOs to start questioning the state's sovereignty, on the one hand, and the benefits that globalization was thought to bring, on the other. While some scholars (e.g., Inglehart, 2000; Carter, 2007) highlight the importance of a new array of post-materialist values that came to the fore in the last few decades of the twentieth century, others (e.g., Edwards, 2008; Korten, 2006; Khor, 2001; Speth, 2008) dwell on the necessity of establishing a new model of development that both counterbalances what they deem undesired effects of globalization on the state's sovereignty and fulfills the state's obligations. Other critics (e.g., Kjellén, 2008; Dobson, 2016; Dale, 2001; Sydee & Beder, 2009) warn that economic globalization has eroded the state's sovereignty away without offering an alternative mechanism that can fulfill the state's duties.

The spreading frustration and dissatisfaction with both the national governments (Peterson, 2002) and mechanisms of global governance (Robbins, 2009; Chasek, Downie, & Brown, 2010) has also led to mainstream distrust of the viability of these "national and local governments and politicians [that] were seen to be unresponsive to people's needs, geared to short-term self-interest, beyond influence and unlikely to act on those social and environmental trends that provoked much anxiety and pessimism" (Martin & Huckle, 2001, pp. 243–44). Some think-tanks and activists in North and Latin America, as well as in other parts of the world, have called for a new system that fulfills the state's obligations toward its citizens while at the same time is able to transcend the states' rather myopic vision of global issues such as the environmental issues and development concerns. Gary Sampson, for instance, points out that "the growth of global environment agreements led to a search for long-term strategy that would facilitate integrated action on the part of a number of governments and international institutions" (2005, p. 20). Recent global environmental challenges such as the depletion of the ozone layer and the alarming rates of global warming also increased post-industrial societies' readiness to embrace a new kind of development that is more responsive to the current social and ecological concerns. "What is needed (and has not yet emerged)," argue Roger Keil et al., "is a new framework or paradigm, that will allow humankind to lighten its 'ecological footprint' while reforming the inequities within and between countries" (1989, p. 12).

Taken together, government's development strategies, deteriorating environmental conditions, and the effects of globalization on the state's sovereignty have all caused ordinary people in industrialized countries to identify with the concept of sustainable development once it was set forth in global debates in UN summits starting from the 1980s onwards. This has also generated a growing conviction among researchers that single-issue environmental regimes are no longer enough to adequately address the wide range of intertwined environmental and developmental problems of the late twentieth and early twenty-first centuries. Consequently, a holistic approach that highlights the connections between economy, society, and the environment in addressing these problems has been thought of as an essential alternative to get out of the current developmental impasse. However, it would not have been possible for these aspirations to spread without an interconnected active global society to promote them.

A CONCEPTUALIZATION OF THE GLOBAL CIVIL SOCIETY (GCS)

As a response to the untrammelled waves of industrialization and urbanization in the developed countries, a new set of "post-materialist" values came into being, emphasizing more social equity and the preservation of the environment. These "post-materialist" values have been largely adopted and popularized by what is referred to as the New Social Movements (NSMs)[18] through their different modes of activism that shaped the late twentieth and early twenty-first centuries. In the United States, for instance, calls for change came mostly from intellectuals who launched a scathing critique of the capitalist model of economic growth which, they argue, is not responsive to important issues such as environmental protection and social equity. Thanks to various large-scale NGOs, a new notion of "Global Civil Society" has been largely promoted through a set of global networks which provided an incubator for the notion of sustainability. Within this context, my aim in this section is to examine to what extent the Global Civil Society has consolidated the emergence of the project of sustainable development as an alternative to the conventional mode of development and shed light on the specific role played by the NSMs and NGOs in popularizing this new vision of development.

The Emergence of Global Civil Society (GCS)

Hitting unprecedented rates during the closing years of the second half of the twentieth century, the rapid processes of industrialization and urbanization in North America and Western Europe led to renewed concerns about the environment. These concerns became prominent especially in the industrialized nations toward the end of the 1960s before this wave swept many other parts of the world by the end of the 1970s including the former Soviet Union following Glasnost in the late 1980s (Thomas, 1992). This new wave of dissatisfaction with the existent economic and social policies was translated into new forms of activism by different groups such as peace movements, women's movement, the environmental movement, and the students' movement, among others, which theorists refer to as New Social Movements (NSMs). Thanks to advanced communication technologies, these new forms of activism found a favorable climate to initiate a global network of social and environmental activists that gave shape to what is referred to as the Global Civil Society (GCS).

By the turn of the century, these NSMs noticeably broadened their agenda, challenging whole dominant ideologies and aiming to change centuries-old patterns of governance and economic policies. The environmental movement, for instance, has been regarded by many observers (e.g., Blewitt, 2008; Carter, 2007) as one of these NSMs, with a whole new set of social and philosophical values that political scientist Roland F. Inglehart (2000) refers to as "post-materialist" values. According to some views (e.g., Speth, 2008; Dale, 2001), affluence, especially in the rich industrialized countries, has given rise to a post-materialist way of thinking associated with these new values. In his landmark book, *The Silent Revolution: Changing Values and Political Styles among Western Publics,* Roland F. Inglehart referred to this shift in the values of post-industrial societies as the "silent revolution." Explaining this culture shift, Inglehart argues that generations born in modern post-industrial societies firmly believe that the rise in the material standards of living especially in the West can only satisfy a certain set of material needs at the expense of other "post-materialist" needs (2000, pp. 222–225).

The post-materialist view has also gained currency among some politicians and decision-makers who expressed their societies' need for adopting a new approach to Western lifestyles. Former French Prime Minister Lionel Jospin, for example, puts it succinctly as follows: "we have to accept a market economy, but we should not accept a market society" (as cited in Kjellén, 2008, p. 23). Likewise, former British Prime Minister Tony Blair confirms in a BBC interview that "the time has come in Europe for a renewed European social model which is about how you can buy dynamism and social justice in a model global and technological age [. . .] I do talk about Social justice, community, [and] opportunity for all." By the same token, the Secretary-General of the Rio Conference 1992, Maurice Strong, bluntly declared in his speech at the UN Headquarters that "if the market economy cannot solve the problems of social injustice and environmental deterioration, then it will not last" (as cited in Kjellén, 2008, p. 23). These declarations, among others, reflect a conviction among both intellectuals and the general public in the post-industrial societies that the materialist ethics of growth underpinning their current paradigm of development need to be reconsidered.

The Role of the NSMs in disseminating these post-materialist ethics has been the focus of intensive scholarly studies. Adrian Martin and John Huckle point out, for instance, that unlike "old" social movements which were mainly working-class labor movements struggling to improve their working conditions and wages, the NSMs are "historically distinct because they transcend class-based social organization" (2001, p. 131). Through NGOs, pressure groups, and other forms of activism, NSMs constitute today the backbone of a new emerging global community dubbed Global Civil Society (GCS). In the literature, the term Global Civil Society has often been used "to refer to a diverse and diffuse range of actors, campaigns, and events such as NGOs and citizen groups and the battle at Seattle" (Choudhary, 2004, p. 2). In his article "Interpreting Global Civil Society," Robert Taylor notes that the concept of GCS came out as "a kind of catch-all term for non-governmental organizations (NGOs) or social movements, of all shapes and sizes, operating in the international realm" (2002, p. 339).

Asserting that excessive consumption in their societies is destroying the environment while failing to satisfy non-materialistic needs such as reviving spiritual affinity with nature, different actors in the GCS have endorsed the growing demand for an alternative paradigm of development. Observers (e.g., Pichardo, 1997; Fisher, 1996) note that the popularity of the NSMs has played an important role in giving shape to the calls for an alternative model of development through various forms of activism. Explaining this need for a whole paradigm shift, Adrian Martin and John Huckle contend that "as the industrial model of social progress was progressively exposed for its failures to bring harmony within society and, most pertinently, between society and natural systems, the Enlightenment ideology was ripe for challenge" (2001, p. 133). With a new set of post-materialist ethics, the GCS has constituted, therefore, a propitious context in which the new alternative came into being. Moreover, the emergence of a Global Civil Society as a framework for activism for a wide array of NSMs through NGOs, and other organizations and groups, signaled an important juncture in the evolution of environmentalism. Within this new framework, it is now possible for these activists not only to express their dissatisfaction with what they consider as the excess of the capitalist model of growth, but also to interact among themselves and seek an alternative. The socio-economic changes that underpinned the inception of post-materialist ethics have also shaped the formulation of the GCS as a global framework for activism. Against this backdrop, the image of the wealthy Western society changed from a bountiful bonanza of material wealth to a society with new global threats dubbed "risk society."

Exigencies of the "Risk Society" and the Emergence of New Ethics of Development

While the environmental movement was mostly inseparable from issues of local livelihood and people's struggle with poverty in the developing countries, post-materialist ethics were certainly born out of affluent consumer societies in industrialized nations. In essence, these values constitute a real challenge to the predominant socio-economic model of development in these countries and to the fundamental principles of neoliberal capitalism as a whole. With their aspirations going beyond material well-being, young generations of today's post-industrial society are rather disillusioned with their way of life that not only abuses nature systematically but also entails new kinds of global threats, namely ecological threats. Disgruntled with the current model of development, these activists have launched a scathing critique of this paradigm that precipitated the emergence of the risk society they live in.

NSMs' growing activism has been partly a response to the environmental abuses of the late twentieth and early twenty-first centuries and a reflection of the subsequent decline in confidence in the capitalist economies and modes of development. Despite unmistakable signs of affluence in the modern, industrialized societies, these environmental abuses took on enormous cultural significance and new intellectual dimensions. This juncture in history is, therefore, largely characterized by "the transformation of industrial society into *risk society*, a state that is characterized by a new breed of risks" (Martin & Huckle, 2001, p. 158). Unlike the "old risks" which include diseases, earthquakes, floods, droughts and so on, the "new risks" are believed to be of global dimensions, including nuclear threats, global ecological disasters, and the scarcity of vital natural resources such as fresh drinking water and depletion of the ozone layer. In his landmark book, *Risk Society: Towards a New Modernity*, German sociologist Ulrich Beck writes: "The risks and hazards of today thus differ in an essential way from the superficially similar ones in the Middle Age through the global nature of their threats (people, animals, and plants) and through their *modern* causes. They are *risks of modernization*. They are a *wholesale product* of modernization, and are systematically intensified as it becomes global" (1992, p. 21).

Global as such, these new risks obviously are characterized by fewer spatial and temporal boundaries, for their impact can affect the whole planet regardless of where the original causes are. Indeed, within the risk society, "there is no concrete enemy, the threat is nowhere and everywhere [. . .] within the very fabric of our societies and lifestyles, often linked to material progress" (Kjellén, 2008, p. 40). Distinct from old ones both in nature and magnitude, these new types of risk have challenged the whole notion of affluence that industrialized nations have long prided themselves on. In addition, the risk society is characterized by another equally dangerous global phenomenon—what is referred to as "organized irresponsibility." In fact, this expression refers to modern governments' efforts to conceal the real causes and consequences of environmental hazards both in the developed and the developing countries (Blewitt, 2008). The notion of "organized irresponsibility" is particularly evident when these governments attempt to shirk any responsibility for environmental degradation and heap the blame on isolated "human errors" rather than admitting serious flaws in these governments' economic policies and management strategies.

What is alarming about the risk society is that governments seem to be poorly equipped to deal with the new type of threats as many decision-makers[19] have little readiness to sacrifice any aspect of affluent lifestyles in the developed countries to solve such global environmental problems. Bo Kjellén takes the discussion in yet another direction, arguing that understanding the different social, environmental, and political concerns of the risk society and translating them into effective strategies necessitates the establishment of a new type of diplomacy. "The absolute character of the threats, the need for a broad vision, and the primacy of the long-term," asserts Kjellén "are defining elements for the very concept of the new diplomacy for sustainable development" (2008, p. 44). Thus, the critique expressed in the risk society discourse clearly echoes much of what the project of sustainable development is all about. The call for a new diplomacy is also a clear sign that there is an urgent need for a development model with viable strategies that can bridge the gap between the decision-makers and the ordinary citizens.

In a context of a risk society and armed with a new set of post-materialist values, NSMs strive to bring morality and a genuine sense of responsibility to bear on economic and political decision-making within the frame of what is referred to as "reflexive modernization." In the literature, this expression refers to applying a critical approach to the contradictions and flaws in the economic and environmental policies of the current Western socio-economic model of development. NSMs' activists assert that putting new reflexive modernization into practice hinges essentially on choosing the right model of development which can both replace the current capitalist model of economic growth and at the same time fill the void resulting from the weakening of nation-state sovereignty and the overwhelming drive of globalization.

What I consider central to this discussion is that these NSMs clearly transcend the issue of defending the environment or nature per se and assume a broader, more sophisticated role. In response to extreme poverty, continuous destruction of their local livelihoods, social marginalization, and political exclusion, activists in these NSMs have gone so far as to question the dominant economic system and its harmful effects not only on environment but also on society, culture, and local identity (Pichardo, 1997). For these activists, the protection of the environment represents just a starting point from which they launch a new criticism "against neo-liberal policies and state centralization and authoritarianism, [. . .] demand direct participation in decision-making regarding public policies, and claim new rights of access to, and control over, the common environmental resources of their locale" (Leff, 2000, p. 68). According to this view, new forms of presentation and the application of democratic values to environmental and social problems of their local community are desperately needed, especially in disadvantaged areas in both developed and developing countries.

Many of the early demands expressed by environmentalists and activists in the NSMs has constituted, in my view, a foundation for the project of sustainable development, thus reflecting a bottom-up process of social, environmental, and political activism for change. Even the new approach to ecological concerns is in fact far from the conventional single-issue campaigns that characterized the environmental movement in its early years. Put in other terms, the activism of these NSMs has matured from limited demands for environmental protection and better living standards to the necessity of establishing a new holistic model of growth sensitive to people's local needs and indigenous culture. In his article *Sustainable Development in Developing Countries: Cultural Diversity and Environmental Rationality,* Enrique Leff sheds light on this issue:

> These emergent sustainable development movements integrate "environmental rights" with new demands for democracy and autonomy, that is, for a more direct appropriation of nature based on consensual decisions of popular organisations and communities themselves. These demands oppose centralized decision-making and hierarchical structures, opening up a more decentralised and democratic process. Sustainable development led by such principles in grass-roots social organizations is mobilised by cultural values which depart from a unidimensional conception of progress in terms of technological productivity. (Leff 2000, p. 68)

The social and political activists of the NSMs also reject the prevailing mechanisms of political representation and ask for more equity. The kind of equity they aspire to achieve is by no means limited to a more just distribution of environmental costs or compensation for environmental damage or even a bigger role in the prevalent economic and political system. Their chief objective actually mounts up to a new socio-economic system with new ethics and modes of production and consumption that would definitely reflect their belief in the project of an entirely new sustainable development model of growth. "What is (implicitly or explicitly) being called into question in various ways by these movements [i.e., NSMs]," explains Bina Agarwal, "is the existing development paradigm—with its particular product and technological mix, its forms of exploitation of natural and human resources, and its conceptualization of relationships among people and between people and nature" (1998, p. 213). Above all, these movements have exhibited a strong will to question the established political, economic, and social order and to expose what they see as the "fallacy" of the capitalist model of economic growth.

NSMs' activism has also fed into the identity quest of some American activists from indigenous social backgrounds. Some of these activists started, for instance, redefining their ethnic identities and establishing autonomous organizations and independent communities. Michael Silverstein notes that activists in the environmental movement did not want to miss the "chance to join a movement that not only promised to save the world, but that permitted rejection of the acquisition ethic that dominated the lives of their parents" (1993, p. 12). Thus, raising the identity issue has led to a "cross-fertilization" of the environmental and indigenous peoples' movements, which gave both parts more empowerment to assert their rights in demanding a more sustainable model of development and their historic legitimate rights to regain control over natural resources of their motherland (Leff, 2000). To my mind, this factor adds yet another element that enriches and broadens the new project of sustainable development across race and gender.

Amid this social and intellectual unrest stirred by NSMs' intensifying activism, many views (e.g., Dale, 2001; Speth, 2008; Hart, 2009; Korten, 2006; Hawken 2001, among many others) assert that the "moral void" that the predominant capitalist paradigm of growth created can be alternatively filled by the new ethics of sustainability as defended in the project of sustainable development. Adrian Martin and John Huckle, for instance, contend that this new morality actually stems from the NSMs, putting it as follows: "The emergence of NSMs, and especially the environmental movement, signals the emergence of a new morality. The space for such a new morality has been opened up by a loss of faith in the modern project. NSMs are seen as evidence that this moral void is being filled by new commitments to universal norms based on social and environmental justice" (2001, p. 161).

All in all, the formulation of the GCS came as a culmination of a proliferation of NGOs, pressure groups, and other types of civil society organizations that effectively use the latest breakthroughs in communication technology to interact globally. Within the frame of the GCS, the emerging NSMs have succeeded in popularizing their own causes and raising public consciousness of what they consider as the excesses of the predominant socio-economic paradigm of growth. Alarmed by eye-openers such as the ecological disasters at the turn of the century and the growing literature about the emerging risk society, activists in these NSMs called for an alternative to this paradigm of growth and advocated a new set of post-materialist ethics. As the moral void in post-industrial societies grew more obtrusive, the general characteristic features of the new paradigm of development started to take shape. The conceptualization of this new paradigm, however, is laden with controversies about definitions and theoretical clashes between different schools of thought that all claim to be the "founding fathers" of this emerging alternative.

THEORETICAL AND CONCEPTUAL EXPLORATION OF SUSTAINABLE DEVELOPMENT

As a relatively new area in development studies, sustainable development studies incorporate two big areas of study—the environment and development. Environmental studies in general, and writings about sustainable development in particular, draw on multiple other disciplines such as ecology, economics, sociology, and politics. This complex interplay of disciplines makes the formulation of one academically rigorous and unbiased definition of sustainable development a very difficult task. As no one definition can meet the requirements of all these fields, defining sustainable development has been the subject of a heated debate ever since the inception of this concept. Thus, my primary aim in this section is to launch a thorough theoretical and conceptual exploration of this new concept that has gained momentum in many academic and political debates worldwide.

In the process of exploring the meaning and dimensions of this new project, my aim is also to highlight the far-reaching repercussions that the controversy over defining sustainable development has had on its integrity and evolution. Examining the various definitions of this new concept would certainly lead us to what came to be known as the authoritative definition advocated by different UN conferences, namely the *Brundtland Report*'s definition. Hence, my ultimate aim is to discuss the validity of this definition and criticize its applicability in the light of all the contemporary challenges that this project faces nowadays. The wide spectrum of definitions of the concept of sustainability has resulted in a serious obfuscation entailing many misunderstandings, frictions, and clashes between different schools of thought in political, economic, and developmental studies. The confusion and misinterpretations resulting from many discipline-biased definitions have, in fact, been lingering ever since this concept came into being.

The Inception and Evolution of the Sustainability Discourse

With the maturing and expansion of the environmental movement, the concept of sustainability has gradually become the backbone of this movement's approach to ecological and developmental concerns (Caradonna, 2016; Robertson, 2014). When conceptualizing sustainability, however, I believe it is essential to point out that the different disciplines and conflicting perspectives underlying this concept have resulted in a large number of definitions. In economics, which is one important part of environment-development studies, for example, human beings are seen as rational self-interested individuals working to ensure their material well-being whereas nature is considered as an instrument to achieve this well-being. Definitions from this discipline, therefore, tend to place human beings as the core and nature as the periphery. By contrast, in ecology, which is also an integral part of environment-development studies, human beings are regarded as one species, among many others, that make integral parts of nature. In the literature, this duality is referred to as the "ecocentrism-technocentrism" divide (Elliott, 2000; Bakari, 2017).

Before discussing the different definitions given to sustainable development, I would like first to reflectively examine the particular social, political, and environmental circumstances in which this concept was forged, and the array of problems and challenges it addresses. To begin with, the discourse on sustainable development dates back to 1974 when the concept of a "sustainable society" was discussed at the Conference on Science and Technology for Human Development convened by the World Council of Churches[20] in Bucharest, from June 24 to July 2 (Dresner, 2002). At this conference, scientists, environmentalists, and politicians highlighted the importance of many factors deemed vital for a sound model of development such as the equitable distribution of scarce resources, an opportunity for all to participate in social decisions, the need for limiting the emission of pollutants, and the sound use of technological innovation in order to conserve non-renewable resources. The first mention of the concept of sustainability at this conference gave priority to social needs for equity, democracy, and the alleviation of poverty before even speaking about environmental issues.

This concern for social equity and human development has gradually shaped the core of sustainable development as a paradigm of growth in the endless process of defining this project whether in the development discourse literature or at conferences of IGOs such as UN conferences and NGOs. This approach to a sustainable society struck a chord with a large proportion of scholars and activists precisely because it tackled the South's concerns with development, poverty, and social equity on an equal footing with the North's concerns with the environmental and ecological conservation. Spotlighting the notion of sustainable society, Simon Dresner writes:

> Like the United Nations, the World Council of Churches was very much influenced by the developing world. Many developing world clergymen thought that the environment was a distraction from justice and development. They saw environmentalism as a "bourgeois" concern. The idea of a sustainable society—one that would not self-destruct—sounded more serious and also had less tension with the concern for justice. (Dresner 2002, p. 30)

Few years later, the term "sustainable development" started to spread in public debates starting from 1980 when it was mentioned in a document entitled *World Conservation Strategy* published by the International Union for the Conservation of Nature and Natural Resources (IUCN).[21] This document stressed the necessity of achieving a new model of development through the conservation of natural resources and promoting ecological sustainability. Critics (e.g., Baker, 2006), however, point out that the focus of this report was largely limited to pure ecological concerns without linking sustainability to wider social and economic issues. Seven years later, the concept of sustainable development gained momentum as the World Commission on Environment and Development (WCED) accentuated the links between the social, economic and ecological dimensions of development in its famous report, *Our Common Future*, which gained widespread popularity. Taking its label from WCED chairman Gro Harlem Brundtland, then Norwegian prime minister, this report is widely referred to as the *Brundtland Report*. In this document, the participants stated their vision of the new model of development as follows: "We came to see it [i.e., development] not in its restricted context of economic growth in developing countries. We came to see that a new development path was required, one that sustained human progress not just in a few places for a few years, but for the entire planet into the distant future" (WCED, 1987, p. 8).

Combining the two concepts of "development" and "environment" that had been studied and examined separately for decades, the *Brundtland Report* signaled the beginning of the sustainability discourse in the last few decades of the twentieth century. In this report, sustainable development is defined as "development that meets the needs of the present without compromising the ability of future generations to meet their own needs" (WCED, 1987, p. 43). According to many critics (e.g., Portney, 2015; Baker, 2006; McNeill, 2000; Schrijver, 2008), this definition has become the most widely used definition of sustainable development and gained authoritative status as it was adopted by many UN organizations, IGOs, NGOs, and international financial organizations such as the World Bank. Nico Schrijver (2008) further asserts that the concept of sustainable development has become a prominent issue in international law concerning global ecological problems, natural resources, energy, health, international trade, and security. Other critics (e.g., Dresner, 2002) contend, however, that the vision underpinning this definition of sustainable development in *Our Common Future* echoes much of what was advocated by the World Council of Churches especially regarding a new concern for a combination of the development and environmental concerns.

According to the *Brundtland Report*, sustainable development stands for a "new development path [. . .] that sustain[s] human progress not just in a few places for a few years, but for the entire planet into the distant future" (WCED, 1987, p. 4). As such, this concept seems to have encapsulated some of the values and ethics that have been popularized by the NSMs since the 1970s. However, sustainable development soon became one of the most controversial concepts in the closing decades of the twentieth century. In her book, *An Introduction to Sustainable Development*, Jennifer A. Elliot argues that there are more than seventy definitions of sustainable development currently in circulation (2000, p. 6). These different definitions are certainly the outcome of different interpretations and perceptions of how economic growth and the protection of the environment can be combined in one model of development.

By the late 1990s, the term sustainable development gained currency in global politics and academic arenas, engendering endless debates among scholars and politicians who tried to conceptualize this new model of human growth (Robertson, 2014). As a new concept, sustainability exposes and tackles weaknesses of the current political, economic, and social systems, especially in the industrialized countries. Politically, it aims at securing effective bottom-up citizen participation in decision-making, while it tries, at the same time, to build an economic system that avoids tensions arising from unbalanced modes of growth at the expense of the environment and social issues (WCED, 1987, p. 65). Socially, it aims at achieving both "inter-generational" and "intra-generational" social equity by securing a decent and environment-friendly way of life for different segments of society, ethnic minorities, and races in the same society and between different generations. The discourse on sustainable development has also generated a paradigm shift from what is usually considered as "nationally demarcated environmental problems" over which the state would usually have control to the idea of a global environmental and developmental crisis that can be managed only at a global scale (Hettne, 2008, p. xvi).

The discourse of sustainable development has gone through different phases that marked its maturity after the 1987 *Brundtland Report*. In the beginning of the new millennium, the meaning and scope of sustainability developed and expanded to include more social, cultural, and economic concerns which enriched the essence of this emerging concept. In September 2015, for instance, world leaders attended a special summit at the United Nations in New York to adopt Agenda 2030, which entails a set of 17 Sustainable Development Goals (or SDGs). As a matter of fact, this set of goals succeeds the eight Millennium Development Goals (MDGs),[22] which were forged in 2000, agreed upon by governments in

2001, and were due to expire at the end of 2015. Officially, the SDGs were declared in paragraph 54 United Nations Resolution A/RES/70/1 of 25 September 2015 (Dodds, Donoghue, & Roesch, 2016). Applicable to all countries, these goals constitute a holistic framework, aiming to eradicate poverty and deprivation, grow economies, protect environment, and promote peace and good governance. As such, the SDGs stand for a universal set of goals, targets, and indicators that UN member states will be expected to use to frame their agendas and political policies over the next fifteen years.

Unlike the MDGs, which were drafted by a group of experts behind closed doors in the UN headquarters, the SDGs came as the fruit of the largest UN consultation program in its history to gauge opinion on what sustainability should include. In essence, establishing these post-2015 goals was an outcome of the Rio+20 summit in 2012, which mandated the creation of an open working group to come up with a draft agenda. With representatives from seventy countries, this open working group had its first meeting in March 2013 and published its final draft, with its seventeen suggestions, in July 2014, and then was presented to the UN general assembly. Member state negotiations followed, and the final wording of the goals and targets, and the preamble and declaration that comes with them, were agreed upon in August 2015. Alongside the open working group discussions, the UN launched a series of "global conversations," which entailed eleven thematic and eighty-three national consultations, and door-to-door surveys. The UN also conducted an online "My World survey" asking people to prioritize the areas they would like to see addressed in the goals. The results of the consultations were fed into the working group's discussions (Dodds, Donoghue, & Roesch, 2016).

Though regarded by some scholars such as Ann Dale (2001) and Neil Carter (2007) as a sign of the richness of literature on sustainability, the proliferation of definitions of such a recent concept is considered by many other critics (e.g., Portney, 2015; Blewitt, 2008; Robinson, 2004) as an indication of its vagueness. This vagueness has indeed caused sustainable development to become one of the most contested concepts over the recent years as I will demonstrate in the following section. While asserting that "the idea of sustainable development is fraught with contradictions," Michael Redclift admits that "like motherhood, and God, it is difficult not to approve of it" (1993, p. 3). Still, other critics such as Desmond McNeill contend that "the term sustainable development is only two-thirds complete, for the social dimension is not explicitly included" (2000, p. 117). As a normative concept, sustainability subsumes an unmistakable notion of fairness of access to basic natural resources and an equal right to decent living standards not only for all segments of society, but also for generations living now and those yet to come. Despite its wide popularity among scholars, economists, and environmentalists, the concept of sustainability seems to be excessively open to various, sometimes conflicting, interpretations. In addition, this concept has become part and parcel of a bigger debate about development and growth which is laden with numerous controversies. The vagueness of the concept of sustainable development is, therefore, in part a reflection of the controversy over the meaning of the broad notion of development and the best way to achieve it.

One of the most fertile sources of reflection for researchers today is the question of how far the objectives of sustainable development can be achieved within the prevailing socio-economic paradigm of development. Despite its worldwide popularity, the concept of sustainability has been received with a lot of skepticism and suspicion ever since its inception. This skepticism has come from environmentalists, politicians, and economists alike. Suspicions have intensified even more when the concept was widely accepted and popularized among politicians and was taken up as a slogan by many governments and NGOs during the last few decades. Many criticisms have been voiced in the literature about the hidden agenda behind the project of sustainable development. Allan Holland points out, for instance, that "development and growth, which are creatures of the market economy, are being offered, under the banner of sustainable development, as a cure for the very ecological crisis that they have served to bring about" (2000, p. 3). Sharing the same view, Susan Baker pointedly argues that "the discourse on sustainable development is seen to share characteristics of colonizing discourse, becoming another example of a Western style for dominating, restructuring, and having authority over the Third World" (2006, p. 160). As a matter of fact, many scholars (e.g., Carter, 2007; Dobson, 2016; Baker, 2006; Connelly & Smith, 1999) voice also their suspicion that while sustainable development appears to be imposing constraints on business and industrial sector, it, in fact, covers for and even supports more industrial growth.

Globally, the debate on sustainable development has been a fertile ground for mutual suspicion between the North and the South. On the one hand, the South denounces Northern sustainability strategies as intentional constraints designed to hinder their economic growth and make them pay for an "environmental" bill that they hardly benefited from (Baker, 2006; Elliott, 2000). Decision-makers in the North, on the other hand, argue that sustainable development strategies in the South are not strict enough to stop environmental degradation and alleviate global environmental problems (Chasek, Downie, & Brown, 2010; Leff, 2000). Though this issue was a focal point of discussion at the Conference on Environment and Development held in Stockholm in 1972 and the Earth Summit at Rio de Janeiro in 1992, very little improvement has been achieved so far. Even diplomats who had first-hand experience in the negotiations about reaching a definition of sustainable development admit that they "had doubts and misgivings about the concept of sustainable development," which "seemed more of a convenient political slogan than a basis for real action" (Kjellén, 2008, p. 4).

For the most part, sustainable development has triggered numerous heated debates about its essence and validity within the contemporary socio-economic paradigm of development. Some scholars (e.g., Dresner, 2002; Redclift, 1993), for example, liken it to universal concepts such as "liberty" or "justice" that would never cease to be the hot topic of political, cultural, and philosophical discussions. In his book, *The Green Economy,* Michael Jacobs also argues that like liberty, social justice, and democracy, sustainable development is one of the "contestable concepts" that "have basic meanings and almost everyone is in favour of them, but deep conflicts remain about how they should be understood and what they imply for policy" (1991, p. 60). This perspective is equally shared by Allan Holland, who highlights the controversial nature of this concept, pointing out that "there is a conflict at its core [. . .] that explains its contested status" (2000, p. 9). On the other hand, some other critics assert that: "There is no simple, single path to, or formula for, sustainable development. Each development must be considered in the light of the prevailing social, economic, physical and, sometimes, political environment" (Hulse, 2007, p. xv). Ultimately, Joseph Hulse asserts that sustainable development must be conceived of more as "a process of change" than as "a fixed state of harmony" (2007, p. 12).

By and large, the very essence of the concept of sustainability contributes significantly to the contested status that has become one of its prominent characteristic features. The inner conflict of sustainable development manifests itself twofold: It is a conflict between ensuring the human welfare through continuous economic growth and conserving the environment, and it is also a conflict between meeting the needs of present generations and preserving enough resources for future generations, too. At a larger scale, it is a conflict between the local and the global aspects of governance. Some observers point out that "economists have been at pains to make sense of the elusive condition for sustainability," arguing that "various interpretations of this definition have consequently emerged, differing along the disciplinary lines of ecology, economics, philosophy and others" (Ikeme, 2000). This inner conflict mirrors also some wider conflicts about the meaning of contemporary concepts such as "development" and "growth" and on what basis they can be defined. This issue will duly be discussed in later sections.

On the whole, the inner conflicts of this emerging project have had such far-reaching consequences that cast their shadow on the evolution of sustainable development and its interaction with other phenomena such as globalization and changes in global politics. What underlies these inner conflicts is the contradiction between different disciplines that inform the discourse on sustainability, which resulted in a noticeable proliferation of definitions of this concept. However, neither the purpose nor the scope of this book allows me to examine all the numerous and conflicting definitions given to sustainable development. I will, therefore, limit myself to examining one definition that has achieved an "authoritative status" in development studies and political forums, namely what came to be known as the Brundtland definition of sustainable development.

An Overview and a Critique of the Brundtland Formulation of Sustainability

The publication of the WCED report, *Our Common Future,* in 1987 signaled a very important juncture in the evolution of the project of sustainable development. Thanks to this report, the links between the environment on the one hand, and the social, economic, and ecological dimensions of development on the other were officially addressed and debated at a global scale. Not only did the Brundtland formulation of the concept of sustainability popularize this alternative paradigm for development, but it also gave it a new global dimension. Categorically, the *Brundtland Report* summed up many aspects of sustainable development in one succinct definition that has achieved authoritative status. My primary aim in this section is twofold: First, I want to spotlight the different aspects of this definition and examine the validity of the authoritative status it has achieved; and secondly, I want to contextualize this definition within the overall formulation of this concept in the WCED document.

Defining sustainable development as a "development that meets the needs of the present without compromising the ability of future generations to meet their own needs" (WCED, 1987, p. 43), the *Brundtland Report* clearly articulates the integral link between the needs of people today and those of future generations. This link constitutes, in essence, a very important characteristic feature of this new concept that seeks to ensure "inter-generational" equity. As for today's generation, this report states that sustainability "contains within it two key concepts: the concept of 'needs,' in particular the essential needs of the world's poor, to which priority should be given; and the idea of limitations imposed by the state of technology and social organization on the environment's ability to meet present and future needs" (WCED, 1987, p. 43). Implicit in this formulation of this concept is the notion that industrialized countries consume excessively much more than their needs. Priority in development is then given to poor communities so that a minimum of well-being is ensured for these disadvantaged people.

With its high emphasis on the capacity of humankind to act collectively to preserve the environment and reach an ecologically sustainable form of development, the Brundtland version of sustainable development can be considered an optimistic view. It is optimistic with regard to its strong hope that the ability of modern technologies can reverse the damage done to the environment and come up with new ways of achieving an environment-friendly economic growth. However, what the Brundtland vision advocates is more than just achieving economic growth and protecting the environment. In essence, this approach also calls for social and cultural changes that can lead to a fundamental change in the predominant lifestyle in the industrialized countries. Ultimately, this vision advocates a kind of holistic approach to development that basically meets human beings' different material and psychological needs, stressing that "sustainable development is a process of change in which the exploitation of resources, the direction of investment, the orientation of technological development, and institutional change are all in harmony and enhance both current and future potential to meet human needs and aspirations" (WCED, 1987, p. 46).

For the most part, the *Brundtland Report*'s formulation of sustainable development implicitly challenges the conventional understanding of growth and asserts the right of the developing countries to follow an environment-friendly path of development. Embracing such a different approach to growth, the report articulates that "growth must be revived in developing countries because that is where the links between economic growth, the alleviation of poverty, and environmental conditions operate most directly" (WCED, 1987, p. 51). Optimistic as it is, the Brundtland formulation of the concept of sustainable development duly highlights the ecological limits to growth and stresses the necessity "to adopt lifestyles within the planet's ecological means" (WCED, 1987, p. 9), thus making of the preservation of a balanced ecosystem a bottom line that should not be exceeded. By and large, the environment in this approach is seen as a "natural capital" vital for human survival and development.

Politically, the *Brundtland Report* goes beyond just addressing causes of unsustainable modes of development and advocates a number of strategies aimed at making patterns of mass consumption and production compatible with sustainability. According to this document, the project of sustainable development aims essentially at creating a political consensus that encourages concerted international efforts to implement sustainable development at the national, regional, and the global levels. By doing so, WCED states that the establishment of a political framework in which a potential integration between environmental concerns and developmental strategies into a new development paradigm is not only possible but urgently needed (1987, p. 65).

At the economic level, this new paradigm seeks basically to refute the perception that the protection of the environment can be ensured only at the expense of economic growth and development in general. By and large, the *Brundtland Report* advocates a new paradigm that provides important guidelines for development such as the necessity to change the current model of growth, making it less energy intensive and more socially equitable, not to mention the necessity to harmonize environmental and economic considerations in decision making. While it urges curbing population growth to sustainable levels commensurate with available resources, this report stresses the idea of dealing with demographic problems in a context of poverty elimination and enhanced standards of living (WCED, 1987, p. 65). When it comes to industry, this paradigm aims at "producing more with less" through the promotion of "green industry" and "ecological modernization" in the economy. According to WCED, the industrial sector in general—and TNCs in particular—are to assume full responsibility for environmental protection and clean-up, the promotion of better working conditions, and a more equitable distribution of income (WCED, 1987, pp. 20–21). As a matter of fact, this document presents solutions for ensuring food security by supporting subsistence farmers and addressing inequality in access to food, while reducing agricultural subsidies and protection in the North. It also highlights maintaining biodiversity for moral, cultural, and scientific reasons in order to conserve the natural resources base. As for energy issues, sustainable development aims at ensuring economic growth in a less energy-intensive way by developing alternative "green" energy systems. Furthermore, this new paradigm of development addresses the challenge of urban growth and advocates developing settlement strategies to guide urbanization and provide adequate social services (WCED, 1987, p. 46).

In the light of this brief reading of the WCED vision of sustainable development, I would like to pinpoint a number of factors that helped promote the Brundtland formulation of this project as a dominant, authoritative vision both in the literature as well as among international institutions such as the UN and global summits. First of all, the Brundtland formulation of sustainable development has for the first time, at least officially, bridged the gap between two different, often conflicting concerns, that is, development and the environment. The Brundtland vision popularized this reconciliation between the environmental concerns and developmental issues on an unprecedented global scale. As a matter of fact, the combination of environmental and developmental concerns came at a critical time when the issue of environmental degradation was increasingly gaining momentum in the global political agenda. As such, the *Brundtland Report* claims to offer an alternative model of growth at a time of growing concern about the insufficiency of the contemporary state's institutions and policies to deal with the new kinds of global environmental problems. Critics point out that one main strength of this report is that it not only helped popularize a new model of development that criticizes and diverges from the conventional model of development, but also presented it "in the right place at the right time" (Dresner, 2002, p. 36). Given the novelty of WCED approach, I strongly believe that this report is a landmark in the evolution of this project. Underlining this important role of promoting sustainable development as a global project, Susan Baker argues that "the Brundtland reconceptualization of the environmental problematic, from how best to manage pollution to how to promote sustainable development, contributed to the increased need for new arrangements for global environment management" (2006, p. 52).

Born out of conflicting concerns about development and the environment, the WCED formulation of sustainable development is widely considered as the official birth date of this new project. This new comprehensive and unorthodox approach to development and environment has achieved an authoritative status because of its novelty. Despite achieving such an outstanding, authoritative status in international politics and global development debates, the Brundtland model of sustainability can be criticized for different weaknesses and ambiguities. These weaknesses range from the very ambiguous wording of the definition that came in the WCED to the grotesque mismatch between what the definition conveys and what is really happening in the current model of growth. The following section conveys much of the critique of this formulation.

In my critique of the UN formulation of sustainable development, I find it essential to dwell on the three major themes that this vision is based upon. The first major theme in this report is the necessity to achieve sustainability through more economic growth; the second one is that the limits to economic growth are rather relative, not absolute, as humans can always rely on science and technology both to make economic growth possible indefinitely and to prevent or reverse any inherent environmental damage that happens; and the third theme is the belief that more social equity and poverty alleviation can be achieved through more economic growth. My ultimate aim in this critique, therefore, is to examine the solidity of this approach as a foundation for sustainability and its impact on its evolution.

To begin with, the WCED vision of sustainable development can be criticized for its huge focus on economic growth as one of its primary goals. Although the *Brundtland Report* emphasizes "the possibility for a new era of economic growth, one that must be based on policies that sustain and expand the environmental resource base" (WCED, 1987, p. 1), it seems to uphold such an instrumental vision of nature when dealing with developmental issues. For instance, throughout its formulation of the concept of sustainable development, this document barely attaches value to nature per se, but rather considers it as an instrument that can be used to achieve human development and boost economic growth. For many critics (e.g., Dobson, 2000; Lee, 2000; Dresner, 2002), sustainability as promoted by WCED is not very different in its approach to nature from the conventional capitalist model of growth, for both of them use nature instrumentally to achieve human welfare. Keekok Lee (2000), for instance, draws attention to the common preoccupation of the *Brundtland Report* and the current paradigm of growth with material development, highlighting that these two models are unreservedly "human-centered" and for all intents and purposes are devoted to managing nature to achieve human well-being.

Underpinning the Brundtland sustainability formulation, the rather instrumental use of nature to serve human needs—widely referred to as the "anthropocentric" perspective in the literature—has had a far-reaching impact on both the credibility of this new project and the potential for its success in the future. In fact, the *Brundtland Report* puts it quite overtly that protecting nature is important simply because nature endows humans with the valuable potential resources necessary for economic growth. This view is particularly conspicuous in the report's focus on the primacy of economic growth rather than on the protection of nature, stating, for example, that "the loss of species and subspecies, many as yet unstudied by science, deprives us of important potential sources of medicines and industrial chemicals" (WCED, 1987, p. 35). Andrew Dobson further contends that this instrumental approach is inextricably related to the focus on economic growth as both desirable and necessary for all countries, constituting one major pillar in the Brundtland vision of sustainable development (2000, p. 55).

The second major theme I find particularly relevant to the critique of the formulation of the concept of sustainability in the *Brundtland Report* is the belief that the limits to economic growth are relative rather than absolute (WCED, 1987, pp. 8–10). Although the report admits that "ecological limits" to current patterns of economic growth do exist, it clearly urges for a more effective use of science and technology not only to stop and reverse environmental damages, but also to find substitutes for depleted natural resources in order to ensure a continuous economic growth (WCED, 1987, pp. 44–45). The report, however, fails to address some important issues such as the rising scientific uncertainties as to how to stop and reverse environmental damage and the lingering problem of technology transfer from the developed to the developing countries.

The *Brundtland Report* also fails to take on board the time and space limits of applying such technological solutions to global environmental problems such as ozone layer depletion or biodiversity loss, which ultimately compromised its applicability at the local, regional, and global scales. Within this context, the report can also be criticized for falling short of clear-cut, feasible targets to be met in the future. The text of the report itself does not set definite targets for the protection of nature and the maintenance of the natural recourses base, which implies that this document did not attach enough importance to the issue of the implementation of any measures to conserve or protect nature, scarce as they are. "If part of the project of sustainable development is the maintenance of biodiversity, and if, even in the absence of specific targets, we can say that, overall, biodiversity has been in decline," argues Andrew Dobson, "then we seem entitled to conclude that sustainable development is failing in this particular objective" (2000, p. 50). This imprecision in defining clear steps as to how to protect nature has had a negative impact on the solidity of this emerging project especially among hardliner environmentalists.

The third theme in this critique is the WCED report's presumption that social equity and the alleviation of poverty can be promoted through more economic growth while at the same time it warns the developing countries against replicating the Western model of economic growth. On the one hand, the *Brundtland Report* states clearly that growth has to be boosted in developing countries to alleviate poverty and safeguard the environment (WCED, 1987, p. 51), but it pointedly warns the South that "the simple duplication in the developing world of industrial countries' energy use patterns is neither feasible nor desirable," on the other (WCED, 1987, p. 59). Thus, the Brundtland vision of sustainable development model implies that people in the industrialized North can still enjoy their affluent lifestyles with minor changes to care for the environment whereas people in the South are not entitled to the same degree of affluence and industrialization to avoid causing the same environmental damage that the North had caused. The developing countries, therefore, have to follow another path of development that is still lacking any feasible strategy of implementation, and exists only in embryonic form in the WCED document.

The report's vision of the type of growth required in the South exposes, in my opinion, an even more serious inconsistency. According to this document, affluent nations are required to adapt their lifestyles to fit within the ecological limits of planet Earth, while poor countries are asked to follow a "green" model of economic growth that can only meet their basic needs such as food, shelter, and health, being their "legitimate aspirations for an improved quality of life" (WCED, 1987, p. 43). On the surface, the *Brundtland Report*'s accentuation on meeting these basic needs seems to be a positive step on the side of the South, yet equating the wealthy nations' lifestyles, which have gone way beyond their subsistence needs, with the poor nations' basic needs seems far from fair. By equating the wealthy lifestyles of the North to the basic needs of the South, this approach contributes also to the perpetuation of the current gross inequities between the affluent and the poor nations of the world. Equating the South's basic needs with the North's current lifestyles would also be another factor that corrodes the integrity of sustainable development and stirs up mistrust between the North and the South. This inconsistency, therefore, underlines much of the apprehension and mistrust that the project of sustainable development faces, especially from the South's perspective as the lingering suspicions about the novelty and bias of this new project were further nurtured. "It looks as if the Report endorses the priority of the wants of the affluent over the basic needs of the non-affluent," contends Professor Keekok Lee of Lancaster University (2000, p. 42). Ultimately, this type of inconsistency raises serious questions about the report's genuine understanding of the differences between the concepts of "needs" and "wants" in its now authoritative definition of sustainable development.

The WCED version of sustainability is also vulnerable with regard to the link it establishes between boosting an ongoing economic growth and the alleviation of poverty. A close reading of the formulation of sustainable development in the *Brundtland Report* shows that it sets forth as one of its premises the alleviation of poverty through economic growth whereas it claims that "poverty itself pollutes the environment" and that "those who are poor and hungry will often destroy their immediate environment in order to survive" (WCED, 1987, p. 28). This claim can be called into question in many respects: First, though we cannot deny that poverty might be a direct or an indirect cause of abusing the environment in some cases, especially in the poor developing countries, this description does not apply to the environment-poverty relationship worldwide. For example, linking environmental degradation to poverty is not accurate in many parts of the developed countries where poor people do not have to abuse their environments in order to survive. Thus, the premise that poverty causes environmental degradation is only true in particular parts of the world—mostly in the least developed countries of the South—and under certain conditions where people have no other option but to abuse their local environment to survive.

Scientifically, establishing a strong link between poverty and environmental abuse is still far from certain yet and has not been examined in all its dimensions by researchers to date. Some environmental studies (e.g., Leff, 2000; Redclift, 2000), for instance, provide strong evidence that there exist many extremely poor communities in Africa and Latin America that are maintaining very high standards of sustainability for their local environments and living in complete harmony with nature. In addition, most of the time, it is wealth, not poverty, that causes the direst environmental problems. Some critics (e.g., Dobson, 2000; Baker, 2006; Khor, 2001) further argue that any unbiased study of the poverty-environment relationship will expose the responsibility of the North in this degradation. "Such a study," asserts Andrew Dobson, "would make it clear that many environmental problems are caused by wealthy styles of life rather than poor ones, and this would be a useful political corrective to the handy view (for wealthy Westerners/Northerners) that most of the world's environmental ills are due to the activities of poor people" (2000, p. 53).

Another weakness in the WCED formulation of sustainable development is the relatively cursory and homogeneous approach it adopts in advocating and popularizing this new model of development. With the purpose of building international consensus, the *Brundtland Report* tried to come up with a formulation that would be acceptable to as many politicians, economists, activists, thinkers, and citizens as possible, which resulted in many vital nuances and theoretical differences being sacrificed for the sake of forging the desired international consensus. In his recent book, *A New Diplomacy for Sustainable Development: The Challenge of Global Change*, Bo Kjellén criticizes this rather open-ended definition, putting it as follows: "The sweeping character of the expression meant that efforts of interpreting it more in detail or to make it operative would lead to difficulties. [. . .] Probably any attempt to move beyond Brundtland's definition would raise scientific questions and even ethical and political dilemmas" (2008, p. 4). As a consequence, this discursive formulation of a widely acceptable definition of sustainable development has consolidated the growing suspicions about this new project.

The WCED also fails to take account of the notion that the discourse on sustainable development "cuts across diverse cultural perceptions and divergent economic and social interests" (Leff, 2000, p. 62). Attempts by WCED members to make of sustainable development a consensual concept made their conceptualization seem rather shallow and raised many suspicions. "It is this seeming desire of the Brundtland Commission to tell people they could have everything they wanted and that nobody would have to make sacrifices," argues Simon Dresner, "that explains both its political popularity for squaring a circle and the suspicion it is viewed with by the more sceptical" (2002, p. 36). The unmistakable emphasis on the necessity of continuous economic growth and on the benefits of the free-market economy that characterizes the WCED approach to sustainable development has also made it the subject of suspicions that it is simply a reflection of a Northern hidden agenda. "Although the relationship between debt and poverty was recognized in Agenda 21," some critics argue, "most of the text celebrated the free market; much of the debate and final documentation was based on free-market ideals, [. . .] [which] highlights the continued international domination of the North and Bretton Woods institutions" (Connelly & Smith, 1999, p. 205).

In the light of this critique, I believe that, on several occasions, the Brundtland version of sustainability engages in shallow generalizations that tend to promote the Northern model of economic growth and lifestyles while criticizing Southern poor nations' attempts to achieve development. The report states as a fact the notion that poverty in the South produces environmental degradation and overlooks the situation when the poor have usually no option but to abuse their environment to survive. This double-standard outlook is indicative of two things: First, sustainable development paradigm as formulated by the WCED is meant first and foremost to maintain development in general, and particularly in the North, and not to promote environment protection per se. Secondly, this formulation of sustainable development aims at achieving two disparate goals, namely ecologically accepted yet affluent lifestyles in the North, and subsistence-level livelihoods that barely afford sheer basic needs in the South.

Everything considered, this document has some strengths and weaknesses: For example, this report does acknowledge the South's right to develop with regard to combatting poverty, disease, and impoverishment. It also contains a strong argument for reforming the prevailing structures of existing political and economic systems so as to achieve sustainability. On the other hand, the unmistakable priority given to continuous economic growth over protection of the environment coupled with its unabashed instrumental approach to nature undermines the very basis of this emerging project as a new alternative paradigm for sound human development. Many of the inconsistencies I have pointed out call into question the *Brundtland Report*'s claim that its model of sustainable development is a "global" project. The importance of this critique, in my view, is that it provides an insight into some theoretical contradictions that the project of sustainable development is based upon, and it highlights some features of this project that are widely regarded as a challenge to the contemporary socio-economic paradigm of growth.

Sustainable Development as a Challenge to the Current Socio-economic Paradigm of Development

The new project of sustainable development came as a real challenge to the current paradigm of development that has prevailed in most countries since the Industrial Revolution, and predominated in the post-Cold War years. Not only does sustainable development challenge this conventional model on various levels including economic growth, social equity, and the protection of the environment, but it also questions this model's efficacy in achieving development and its responsiveness to the needs of post-industrial societies. One of the major challenges to environmentalists today is that this new project aims not at reforming the current socio-economic model of development, but rather at establishing a new model that claims to be fully responsive to people's needs within the ecological limits of their natural environment. As I elaborate on the many points that the two paradigms clash over, my aim is primarily to underline the degree of incompatibility of the two models of development and investigate the root causes behind this divergence. I also want to portray the interaction between this new project and the economic and social context that witnessed its inception and evolution.

With the intensification and globalization of environmental problems, the viability of the contemporary model of development has been called into ever more doubt in a post-industrial society whose concerns are no longer limited to material wealth. Sociologist Philip McMichael, for instance, launches a scathing criticism of today's socio-economic development paradigm in the industrialized countries, pointing out that "the consequences of agro-industrialism—landlessness, hyper-urbanization, and environmental deterioration—reveal the shortcomings of the development paradigm's underlying belief in inexorable technological progress" (2007, p. 216). Unlike other development discourses which, to different degrees, identify with the process of development in the industrialized countries and consider it a model for the rest of the world to emulate, a new discourse declares that sustainability, not "hyper-growth," should be "a goal not just for the developing countries, but for industrial ones as well" (WCED, 1987, p. 4).

Globally, the project of sustainable development seeks to achieve a two-fold goal. Firstly, it aims at curbing and reversing the environmental degradation caused by the process of industrialization and economic growth, especially in the North (WCED, 1987, pp. 8–9). Secondly, this project aims at slowing down the South's population growth, which is considered as one of the principal causes of depleting natural resources and slowing any rise in the living standards in developing countries. In addition, this paradigm is based on an important principle that consumption habits and extravagant affluent lifestyles in the rich North are not to be transferred to the entire world (WCED, 1987, pp. 49–50). With regard to the North-South relations, the promotion of sustainable development as a new paradigm of development involves also two main goals: first, the elimination of the barriers to a sustainable mode of development in the South; and secondly, the reduction of the high consumption levels in the industrialized countries (WCED, 1987, pp. 50–51).

Politically, the sustainable development paradigm can be considered as a real challenge to conventional forms of development and theories of modernization that have prevailed for long. Unlike other common single-issue environmental regimes[23] that were formed in the last few decades of the twentieth century, sustainability comes as a comprehensive approach that seriously questions the structure of the global political and economic systems. Critics James Connelly and Graham Smith point out that "the principles and implications of sustainable development can challenge the very structures of the global political and economic systems far more than the environmental regimes developing in response to separate problems" (1999, p. 184). Thus, neoliberal economic approaches that envisage development as speeding up the process of industrialization and economic growth are increasingly being called into question. Precisely, modernization theories that gauge society's development based on the degree of its sophistication in terms of labor specialization, openness of markets, and urbanization rates are now being widely rethought.

Above all, the new discourse of sustainability emerged as a critique of the capitalist development model with its different theories and variants. As such, this discourse aims at exposing what some environmentalists and scholars[24] see as defects of the current Western socio-economic model of growth and point out its dire consequences such as rising unemployment, irreversible environmental degradation, and financial crises in the industrialized countries as well as the ineffective development strategies in the developing countries. Because of all these discrepancies, the project of sustainable development has been considered by some critics as "necessarily radical because it challenges some of our most basic and entrenched ways of seeing, understanding and acting within the world" (Connelly & Smith, 1999, p. 1). Theoretically, the sustainable development model challenges many of the basic assumptions in the predominant socio-economic development paradigm, especially its instrumental use of nature, the way economists define progress and development, and even the political and social mechanisms of how public policy is made and implemented. Reflecting on the conventional vision of development, German scholars Egon Becker and Thomas Jahn contend, for instance, that "until very recently development was largely equated with industrialization, and mean per capita income was regarded as the most important indicator of the degree of development attained by a national economy" (1998, p. 70).

Unlike the holistic vision of development in the sustainability discourse, the current capitalist model of development, environmentalists argue, defines progress in a rather limited way and measures it primarily in terms of more material wealth in society, increased domination over nature, and the subsequent overuse of its resources to provide luxury for humankind. James G. Speth, for instance, contends that domination of nature is seen as a key indicator of human progress in the current model of development (2008, p. 57). Therefore, using more natural resources such as oil, gas, and coal to produce energy, boost patterns of production, and stimulate more consumption is considered a healthy sign, reflecting ongoing progress and economic growth. In the process, however, nature is reduced to nothing more than a necessary resource in a model of development that "values nature only in terms of the use that these resources have for human beings" (Baker, 2006, p. 3). Nature is denied any "intrinsic value" of its own, and it is given only an "instrumental value" proportionate to the degree of its usefulness in meeting human beings' needs.

With rates of environmental degradation going higher constantly, many critics (e.g., Dale, 2001; Robbins, 2009; Blewitt, 2008) deplore the notion that non-human forms of life are either denied separate entity or valued instrumentally as is the case with nature in the current capitalist paradigm of development. In addition, the understanding of the concept of development as primarily reflected in the subjugation of nature and the mastery of science and technology has been the subject of harsh criticism: "Utilitarian materialism underpinned by science and technology will see humankind right," argues Keekok Lee, "but nature, whether as whole plants and animals or as seeds and eggs/sperms—indeed even as segments of DNA—is regarded only as providing actual or potential raw resources to enter into the processes of production" (2000, p. 39). For environmentalists, this instrumental view of nature stands in stark contradiction with the sustainable development discourse that views nature as holding an intrinsic value, and therefore as worthy per se of being preserved rather than as a resource base for human use. An in-depth discussion of the Man-Nature relation in both paradigms will be my focus in later sections.

The debate on the growth-nature relationship has, in fact, flared up in the last few years. On the other hand, environmental degradation is assumed by neoliberal economists and thinkers (e.g., Sagoff, 2000; Bhagwati, 2007) to be an inevitable consequence of development that can be healed by modern technology or accepted as a kind of trade-off between economic growth and a sound environment. Counterbalancing this view is environmentalists' belief that there are certain limits to growth that humans should not ignore. Thus, this project advocates a whole restructuring or a new formulation of developmental strategies so as not to exceed the carrying capacities of planet Earth. Because it rejects the notion of limits to growth, the neoliberal capitalist development model, from an environmentalist viewpoint, is based primarily on an individualistic drive for consumption and promotes an ethic of self-realization at the expense of nature. Actually, consumption is regarded as the most important factor contributing to human welfare, which is usually measured by the standards of living according to "the amount of disposable income that an individual has to purchase goods and services" (Baker, 2006, 3). Other views (e.g., Sachs, 2015; Carter, 2007; Kütting, 2004; Speth, 2008) also point out that, by nourishing the unrelenting drive for economic growth, encouraging more consumption, and celebrating individualistic ethics of material individual achievement, this model serves to erode important social values like communal solidarity and common responsibility in society, thus indirectly increasing social inequality and widening the gap between the haves and the have-nots.

Economic growth and industrialization in the North have also been based in large measure upon exploitation not only of the developed countries' own natural resources but also of those of the developing countries. Some critics (e.g., Dale, 2001; Elliott, 2000; Sachs, 2015) assert that as a result of this energy-intensive mass consumption model of development, developing countries have experienced dire environmental degradation and resource impoverishment as well as economic dependency on the North. Though scientists have confirmed that it is impossible for the Earth's finite natural resource base to survive the wave of intensive exploitation required to replicate today's model of growth, many developing countries are still trying to achieve economic development by following the Western model. Thus, unlike the paradigm of sustainable development, the current model of development cannot be exported to countries seeking industrial growth today, nor can it be reserved for future generations.

The capitalist model of development is also criticized for being blind to the natural limits on economic growth. Many critics (Portney 2015;

Dale, 2001; Edwards, 2008; Speth, 2008; WCED, 1987) point out that the carrying capacity of the planet and the inability of its ecosystem to absorb all the negative effects of intensified human activities pose rigid limits to economic growth today. In fact, many of these critics decry the current capitalist model of development as both exploitative and unsustainable, arguing that "a capitalist society is dependent on the domination of ecosystems and people; constant economic growth; and neglecting the organism-environment relationship" and warning that "capitalism requires the continuation of many unsustainable practices" (Hartmann, 1998, p. 345). Sustainable development, on the other hand, focuses on the collective quality of life of the community as a whole rather than on the standards of living of a privileged segment or the elite in society. Precisely, a sustainable development model attaches great importance to quality of life and social equity not only for the present generation but also for generations to come (WCED, 1987, p. 46).

As the project of sustainable development evolves and the consensus on sustainability broadens, the features of incompatibility between this project and the current neoliberal capitalist model of growth become clearer to observers. This new project represents a challenge to today's dominant model of growth because these two models of development entail radically different approaches to development, society, and nature. Underpinning this divergence is a whole set of ethics associated with the discourse of sustainability that seeks to reverse today's materialist ethics. Within this context, I believe it is essential to hammer home the idea that the advent of sustainable development was largely a result of an increasing philosophical and ethical tension between two visions of the relationship between humans and Nature. This tension is echoed in art, literature, social theories, politics, history and economics. It is a tension between what is referred to as "immanence" and "transcendence"—the tension between the desire to live as an integral part of Nature and the drive to rise above being a part of Nature to being its master.

In the literature on sustainability, the immanence-transcendence tension has often been portrayed as a clash between two frameworks of thought: a clash between ecocentrism which "reflects immanence by basing ethics and politics on a friendly 'nature' that may be assumed to have value in its own right (intrinsic value)" and technocentrism which "reflects transcendence by basing ethics and politics on the virtues of exploiting 'nature' as a resource" (Martin & Huckle, 2001, p. 19). Hence, ecocentrics tend to regard humans as subject to the ecological laws of Nature because they constitute an integral component with the same degree of importance as other components such as animals, insects, rivers, mountains, and so on. On the other hand, regarding Man as the master of Nature, advocates of technocentrism are fully committed to using Nature instrumentally to achieve more human well-being.

The discourse of sustainability has generally been informed by both ecocentrism and technocentrism. Advocates of sustainable development claim that this new project strikes the right balance between economic growth and environmental protection, between using natural resources and preserving Nature, and ultimately between technocentrism and ecocentrism (WCED, 1987). Jennifer Elliott notes that the ecocentrics, who have little faith in technology and progress associated with modern societies, tend to accentuate spirituality and advocate environment-friendly self-sufficiency whereas technocentrics, who have a strong belief in modern science's ability to solve social and environmental problems are fully committed to on-going economic growth and the exploitation of natural resources (2000, pp. 20–21). By and large, these two trends are reflected in the formulation of sustainable development and the tension between them underlies much of the plight of this new paradigm of development in a context on neoliberal capitalism. For other critics, however, "the philosophical and political challenge is not to choose between immanence and transcendence but to balance the two in a political theory that promotes sustainability and the welfare of both human and non-human nature" (Martin & Huckle, 2001, p. 19).

From an environmentalist point of view, the predominant capitalist model of development is considered a major threat to the natural base for future development. The capitalist commitment to economic growth and material advancement, therefore, is no longer an asset in the new paradigm. On the contrary, making economic growth a nation's paramount priority is, in the view of environmentalists, a serious flaw, and even more so if this priority is maintained at the expense of social equity and environmental protection (Moghadam, 2007; Kütting, 2004; Shiva, 2008). Other critics (e.g., Sachs, 2015; Lubchenco, 2003; Thomas, 1992) cite global threats such as biodiversity loss, climate change, depletion of ozone layer, deforestation, and desertification as global threats to planet Earth caused mainly by the unfettered economic growth in the second half of the twentieth century. In fact, the new sustainability discourse not only opposes certain practices of mass production and consumption in capitalism, but it constitutes the absolute antithesis of this model of development. Spotlighting this contradiction, James Connelly and Graham Smith write: "Contemporary capitalism primarily requires governments to protect private capital and to ensure continued economic growth. Under such conditions, environmental considerations will never be given priority where they conflict with capital accumulation. Sustainable development is at odds with the logic of capitalism" (1999, p. 60).

Socially, this new discourse of development deems it futile to think of development in isolation from its ecological and social consequences, as these deteriorating environmental conditions cause serious negative impacts that erode social and political stability in every society. It follows that this new discourse of sustainable development rejects the idea of equating human progress with the domination of Nature, and decries the instrumental use of it for the sake of creating more wealth and material well-being for humans. According to this new discourse, consumption is no longer the most important aspect of human welfare, and unfettered economic growth is no longer the backbone of development as such (Carter, 2007). Ultimately, there is a whole new lifestyle and mode of development being advocated as an alternative to the conventional model of development: "By showing that the model of development pursued by the Western industrial societies cannot be carried into the future, either in its present forms or at its present pace," argues Susan Baker, "environmentalism makes it imperative for society to construct a new development model" (2006, p. 212). This new discourse, therefore, is unorthodox by nature.

In their critique of the capitalist model of development, advocates of sustainable development (e.g., Sachs, 2015; Edwards, 2008; Speth, 2008; Kütting, 2004) also point out that the current socio-economic paradigm of growth overtly celebrates the individualistic drive for more consumption and the ethics of achieving more material well-being. Contrariwise, sustainable development discourse deplores the culture of mass consumption and the individualistic ethics of material self-realization. It aims rather at achieving social solidarity by including all segments of society in the process of development and by attaching great importance to the protection of the environment. Structurally, it is clearly underscored in the Earth Charter that sustainable development adopts a bottom-up process of building a partnership between sectors such as industry, education, services, and governmental environmental management. Revolutionary as such, "the sustainable development model thus challenges conceptions of development that prioritize individual self-advancement" and "holds that the promotion of the common good takes precedence over the encroachment on the commons by the few" (Baker, 2006, p. 213). Because of all these aspects of incompatibility between sustainable development and the current socio-economic paradigm of growth, I firmly believe that the clash between these two paradigms is first and foremost a clash between two conflicting sets of ethics as well as between two mutually exclusive visions of development.

CONCLUSION

Throughout the last few decades, global politics have undergone fundamental changes that have had a profound bearing on the inception and evolution of the project of sustainable development. Some ecological disasters that took place in the United States, Canada, and former Soviet Union and its satellites also triggered a widespread public awareness of the environmental issue and boosted scholarly interest in conceptualizing new alternatives for modes of growth. Globally, the increasing activism of IGOs and NGOs in the last few decades has had a profound effect on the evolution of environmental politics which brought the environmental issue to light. As a result, the environmental issue came to the fore as a high-profile issue on the global political agenda among other issues such as nuclear threats, terrorism, and economic recessions. Besides, the last decades of the twentieth century were fertile ground for the emergence and activism of NSMs that set the stage for a new paradigm of growth to take shape.

With widening new room for international cooperation following the end of the Cold War and the simultaneous emergence of global ecological challenges, environmental politics successfully developed from catering to single-issue environmental regimes to embracing a new holistic paradigm of growth. The many new actors that entered the arena of global politics have, in turn, brought new dimensions to the environmental issue which became intertwined with the notion of development as a whole. Meanwhile, the advent of globalization and the resulting weakening of the nation-state's sovereignty exposed many defects of the current governance system that failed to rise to the contemporary ecological and social challenges. Altogether, these different factors engendered a wide dissatisfaction with the current paradigm of growth in the post-industrial societies, which now eagerly seek an alternative that would heal the excesses of their model of growth.

A set of global networks constituting the GCS has been also a propitious space for the maturation of the concept of sustainable development. This project, which merges economic, social, and environmental concerns in one mode of development, has been widely regarded as an essential alternative to overcome the current developmental and ecological challenges. Thus, dissatisfaction with the materialist ethics of the neoliberal capitalist model of development and the moral void decried by NSMs constituted a significant prelude to the emergence of the project of sustainable development. The meaning of sustainable development, however, has become the subject of continuous heated debates, which resulted in a proliferation of definitions and interpretations of this new project. Amongst this big number of definitions, the WCED definition has been widely considered as the "official" definition of sustainable development.

Despite the authoritative status the Brundtland definition of sustainable development has achieved, it still contains multiple weaknesses and ambiguities. Hence, a critique of this document is essential for gaining insight into the problematic formulation of this concept. Though it succeeded in catching the attention of different political and economic factions, the *Brundtland Report*'s open-ended formulation of sustainability lacks the precision necessary for being applied in practice. The ambiguity that characterizes the Brundtland formulation of this new project casts a dark shadow on the resilience of this emerging project and limits its potential to effect the necessary changes to achieve sustainability.

As a critique of the current socio-economic paradigm of growth, however, the project of sustainable development has been successful in distancing itself from the excesses of today's lifestyles in industrialized countries. In fact, this project holds a radically different vision of the concept of "development" that stands in contrast to the prevailing materialist ethics of the current paradigm of growth. Within the current context, the discourse of sustainable development is basically unorthodox; all the more so because it differs structurally and theoretically from the capitalist paradigm of growth. This new project seems to clash with the prevailing socio-economic mode of development with regard to fundamental concepts such as growth, Man-Nature relationship, and social equity. Despite all its inner contradictions, then, this emerging project seems to have achieved wide popularity as the new option for development that would be constructed on the ruins of the current one.

For the most part, the environmentalists' critique of the capitalist model of development and the formulation of this new sustainable development paradigm are part of a wider re-evaluation of a long process of modernization as a whole. The deeply entrenched belief in reason, science, and Man's mastery of Nature that developed in the Enlightenment era and was consolidated during the unprecedented economic growth in the last half of the twentieth century is being widely called into question. Underpinning this re-evaluation is a growing doubt about the soundness of the current socio-economic model of growth. The formulation of sustainable development as an alternative model of development comes, therefore, as part of a bigger post-modernist posture of self-evaluation or self-critique that the sociologists Ulrich Beck and Anthony Giddens have labeled "reflexive modernization."

NOTES

1. The term "environmental politics" is used in this book to refer to the national and international governmental negotiations, discussions, decisions, treaties, and policies as well as all other sorts of political activism about the environment, especially at the global level through UN conferences such as the Stockholm Conference in 1972, the Rio Conference in 1992, and the UN World Summit for Sustainable Development (WSSD) in 2002 (Dauvergne, 2005, pp. 13–12). Scholars Pamela Chasek, David Downie, and Janet Brown note that "environmental politics include at least two dimensions: the environmental consequences of the economic or other activity in question and the state and non-state actors involved" (2010, p. 15).

2. In the literature of environmental politics, a "regime" is typically defined as a set of "implicit or explicit principles, norms, rules and decision-making procedures around which actors' expectations converge in a given area of international relations" (Krasner, 1983, p. 2). Scholars Chasek, Downie, and Brown define a "regime" as "a set of norms, rules, or decision-making procedures, whether implicit or explicit, that pro-

duces some convergence in the actors' expectations in a particular issue area" (2010, p. 19).

3. According to the 1969 Vienna Convention on the Law of Treaties, a "treaty" is "an international agreement concluded between States in written form and governed by international law" in which states pledge their "consent to be bound" (as cited in Mitchell, 2003, p. 432).

4. For example, Friends of the Earth was founded in 1969, Earth First!, a radical environmental group, was founded in 1971, and the Environmental Protection Agency (EPA), an independent regulatory agency of the federal government, was created by an executive order of President Richard Nixon in 1970 to support research on environmental quality (US Environmental Agency, 2011).

5. Such as the demonstrations that took place on Earth Day on April 22, 1970 when "20 million Americans took to the streets, parks, and auditoriums to demonstrate for a healthy, sustainable environment in massive coast-to-coast rallies" and "thousands of colleges and universities organized protests against the deterioration of the environment" as well as those demonstrations on Earth Day in 1990, "mobilizing 200 million people in 141 countries and lifting environmental issues onto the world stage" (Earth Day Network, 2011). In the 1988, some 50,000 to 100,000 Latvians, Estonians, and Lithuanians protested against pollution of the Aral, Baltic and Black seas in Eastern Europe in addition to huge demonstrations in Russia against the pollution of Lake Baikal, which supplied 80 percent of Soviet freshwater (Thomas, 1992, p. 31).

6. For a thorough overview of the pioneers of environmentalism in America, see Golden, 2000, pp. 54–7; Marinelli, 1991, p. 1–7; Caradonna, 2016, pp. 21–54.

7. Following the North American Conservation Conference, attended by representatives of the United States, Canada, and Mexico, held at the White House in 1909, a declaration of principles was drafted suggesting that all the nations of the world should be invited to meet in a World Conservation Conference. President Theodore Roosevelt addressed to forty-five nations a letter inviting them to assemble at The Hague for such a conference, but the idea was soon abandoned after he left the White House in March 1909 (Chronicles of America, 2014).

8. Statistics conducted on the membership of selected U.S. environmental NGOs show, for instance, that members of Sierra Club rose from 124,000 in 1971 to 615,000 members in 1992, members of National Audubon Society rose from 115,000 in 1971 to 600,000 members in 1992, members of National Parks and Conservation Association rose from 49,000 in 1971 to 230,000 members in 1992, members of Environmental Defense Fund rose from 20,000 in 1971 to 175,000 members in 1992, members of National Wildlife Federation rose from 540,000 in 1971 to 997,000 members in 1992, members of Defenders of Wildlife rose from 13,000 in 1971 to 77,000 members in 1992, and members of Friends of the Earth rose from 7,000 in 1971 to 30,000 members in 1992 (Bosso, 2005, p. 54).

9. Statistics show that in the early 1990s, there were more than 150 national environmental organizations and 12,000 grassroots groups with a total estimated membership of about 14 million members in the US, about 200 national environmental organizations with a total estimated membership of about 5 million members in the UK, and about 900 environmental organizations with total estimated membership of about 3.5 million members in Germany (Carter, 2007, p. 144).

10. Statistics conducted on the electoral performance of selected European "green" parties in the 1990s show that the green parties got 10.9 percent of the vote in the national election in Belgium, 8.9 percent of the vote in the national election in Luxembourg 7.2 percent of the vote in the national election in France, 6.3 percent of the vote in the national election in Germany, and 5.5 percent of the vote in the national election in Switzerland (Carter, 2007, p. 89).

11. Statistics show, for instance, that less than one-third of the surveyed Americans said they trusted the government in Washington, DC, in 1998 whereas 61 percent of the surveyed Americans said they trusted it in 1966 (Peterson, 2002, p. 95).

12. See Kjellén, 2008; Hart, 2009; Robbins, 2009; Kütting, 2004; Sydee & Beder, 2009.

13. Many critics refer to this particular period in modern American history (i.e., the 1950s and the 1960s) as the era of conformity and sameness. This view is thoroughly developed by notable sociologists and thinkers such as David Riesman in *The Lonely Crowd* (1950), William H. Whyte Jr. in *The Organization Man* (1956), and C. Wright Mills in *The Power Elite* (1956).

14. See Speth, 2003, 2008; Khor, 2001A; Eckersley, 1998; Dale, 2001; Blewitt, 2008; Earth Charter Commission, 2012.

15. Studies show, for example, that more than fifty peace-keeping operations were administered by the UN in the post-Cold War years in troubled regions mainly in Africa, Eastern Europe, the Middle-East, and parts of Asia (Yilmaz, 2008, p. 49).

16. In his seminal article "What Is Global Governance?" scholar Lawrence S. Finkelstein defines this term as "governing, without sovereign authority, relationships that transcend national frontiers" and "doing internationally what governments do at home" (369). He explains that global governance entails "diplomacy and politics within and between states, alliances and coalitions of states; international pressure groups of nongovernmental actors [. . .] feedback loops between international, national, and subnational actors; and institutional procedures and methods that channel inputs and determine their efficacy" (1995, pp. 368–69).

17. IMF statistics show that many developing countries (including Argentina, Bangladesh, Bolivia, Botswana, Brazil, Cameroon, Chile, Colombia, Costa Rica, Cyprus, Dominican Republic, Ecuador, Egypt Arab Rep., El Salvador, Fiji, Ghana, Greece, Guatemala, Guyana, Honduras, India, Indonesia, Iran, Israel, Jordan, Kenya, Korea Rep., Kuwait, Liberia, Malawi, Malaysia, Mali, Mauritius, Mexico, Morocco, Nepal, Nicaragua, Pakistan, Panama, Paraguay, Philippines, Singapore, Sri Lanka, Syria, Tanzania, Thailand, Trinidad and Tobago, Tunisia, Turkey, Uruguay, Venezuela, and Zimbabwe) spent an average of 3.2 percent of their GDP on welfare services in 1972–74 compared to only 2.5 percent of their GDP in 1994–95 (as cited in Rudra, 2002, p. 412).

18. In the literature, a New Social Movement (NSM) is defined as "a loose-knit organization that seeks to influence public policy on an issue such as the environment, nuclear energy or peace, and which may use unconventional forms of political participation, including direct action, to achieve its aims" (Carter, 2007, p. 84).

19. According to critics, the speech of George W. Bush at the 1992 Rio Conference was, for instance, very shocking and revealed how unwilling many Western leaders were to sacrifice the affluent lifestyles in the industrialized countries and live sustainably. They particularly point to Bush's assertion that "the American way of life is not negotiable" and that "growth is the engine of change and a friend of the environment" as an evident signal of this unwillingness to change (as cited in Vidal, 2012).

20. In their website, this organization defines itself as "a worldwide fellowship of 349 churches seeking unity, a common witness and Christian service" (World Council of Churches, 2012).

21. Established in 1948 in France, the IUCN (Union Internationale pour la Conservation de la Nature) is the world's oldest global environmental network which has more than 1,000 member organizations including more than eighty states, more than 110 government agencies, and more than 800 non-governmental organizations (NGOs).

22. The eight MDGs—reduce poverty and hunger; achieve universal education; promote gender equality; reduce child and maternal deaths; combat HIV, malaria and other diseases; ensure environmental sustainability; develop global partnerships—failed to consider the root causes of poverty and overlooked gender inequality as well as the holistic nature of development. The goals made no mention of human rights and did not specifically address economic development. While the MDGs, in theory, applied to all countries, in reality they were considered targets for poor countries to achieve, with finance from wealthy states. Conversely, every country will be expected to work toward achieving the SDGs.

23. Examples of single-issue regimes (which are environmental treaties about a single ecological issue) include the United Nations Convention on the Law of the Sea (UNCLOS) Convention, Montego Bay, 1982; the Basel Convention on the Control of Transboundary Movements of Hazardous Wastes and their Disposal, Basel, 1989; the Convention on Biological Diversity (CBD), Nairobi, 1992; the Montreal Protocol on Substances That Deplete the Ozone Layer, Montreal, 1989; and the Convention on Nuclear Safety, Vienna, 1994, among many others whose main aim was to protect the environment but were mainly limited to one major issue.

24. See Dale, 2001; Dobson, 2000; Hawken, 1997, 2001; Hart, 2009; Khor, 2001a; Korten, 2006; Speth, 2008; Yeh, 1989.

TWO

Sustainable Development in a Context of Globalization

Incompatible Paradigms

One of the greatest controversies facing economists, thinkers, researchers, and world leaders in the twenty-first century is how to make sense out of two global multi-dimensional phenomena ushering the world into the new millennium, namely sustainable development and globalization. This issue is academically perplexing essentially because the two phenomena seem to have many characteristics in common, but are in essence almost mutually exclusive and based on two conflicting theories of development. Within this framework, my aim in this chapter is manifold: first, I want to demonstrate that the classical theories of development that have guided human growth for centuries are in fact incapable of dealing with the environmental issue as they were developed at a time when the environment was not such an important issue for consideration. Second, it is my aim to examine how this ineffectiveness in dealing with the environmental challenges has characterized the predominant paradigm of growth to date, namely neoliberal capitalism. Ultimately, I want to investigate to what extent this lingering mismatch between the current paradigm of growth and pressing environmental concerns has manifested itself in an intensifying clash between the two emerging projects of globalization and sustainable development.

Before I highlight the different areas that sustainability and globalization clash over, I believe it is essential to identify some recurrent concepts such as "development," "growth," and "globalization." I also find it very important to point out that these new emerging development paradigms share some important structural characteristics that might ease the clash between them if they receive enough academic and scientific attention. However, at this stage, my overall aim remains fundamentally to discuss the different aspects of the clash between globalization and sustainable development and envisage any chances of survival that the latter has in a context of a globalized economy.

THEORIES OF DEVELOPMENT: THE SEEDS OF THE CLASH

Globalization has brought about different changes as well as challenges to current cultural and intellectual debates. As such, the phenomenon of globalization stands out as one of the biggest challenges thus far to sustainable development that is still struggling in a global context overwhelmingly predominated by the liberal capitalist model of growth. To understand the major startling contrasts and rapid changes that globalization has brought about, it is essential, in my view, to examine earlier major economic changes associated with the era of industrialization onwards. To achieve this goal, I am going to touch upon the writings of eighteenth and nineteenth centuries' theorists who studied and analyzed the political, economic, scientific, and social changes of their epoch that served as a solid foundation for their theorizing about development. In the following section, I am going to deal briefly with pioneer theorists such as Adam Smith (1723–90), Karl Marx (1818–83), Friedrich Engels (1820–95), Max Weber (1864–1920), and Walt W. Rostow (1916–2003), who introduced theories of development, that have formed the bedrock of many contemporary development studies to date.

The discussion of the incompatibility between sustainable development and the current socio-economic development paradigm has many far-reaching implications. However, before I delve into such a discussion, I think it is necessary to launch a theoretical and conceptual exploration of related concepts such as development, growth, and globalization, for they constitute some of the most important elements in the clash between sustainable development and the current model of development. In the theoretical exploration of these concepts, I want also to highlight the interdisciplinary feature that characterizes sustainable development as a research area. Indeed, dealing with two major phenomena such as sustainability and globalization would inevitably entail the exploration of many related areas in economics, history, philosophy, social science, political science, and some other relevant fields.

Defining Development: Classical Theories of Development and the Prevalent Notion of Growth

As with most human concepts, the notion of "development" is elusive, open-ended, and controversial. For the last few centuries, theorists, philosophers, and economists have been at pains to formulate a comprehensive definition of what the term development means. As political, economic, social, and cultural perceptions are constantly changing, some new unpredictable variables appear in the equation of development in every phase of history. For some scholars, defining development is rather problematic, for it is inextricably linked to the context where it takes place, and therefore "there can be no fixed and final definition of development; only suggestions of what it should imply in particular contexts" (Hettne, 1994, p. 27). Stressing the importance of the historical context as to when and where the concept of development is defined, Björn Hettne writes: "Development has meant different things in different discourses. Development is still, to my mind, part of the unfulfilled modern project, defined as critical, reflexive, and potentially universal" (1994, p. 27). This notion of development as an "unfulfilled modern project" is echoed in various other writings in development studies such as in Philip McMichael (2017), Jennifer Elliott (2000), and Samuel Huntington (2007).

Other theorists, however, believe that it is possible to define development. In their book, *Theories of Development*, Richard Peet and Elaine Hartwick, for instance, depict their view of development in the following terms: "Development is a founding belief of the modern world. Progress has long since replaced God as the icon of our age. In development, all the modern advances in science, technology, democracy, values, ethics, and social organization fuse into the single humanitarian project of producing a far better world" (1999, p. 1). In fact, this view very much reflects the wider vision of development which is based on the Enlightenment notions promoting the use of modern science and the supremacy of the human mind that brings about the liberation of humankind in two respects: "liberation from the vicissitudes of nature through advanced technology, and self-emancipation, that is, control over social relations, conscious control over the conditions under which human nature is formed" (Peet & Hartwick, 1999, p. 1). According to this view, development can be understood as the most effective way to fulfill human aspirations and satisfy people's needs.

Over the last half of the twentieth century, the capitalist model of economic growth and the application of modern science were prioritized as a successful model for attaining prosperity and as an example for the rest of the world to emulate (Baker, 2006; Elliott, 2000). UN economists and experts, for example, argued that some of the development problems of the developing countries would be solved through a global transfer of technology and open market policies from the North to the South (Elliott, 2000). Commenting on this frenetic zeal for economic growth, Richard H. Robbins puts it as follows:

> In fact, failure to grow can bring our entire economic edifice and the society it supports crashing down around us. To ensure this does not

> occur, we have evolved an economic and cultural strategy designed to encourage and, in many ways, guarantee a flourishing economy. This strategy goes by various terms including "liberalism," "neoliberalism," or "market capitalism." It represents also what is loosely termed 'globalization.' (2009, p. 1)

However, this zeal to follow the Western development model was soon challenged by a number of theorists and think-tanks (e.g., dependency theorists) who argued that both the Western definition of, and strategy for, development are faulty because they focus solely on economic growth at the expense of other social, intellectual, and environmental issues (Fotopoulos, 1997). Other views contend that "the sustainable development model is a challenge to the conventional form of development [which] [. . .] sees development as simply modernization of the globe along Western lines" (Baker, 2006, p. 1). Highlighting the difference between mere economic growth and the concept of development, Neil Carter also maintains that "*development* is a process of transformation which, by combining economic growth with broader social and cultural changes, enables individuals to realise their full potential" (2007, p. 211).

On the whole, more and more views denounce the notion of development as a mere achievement of economic growth and material well-being. Some critics (e.g., McMichael, 2017; Sachs, 2015; Kerbo, 2006; Elliott, 2000; Hart, 2009) point out that the very essence of development differs from economic growth, as it pays more attention to the conditions of production and consumption including several other elements affected by economic activity. The social dimensions of growth, therefore, are increasingly brought to the fore, with more importance attached to issues such as work conditions, labor rights, the protection of the environment, and more equitable wealth distribution. Winner of the 1998 Nobel Prize for economic science, Amartya Sen argues that development should not be defined narrowly as economic growth, putting it as follows: "Development can be seen [. . .] as a process of expanding the real freedoms that people enjoy. Focusing on human freedoms contrasts with the narrower views of development, such as identifying development with the growth of gross national product, or with the rise in personal incomes, or with industrialization, or with the technological advance, or with social modernization" (1999, p. 3). Thus, unlike the notion of development in the capitalist paradigm of growth, the new notion of development that these critics advocate "must encompass not only economic and social activities, but also those related to population, the use of natural resources and the resulting impact on the environment" (Elliot, 2000, p. 13).

For the most part, these post-materialist critiques are highly in tune with the notion of development advocated in the discourse of sustainable development. More importantly, it is to this very juncture of developing an accurate perception of development that the seeds of the clash between the project of sustainable development and the current socio-economic development paradigm can be traced. To my mind, the root causes of this clash between capitalism and the process of globalization on the one hand, and the project of sustainable development, on the other, are brought about essentially by the conflicting conceptions of development that these two vying paradigms are based upon. Hence, defending and popularizing a new notion of development has been the first battle that advocates of sustainable development have to fight. This challenge is highlighted by Ann Dale in the following statement:

> The pervasiveness of "growth" in human societies as a positive and necessary social and economic good for human well-being [. . .] is a main barrier to developing this new [sustainability] politics. Some of these myths are: "to grow is to progress," "to grow is to move forward," and "to do otherwise is to go backwards." Within such a dominant socio-economic paradigm, how does one sell the concept of sustainable development, which, if it is to be meaningfully implemented, means not just "doing more with less" but, ultimately, "doing less"? (Dale 2001, p. 104)

Essentially, challenging the deeply entrenched notion of development as closely related to economic growth is one of the major obstacles facing the project of sustainable development today. For the sustainability vision of development to be put into practice, today's patterns of production and consumption, systems of wealth creation, and the whole fabric of economic growth that has existed for centuries have to be seriously rethought. This dichotomy between sustainable development and the current paradigm of development bespeaks a deeper conflict between the theories of development these two paradigms are based upon. Therefore, comprehending the essence of the main development theories in modern human history gives us a vital insight as to how the current notion of development has been formulated and disseminated. One of the major objectives of theories of development has been to observe, explain, and analyze the shift from "traditional" to "modern" modes of development. Most of these theories are premised on criticisms of the values, conventions, and institutions governing those traditional societies. These theories also shed light on the societal and economic changes transforming communities' perceptions from one dominated by the authority of beliefs, traditions, and superstitions to one based on the application of reason and sciences. Above all, new notions of development were introduced in each phase of history, which had a profound influence on Man's relation with Nature and the human position in the universe.

Although the scope of this section does not allow for an in-depth analysis of every one of the development theories that have existed since the Enlightenment era, I still think it is essential to point out that the overall teachings of these theories are not fully compatible with the theoretical underpinnings of sustainability. In fact, the notion that "nature could be understood and controlled and that life should be organized with a goal of efficiency—termed 'rationalization'" has been a strong tenet in theories of development ever since the Enlightenment era and the Industrial Revolution (Roberts & Hite, 2007a, p. 5). Over centuries, this vision inspired huge efforts on the parts of scientists, thinkers, and discoverers to subjugate Nature and make use of its bounties. This instrumental approach to Nature was indeed one of the pillars of industrialization driven by Enlightenment thought and the craving for more economic growth. One significant example that Gary M. Kroll and Richard H. Robbins point out in this respect is that "when Columbus first saw the forests of the Caribbean, he commented on what wonderful ships masts the trees would make" (2009, p. 247). "The event," they add, "expresses an attitude, or an ideology, by which nature exists to serve the needs of human beings—namely, human beings can and must dominate the natural world" (2009, p. 247).

The classic treatise on economic liberalism and the foundations of the capitalist system was brought to light in Adam Smith's landmark book *An Inquiry into the Nature and Causes of the Wealth of Nations*, published in 1776. Smith's main argument is that in a context of economic growth and stimulating production, "human selfishness" is a universal characteristic, which if left unrestrained, would bring about benefits for the whole society. In chapter II of Book IV, Smith rationally contends that, in a free market, "selfish" individuals would naturally seek the greatest profit for themselves, thus meeting human needs and benefiting the community as a whole. During that epoch of mercantilism, nations strived to protect their own industries by imposing governmental regulations, tariffs, and trade barriers so that their economies would be safe from external competition. Smith, conversely, suggested that the best way to boost the economy and serve consumers' needs was not through such regulations, but rather by giving the forces of free market a free rein. In the same chapter, the impersonal free market force that creates the greatest benefit for the whole society is referred to as the "invisible hand" (1976, p. 477).

On the whole, Smith's main argument is that human selfishness and the concomitant social changes that economic growth and free market forces bring to society would ultimately serve the whole nation in so far as these forces are left unrestrained. According to many observers, this very argument has been the backbone of classic and modern world economics from the era of mercantilism to that of globalization. In their article, "Development and globalization: Recurring Themes," Amy B. Hite and J. Timmons Roberts, for example, point out that "[Smith's] same points will be made again and again as successive periods of change reverberate through the world economy, right up to the current debates over globalization"(2007, p. 5). The classical capitalist notions of unrestrained free market forces and the selfish individualist drive to attain maximum material wealth and well-being will also be prominent, recurring themes in my discussion of the clash between the sustainable development paradigm and the modern capitalist mode of development.

Even theories and ideologies that were meant to counterbalance capitalism did not really pay much attention to the issue of ecological limits of the planet as such. Theorists Karl Marx and Friedrich Engels (1848), for instance, pointedly focused on poverty, social upheaval, inequality, and political crises that the capitalist drive for wealth creation entails. They also tried to understand capitalism, uncover its contradictions, and foresee its inevitable consequences for the community through conceptualization about the relationships between social and economic changes. In Marx and Engels, economic relationships fundamentally shaped people's lives, structured their work relations, and formulated their overall lifestyles and thinking. Above all, they believe that conflict over these relationships underlies social change and that the economy is the backbone of the whole social and political system. Precisely, Marxists regard the capitalist system as inherently flawed because they perceive "wage labor and exchange for profit as an overarching, all-encompassing structure that breeds exploitative economic relationships among individuals, classes, and regions" (Roberts & Hite, 2007b).

In his critique of capitalism, Marx also contends that it hinders people from achieving their full creative potentials and frustrates their aspirations to exercise free will as a fundamental part of their human nature. For Marx and Engels (1844), capitalism not only exploits workers in their daily labor but also makes them feel estranged from the products that they produce with their own hands. This exploitation grows into a dire form of alienation with far-reaching social and intellectual consequences reaching well beyond their workplace. Elaborating on this issue, Marx and Engels write: "All these consequences follow from the fact that the worker is related to *the product of his labor* as to an *alien* object. For it is clear on this presupposition that the more the worker expends himself in work the more powerful becomes the world of objects which he creates in face of himself, the poorer he becomes in his inner life, and the less he belongs to himself" (1844, p. 33). According to this view, capitalism, characterized mainly by conflict and exploitation of labor, is merely a historical stage that bears the seeds of its own demise because its dehumanization of labor would inevitably lead to its replacement by a new social order.

Theoretically, the sustainability discourse, in my view, shares a few important points with Marxism. This new project prioritizes, for example, the need to combat what environmentalists see as "the excesses of capitalism," the need to stop exploitation not only of labor, but also of natural resources, and the need to remedy the social alienation that capitalism engenders. However, the sustainability discourse departs from Marxism in that it considers the exploitation of labor only as one aspect of another kind of exploitation, namely the exploitation of the natural resources. Sustainable development also differs from Marxism, in my view, because it implies that worse than the alienation between the workers and the product they make is the new kind of alienation between the consumer and the whole unsustainable process of production-consumption that constantly depletes the earth's finite resources.

In response to Marx's and Engels's theory of social struggle, German sociologist Max Weber (1864–1920) argued in "The Protestant Ethic and the Spirit of Capitalism" that social change goes beyond economic relationships. He believed that religious currents played a crucial part in the development of capitalism in Europe and should, therefore, be taken into account together with economic factors when analyzing and theorizing about social change. According to Weber (1958), capitalism thrived mainly because of an overriding belief among believers that laziness and idleness were sinful, hence these people's devotion to a divine "calling" that led to the ethic of hard work, investments, vocational specialization, and a constant drive for economic growth. Explaining how capitalism ultimately threw off the cloak of Protestantism and emerged as an independent and secularized drive for economic growth, Weber writes:

> The full economic effect of those great religious movements, whose significance for economic development lay above all in their ascetic educative influence, generally came only after the peak of the purely religious enthusiasm was past. Then the intensity of the search for the Kingdom of God commenced gradually to pass over into sober economic virtue; the religious roots died out slowly, giving way to utilitarian worldliness. (Weber 1958, p. 43)

The spirit of capitalism that Weber theorizes about is going to be particularly important in my discussion of the discourse of sustainable development in a context of neo-liberalism. As I touch upon Weber's analysis of how capitalism threw off the cloak of Protestantism, I find it essential to invoke the notion of the dominance of the materialistic ethics that characterizes the current model of growth. The weakening of the welfare system by the overwhelming waves of deregulation, privatization, outsourcing, and corporate profit-making or "corporatism" is, in my view, merely a reflection of the dominance of this ethic in the current socio-economic paradigm of growth. Within this framework, Jasmin Sydee and Sharon Beder pointedly argue that the work ethic that originally developed from a religious calling later was transformed into a materialistic quest for material success:

> With the rise of capitalism, work came to be valued according to its productivity and wealth-creating potential. Success in business was measured solely in terms of profits. Wealth, as the supposed fruit of hard work, became an indicator of a person's worth and social standing. The emphasis on work as a religious calling was gradually super-

seded by a materialistic quest for social mobility and material success. (Sydee and Beder 2009, p. 260)

The unrelenting quest for wealth creation and the prioritization of economic growth are part and parcel of the overall conflict between the two clashing paradigms of development, namely sustainable development and the current capitalist paradigm of growth. In the light of this rather concise reading of Smith, Marx, and Weber, I want also to highlight the theoretical underpinnings of some prevalent concepts and principles that make capitalism almost totally incompatible with sustainable development. Lastly, this incompatibility comes also as a result of the prominence of some modern theories of modernization that further widen the gap between sustainability and the current socio-economic paradigm of development.

Modernization Theories, Dependency Theory, and Beyond

With the expansion and intensification of industrialization in the second half of the twentieth century, different ideas have been carried forward from Marx, Engels, and Weber's works. Some theorists (e.g., Rostow, 1991; Huntington, 1971/2007) tried to identify the key causes of social change and explore the process of development in a new context of intensified industrialization. In their writings, these theorists place particular emphasis on the possibility of replicating the Western model of development in other countries, deeming varied factors as essential to the process of development. American economist and political theorist Walt W. Rostow (1916–2003), a staunch defender of capitalism, argued, for instance, that wealthy industrialized countries are in a good position to help developing countries modernize their economies provided that these countries follow the Western model of growth. For the developing countries to break out of the cycle of poverty and backwardness, modernization theories suggest that these countries open up their national markets to forces of global free markets, strive to attract vast investments from TNCs, and allow corporate investors free access to local labor and resources (Yeh, 1989; Elliott, 2000).

According to Rostow's theory, all nations go through the same five basic stages of economic growth during their process of development. These stages are, respectively, "the Traditional Society," "the Preconditions for Take-Off" stage, "the Take-Off" stage, "the Drive to Maturity" stage, "the Age of High Consumption," from which societies move to a "Beyond Consumption" phase (1991, pp. 4–16). Rostow's theory, especially his perception of development as a relatively homogenous experience, still influences numerous development agencies' strategies and many nations' economic policies. In fact, Rostow's view gained ascendancy in US foreign policy when he served in the Kennedy and Johnson administrations, and the US agency for International Development Programs based its policies on his analyses of modernization theory. However, many critics (e.g., Yeh, 1989: Baker, 2006; Elliott, 2000) denounce this theory as being simplistic and linear while others contend that it is not based on a solid historical background:

> Such an argument is of course erroneous as it is based on the assumption that conditions for takeoff now and in the nineteenth century were the same and that Britain then and the developing countries now were in comparable situations economically, politically, and socially. Britain was not in the world's periphery when it underwent the Industrial Revolution unlike the developing countries today. Furthermore, it is based on a linear view of time in which development will come to all once they have gone through the right stages or jumped through the right hoops. (Kütting, 2004, p. 99)

According to some other theorists, modernization is also an evolutionary multidimensional process that changes societies at different levels in a complex disruptive way. Harvard political scientist Samuel Huntington, for example, perceives what he calls "the Grand Process of Modernization" as a multidimensional interrelated process of change in society at the social, educational, economic, and political levels: "Modernization is a *revolutionary* process. This follows directly from the contrasts between modern and traditional society. The one differs fundamentally from the other, and the change from tradition to modernity consequently involves a radical and total change in patterns of human life" (1971, p. 57). Although he admits that this process of modernization is a very slow process that occurs in several stages, Huntington asserts that it might entail a process of extremely disruptive and violent phases in the evolution of any society to achieve a stable political and social system (1971, pp. 57–58). Huntington also argues that Modernization originated in Europe and spread to other parts of the world:

> Modernization is a *global* process. Modernization originated in fifteenth- and sixteenth-century Europe, but has now become a worldwide phenomenon. This is brought about primarily through the diffusion of modern ideas and techniques from the European center, but also in part through the endogenous development of non-Western societies. (Huntington 1971, p. 58)

Though criticized for being "ahistorical" and failing "to make distinctions between countries, regions, structural conditions, or specific historical experiences" (Roberts & Hite, 2007a, p. 8), Huntington's theory, still influences many foreign policies and academic approaches to modernization holding the assumption that societies will ultimately modernize into liberal democracies. Notwithstanding, modernization theories' definition and perception of development in general, and Rostow's theory of development in particular, stand in stark contradiction with the tenets of sustainability. Rostow's theory of the "linear" mode of development largely sidelines the issue of the dire environmental degradation caused by Western industrialization and economic growth. By assuming that any country can achieve the same level of growth just by following the linear mode of development that the developed countries undertook, Rostow's theory not only takes the availability of the needed natural resources for granted, but also ignores the systematic damage to the natural environment that has resulted from this process of development. These two issues, among others, have made modernization theories yet another aspect of the incompatibility between the project of sustainable development and the capitalist model of growth. The claims that modernization is essentially a Western concept would also cast a dark shadow on how the project of sustainable development is perceived in the South, thus making it an integral part in the North-South politics.

As a response to the ascendancy of Modernization Theories, a few thinkers, mostly from developing countries, conceived what came to be known as "Dependency Theory." Before I discuss this theory, I find it essential to point out that having been popularized in the developing countries, this theory has had a strong bearing on the evolution of sustainable development, especially against a backdrop of a chronic North-South divide. My chief objective, therefore, is to examine the influence of this theory on the way sustainable development has been tackled in North-South politics, and throw light on the overall impact this influence has had on the development and integrity of this project. Dependency theory was first conceived of and developed by a number of scholars who worked for the Chile-based United Nations Economic Commission for Latin America (ECLA), which was established by the United Nations Economic and Social Council (ECOSOC) in 1948. However, it was the German-American economic historian and sociologist Andre Gunder Frank (1929–2004), who first presented the theory in English. His ideas came as a response to the discourse of Modernization Theory in the 1960s developed by Western scholars such as Rostow and Huntington. Frank's ideas, though controversial, have been very popular among a new generation of scholars who were inspired by what is referred to as Dependency Theory.

According to Dependency Theory, the world consists largely of two parts: wealthy countries being the core or center of the global capitalist system and the poor countries being the satellite or periphery. Because of their vulnerable economies, periphery countries have become more and more dependent on countries of the core as markets for their exports. In general, these peripheral countries are characterized by low wages, poor working conditions, and weak societal engagement exacerbated by undemocratic regimes that undermine independent labor unions and active social movements (Frank, 1969; Cardoso, 1972). The countries of the core, in turn, exploit the countries of the periphery by using their work force as cheap labor, import their cheap raw materials, and thrive on their own larger markets to increase their wealth. Thus, for Dependency theorists, "underdevelopment in the periphery is the direct result of development in the center, and vice versa" (Roberts & Hite, 2007b, p. 70). Overall, Dependency Theory stresses the global nature of the capitalist system, in which both rich and poor countries are interlinked. Accordingly, this prevalent center-periphery relationship both reflects and exposes the inherent hierarchical nature of the capitalist system on the global and national scales. Criticizing modernization theory, Andre Gunder Frank writes: "Our ignorance of the underdeveloped countries' history leads us to assume that their past and indeed their present resemble earlier stages of the history of the now developed countries. This ignorance and this assumption lead us into serious misconceptions about contemporary underdevelopment and development" (1969, p. 76).

Theoretically, Dependency theorists belong to two slightly different schools of thought. The first, as represented by Frank, argues that underdevelopment is not a phase in the development history of the periphery countries but it is rather "a permanent, inescapable condition, only remedied by escaping the entire capitalist system" (Roberts & Hite, 2007b, p. 72). Together with other scholars such as Paul Baran, Theotonio Dos Santos, and Samir Amin, Andre Grunder Frank argues that because it is based on monopolies and unfair competition, the capitalist system denies the countries of the periphery any chance for development or growth. As a matter of fact, these theorists assert that the harder these countries try to engage themselves in this system, the more they become entangled and trapped in what they call an "imperialist stage of capitalism" (Frank, 1969, pp. 82–84). Consequently, while capitalism is bringing about more wealth and further development to core countries, it is also bringing greater poverty and underdevelopment to the satellite countries. Based on this theory, Frank and his followers claim that the only safe option for the poorer nations is to protect their markets and try as hard as they can to disentangle themselves from the exploitative capitalist system dominated by the core (1969, pp. 82–84). Though widely criticized for failing to offer any practical alternative solutions for the periphery and for failing to explain the astonishing development achieved by some satellite countries such as Chile, China, and South Korea, among others, their vision has nevertheless inspired numerous critics and scholars who oppose what they see as the exploitative nature of capitalism (Roberts & Hite, 2007b).

The other school of Dependency Theory is led by the Brazilian sociologist Fernando Henrique Cardoso, who sees the possibility of achieving some degree of development for the periphery countries within the context of their relationship with the core countries. Referring to this type of development as "associated" or "dependent" development, Cardoso contends that "it is necessary to understand that in specific situations it is possible to expect *development* and *dependency*" (1972, p. 92). According to him, although poorer nations are heavily dependent on the core countries, they can still manage to develop, to some degree, by focusing on their domestic industries and empowering their workforces to reduce their economic dependency on wealthy countries. However, Cardoso concurs with the first school of Dependency Theory that throughout their colonial history, wealthy core nations used "imperialist" tactics to keep poorer periphery nations producing cheap raw material and low-value products in order to foster more development and further industrialization in the wealthier countries. On the other hand, Cardoso claims that development is possible for the periphery countries within the framework of the current global economy (1972, pp. 91–94). With regard to the rise of sustainable development, many aspects of this theory are being echoed in the discourse of this new project, which has made it appealing to developing countries in general. This affinity between the two discourses is going to be dealt with in more depth in the section discussing the clash between sustainable development and globalization.

Ultimately, in response to critiques of the weaknesses of Dependency Theory, some theorists have taken their ideas in a new direction and developed a new vision that is referred to as "World Systems Theory." This theory was first elaborated in Immanuel Wallerstein's three-volume book, *The Modern World System*, the first of which was published in 1974 in the USA. Together with other thinkers such as Christopher Chase-Dunn, Peter Evans, and Gary Gereffi, Wallerstein advocates the view that the whole world is interconnected at different intricate levels in the process of development. Based on this notion, they assert that analyzing and defining development requirements at the level of nation-state, though important, is by no means sufficient for establishing an adequate understanding of processes of development throughout history (Wallerstein, 1979). To some extent, however, the World Systems Theory remains but an elaboration on Dependency Theory, in that it keeps the core-periphery hierarchy though it adds another category to it.

Central to the World Systems Theory is the notion of a global system that comprises three main zones: the core, the semi-periphery, and the periphery (Wallerstein, 1979). Although this theory retains the same definitions of core and periphery as in Dependency Theory, it further identifies a semi-periphery category that comprises countries that exhibit features of both rich and poor countries, being the "intermediaries" in the process of the exploitation of the periphery by the core (Roberts & Hite, 2007b). The World Systems Theory admits, therefore, the possibility of poor nations' mobility in the core-periphery hierarchy if they meet development requirements that fit in the world development system as a whole. Development, according to Wallerstein and his fellow World Systems theorists, should be conceived of within the framework of well-defined "totalities" of a capitalist world system: "If we are to talk of stages, then [. . .] it must be stages of social systems, that is, of totalities. And the only totalities that exist or have historically existed are minisystems and world-systems, and in the nineteenth and twentieth centuries there has been only one world-system in existence, the capitalist world-economy" (1979, p. 96).

As such, the World Systems Theory has been criticized for being too economy-oriented, in the sense that economy is assumed to be determining all other aspects of human existence (Yeh, 1989; Roberts & Hite, 2007b). At another level, the whole Modernization project is also criticized by writers such as Martin Khor (2001a), Vandana Shiva (2003, 2009), and Philip McMichael (2017, 2007) as being especially designed to overcome specific economic problems of the developed countries in the aftermath of WWII. This modernization project, therefore, is seen as a mere historical juncture or "a post war construct" in the process of human development rather than being a typical recipe for growth that can be applied at any time to any nation (McMichael, 2007).

To my way of thinking, gaining this insight into the evolution of Dependency Theory is essential to fully envisage some common features between the sustainability discourse and Dependency theories. To begin with, both discourses are launched as a criticism of the capitalist paradigm of growth, and both came as a response to what is considered by critics as the economic and social excesses of this socio-economic model of growth. This common ground would, in my opinion, open up new opportunities for activists on both sides to collaborate on popularizing a new alternative of development. Secondly, both of these discourses aim, to varying degrees, at exposing what is considered as dire effects of uneven economic ties between the North and the South usually referred to as the core-periphery relationship. Equally important, both discourses preach that any initiative of development to be adopted by the South should emanate from the developing countries themselves rather than being exported to them by the industrialized countries given the specific circumstances and conditions of development in each country.

Though from different angles, both Dependency theories and the sustainability discourse tend to view the current capitalist development model as a thinly disguised combination of mercantilism and liberalism under the banner of a new global system. Critics point out that this development model has been exported to the developing countries after the period of decolonization as a flawless recipe for modernization or what Philip McMichael calls "the paradigm of 'developmentalism'" (2007, p. 219). By and large, these two discourses attach a great importance to the bottom-up process of development that celebrates and promotes the indigenous knowledge in societies, local small economic projects, and wide grass-roots participation in decision making as well as awareness raising. Moreover, both discourses claim that the current Western development paradigm is not really global as it claims to be, in part because of its historically specific evolutionary process during the twentieth century, and in part because of the emergence of a new overriding global project—globalization. McMichael, for instance, explains that "the development project was unsuccessful in its own universalist terms. Its failure is both cause and consequence of the rise of a new, alternative project: the globalization project" (2007, p. 219).

Some of the fundamental principles in sustainability, however, are either ignored or sidelined in Dependency Theory. One of the fundamental differences is the absence of any consideration of adjusting the nations' development policies to the ecological limits of the planet in the Dependency Theory discourse. Failing to take the notion of "limits-to-growth" on board, Dependency Theory sounds rather growth-oriented at the expense of other vital goals such as preserving the environment and abiding by the ecosystems' limits. Besides, the social aspect of human development—a vital tenet of sustainability—seems to be relegated to a very peripheral position in Dependency theories. Thus, being essentially growth-centered, Dependency Theory is only partly compatible with the project of sustainable development.

All in all, juxtaposing the two discourses of sustainable development and Dependency Theory leaves us with the following important conclusions: first, although new to the field of global politics, the project of sustainable development has, in fact, some deep roots in the literature of development studies and is relatively compatible with some influencing contemporary theories of development. Secondly, identifying these common features between sustainable development and other theories of development gives us insight as to what chances of success this project has in its fight for survival with the current capitalist paradigm of development especially in a context of an intensifying process of globalization.

Globalization as a Contentious Concept

The phenomenon of globalization is widely perceived of as a new stage in the current capitalist development paradigm, which promotes the dissemination of open market economies and global economic integration. The concept itself is highly controversial and open to different interpretations. Some scholars (e.g., Altvater, 1998; Ikeme, 2000; Parkins, 1996) see globalization as different from the existing development paradigm while others (e.g., McMichael, 2017; Chasek, Downie, & Brown, 2010; Sydee & Beder, 2009) consider it merely as a historical stage that evolved from previous phases of development. Against this backdrop, my aim in this section is to shed light on how the different approaches to globalization in general, and to economic globalization in particular, vary widely among zealous proponents and adamant opponents of this phenomenon. My ultimate aim in this discussion, therefore, is to delineate a clear portrayal of the context that the project of sustainable development has evolved in, and investigate how propitious this context is for the establishment of a new paradigm of development that departs from the predominant one.

The term "globalization" was popularized principally by the American author Thomas Friedman, most notably in his 1999 book, *The Lexus and the Olive Tree: Understanding Globalization,* and his 2005 bestseller *The World is Flat: A Brief History of the Twenty-first Century.* Friedman mainly highlights the dramatic changes that took place at the turn of the century, focusing especially on the instantaneous ability of firms and corporations to globally manage their production and marketing strategies thanks to new breakthroughs in communication technologies. By the end of the 1990s, the concept of globalization came into widespread use and became the subject of numerous heated academic debates. Nowadays, this phenomenon is widely seen as entailing a process of economic, social, and cultural change. Nonetheless, just like sustainable development, globalization has been given many different interpretations, which has resulted in lingering definitional problems in the literature.

In the literature of development studies, the term "globalization" is used in many different ways to stand for different concepts, for "the term means vastly different things to different people" (French, 2000, p. 4). For example, this term is widely used to mean a new state of global interdependence, particularly in relation to issues that have global scale such as nuclear threats, environmental problems, and financial crises. Indian scholar Kameshwar Choudhary defines globalization as "a contemporary process of increasing intense interconnectedness/interactions/inter-dependence/integration across borders/state and communities (local/national) in different spheres of human life—economic/financial, technological, social, cultural, and political" (2004, p. 4). Sharing the same view, Colin Parkins points out that this overwhelming phenomenon "refers to a unifying process of social change, or a way of seeing social relations, that takes in the world as a whole. As such it goes beyond forms of analysis centered on social relations within and between national societies and tries to identify structures and processes that exist at a global level" (1996, p. 69). Globalization is also used to refer to the growth of a new form of increasingly homogeneous global culture, which is seen by many critics[1] as a direct or indirect threat to indigenous cultures especially in the developing countries. "Sometimes described as the 'McDonaldization' of culture," argue these critics, "globalization has been widely criticized for acting as a blanket culture that smothers differences and diversity in a sea of homogeneity and sameness" (Sydee & Beder, 2009, p. 255).

At the economic level, globalization is widely defined as "an economic process that entails the rapid movement of products and people around the world" (Kroll & Robbins, 2009, p. 167), or "the trend of increasing integration of economies in terms not only of goods and services, but of ideas, information and technology" (Ikeme, 2000). Globalization is also regarded as a phenomenon underlying international trends such as trade liberalization, free capital mobility, and the empowerment of transnational corporations (TNCs). As an overwhelming economic and financial trend, the economic aspect of globalization is bringing about the emergence of a qualitatively new world economy characterized mainly by a continuous expansion and capital flow based on global open-market economic strategies. As a consequence, globalization is perceived simply as an extension of capitalism in modern history. Jasmin Sydee and Sharon Beder argue, for instance, that "globalization is a natural extension on the wealth and power-acquiring tendencies of capitalism. The trend toward the concentration of economic power began in the United States at the end of the nineteenth century when a wave of business mergers created several very large corporations" (2009, p. 261).

From other viewpoints, globalization is seen as based on an international network of economic strategies led by WTO, the IMF, the World Bank, and G8 summits, and is heavily influenced by regional trading blocs such as Asia-Pacific Economic Cooperation (APEC), the European Economic Community (EEC), and North American Free Trade Agreement (NAFTA) (Blewitt, 2008). Spotlighting the growing influence of these financial institutions, Gary M. Kroll and Richard H. Robbins point out that "three institutions—the World Bank, the International Monetary Fund, and the World Trade Organization—represent in myth and reality the economic processes of globalization" (2009, p. 225). On the other hand, other critics argue that "it is too narrow a definition to equate globalisation with the internationalisation of economies," pointing out other aspects of globalization that can be felt in society, politics, ecology, and culture (Gruber, 2004, p. 112). Globalization is also regarded as both a cause and consequence of the information technology revolution that the world has been witnessing ever since the closing decades of the twentieth century. The development of electronic communications and information networks has both empowered globalization and been empowered by it as unprecedented breakthroughs in telecommunication technology have done away with physical barriers in the economic, financial, and also intellectual fields (Baldwin, 2016; Blewitt, 2008).

As with sustainable development, the concept of globalization is understandably open to different interpretations and has numerous definitions. In his preface to *Sustainable Development in a Globalized World*, Björn Hettne asserts that "there is still a lack of clarity about the concept of globalization, [and] even [a] debate about whether globalization really exists," though he admits that "globalization defines a growing transnational arena in which limited nation-state control operates and where players other than state players assert themselves" (2008, p. xi). Likewise, Colin Parkins pointedly explains that "the idea of globalization [...] has a variety of meanings and it is consequently difficult to accept or reject in its entirety" (1996, p. 72). As such, globalization has recently been one of the most contentious issues in contemporary political discourse. The term itself has been understood in so many different senses that it has practically lost any precise meaning in political and economic debates. "Not only have different meanings been ascribed to the phenomenon generally referred to as 'globalization,'" conclude some observers, "but also it has become one of the most widely used yet imprecise terms in political and economic debates" (Jegede, 2001).

The heated debates about globalization seem to be endless. For some scholars such as Baldwin (2016), Choudhary (2004), and Ikeme (2000) globalization is defined as the intensification and acceleration of global interconnections in all aspects of life, while others (e.g., McMichael, 2017; Blewitt, 2008) see it as a precise condition in which the world achieves a fully integrated global market. Still, other critics (e.g., Kelbessa, 2001) argue that what is termed "globalization" is in fact far from global as such; all the more so because it refers to economic, social, or political phenomena that affect only specific regions of the world. By the same token, Gabriela Kütting maintains that "the use of the tem globalization to describe the political and economic changes since the 1970s is an exaggeration and that we can only talk of partial globalization or of a globalizing process" (2004, p. 5). Not only do the origins, definitions, and inception of globalization remain controversial, but scholars are also widely divided as to its economic, social, and cultural effects on the individuals, nation-states, and societies. Some interpretations of globalization (e.g., in Krugman & Venables, 1995; Bhagwati, 2007; Norberg, 2003/2007) have mainly focused on its positive economic effects in terms of trade liberalization, the free flow of capital, and the overall economic growth that the globalized economic system offers. Other approaches,[2] however, have dwelt on the negative economic, cultural, and ethical impacts of globalization especially on poor nations and indigenous communities who have been culturally marginalized and economically sidelined.

Still, other views contend that globalization cannot be defined solely in terms of global economic integration, pointing out that "a qualitative shift in the mode of social organization that marks a historic transition in the capitalist world order" is taking place (Roberts & Hite, 2007b, p. 157). This qualitative shift has had one important implication for governments' sovereignty and people's livelihoods, namely that both the nation-state and its people no longer retain full control over vital economic and political decisions that shape their lives. Other observers (McMichael, 2007) decry what they consider as unjust "economic relations" imposed by globalization which put tremendous power in the hands of a new "global ruling class" of politicians willing to implement unfettered open market economies and executives of big business.

In the light of this brief conceptualization of globalization, some characteristic features of this phenomenon can be highly indicative of its mismatch with the project of sustainable development. Though pulling in opposite directions, these two phenomena do share a number of common structural and theoretical underpinnings. However, before dealing with these common characteristics and analyzing their implications, I think it is essential to draw upon the main approaches to globalization and highlight the approaches that I find most relevant to this research. Gaining an insight into these approaches to globalization will not only help us determine what characteristics are common to the two discourses—globalization and sustainable development—but also reveal much about what potential there is for harnessing the powers of globalization to serve sustainability.

As a controversial phenomenon, globalization has, no doubt, been understood to stand for different ideas and conflicting concepts over the recent years. My focus, however, is going to be on four main theoretical approaches to globalization that have predominated in the recent literature. Because the scope of this section does not allow for a lengthy examination of these approaches, I am going to briefly refer to the most prominent features of globalization in each approach. These approaches are defined by Leslie Sklair (2007) as the "world-systems" approach, the "global culture" approach, the "global society" approach, and the "global capitalism" approach. Sklair argues that the first approach is principally "based on the distinction between core, semiperipheral and peripheral countries in terms of their changing roles in the international division of labour dominated by the capitalist world-system" (2007, pp. 236–37). Essentially, this approach is inspired by the World-Systems Theory as presented by Immanuel Wallerstein and his followers. Though it did not define and discuss globalization overtly, this theory constitutes an important theoretical framework for researchers who study globalization from a global perspective. Some scholars (e.g., Roberts & Hite, 2007b), nonetheless, criticize this theory for being too "economistic" usually at the expense of culture and other aspects of human life. Other critics (e.g., Robertson, 1992) also contend that cultural factors were not given enough weight in Wallerstein's World Systems theory, which is heavily based on economic factors such as the international division of labor. As a consequence, this theory is usually criticized as incapable of dealing with cultural and social issues adequately.

Unlike the World-Systems approach, the global culture approach focuses primarily on the problems and paradoxes that a "homogenizing mass media-based culture poses for national identities" and indigenous cultures (Sklair, 2007, p. 238). According to this approach, cultural issues are to be prioritized over political and economic factors in approaching globalization (Robertson, 1992). Most importantly, this approach focuses primarily on addressing the question of how national identities and indigenous cultures can survive in the age of an emerging global culture. It also examines the consequences of the rapid growth of mass media communication and the emergence of what Marshall McLuhan notably called "the global village." This approach pays special attention to the cultural effect of the broadcasting through corporate mass media of identical images and products to people around the world. There are also many other variants within this approach that cut across disciplines and schools of thought, but they all tend to focus on the degree of autonomy that local cultures can achieve in the face of what these critics see as an overwhelmingly powerful, omnipresent global culture.

The struggle between local and global cultures is echoed in contemporary approaches to globalization such as the "global society" approach, which is closely related to the "global culture" approach. Like Anthony Giddens, theorist Roland Robertson argues, for instance, that concepts such as global consciousness or planetary consciousness are typical of a modern era which is different from any other previous phases in history (1992, pp. 8–9). Leslie Sklair further contends that "ideas of space-time distanciation [. . .] and of time-space compression [. . .] illustrate how processes of globalization compress, stretch and deepen space-time for people all over the world thus creating some of the conditions for a global society" (2007, p. 240). In their global society approach to globalization, these views reiterate the belief that the power and influence of the nation-state is continuously decreasing in the face of the overwhelming power and increasing significance of "supra-national" and "global" systems of governance. Because of these processes of change brought about by technology, science, industrialization, and cultural openness, some kind of global society with common universal values is emerging for the first time in the history of mankind, concludes Roland Robertson (1992, pp. 8–9).

The fourth approach to globalization is the global capitalism model, which attaches great importance to the predominant forces of the now global capitalist system as the custodian of globalization. According to this approach, globalization represents "a concept of the global that involves more than the relations between nation-states and state-centrist explanations of national economies competing against each other" (Sklair, 2007, p. 241). Adherents to this approach claim that the current capitalist system constitutes a solid foundation for a new global era characterized by some "transnational practices" performed by "non-state actors" that attach little importance to traditional state borders. Precisely, globalization manifests itself in three main global spheres—the economic, the political, and the cultural/ideological. Sklair identifies the "transnational corporation" as the predominant power in the economic sphere, "the transnational capitalist class" as the major power in the political sphere, and "the culture-ideology of consumerism" as the main power in the cultural/ideological sphere (2007, p. 242).

The global capitalism approach is especially concerned with how some phenomena such as increasing corporate political power and consumer culture coalesce to transform the world economically, politically, and culturally within the specific norms of the new global capitalist system. The "culture-ideology of consumerism" typical of the new global capitalist system prioritizes the ethics of consumerism and nourishes the drive for ever-increasing consumption in society without necessarily ensuring an adequate income for individuals to buy products (Sklair, 2007, p. 242). For many critics (e.g., Edwards, 2008; Robbins, 2009; Kütting, 2004; Speth, 2008), this new system of global capitalism creates an unrelenting desire to consume more in contemporary postindustrial societies while simultaneously it consistently weakens the state's ability to attend to the underprivileged and ethnic minorities through the welfare system.

To my way of thinking, each of these four approaches to globalization can be criticized for some weaknesses. World Systems theory, for example, places emphasis mainly on the economic aspect of globalization while minimizing the importance of political and cultural factors. Nevertheless, this approach is widely considered the most "realistic" one as globalization itself is most often interpreted as an economic global system that subsumes national and regional economies under the umbrella of the global capitalist economy. The globalization of culture approach, on the other hand, tends to be more culture-oriented, playing down the economic dimension while throwing more light on the cultural aspects of globalization. The world society approach is an attempt to reconcile the cultural and the economic effects of globalization in one view. Finally, the global capitalism approach is criticized for prioritizing the global capitalist system while relegating other economic systems to peripheral status.

By and large, Sklair's identification of these three spheres is particularly important in my discussion of the clash between the project of sustainable development and the current capitalist paradigm of growth. However, I find it essential to place more emphasis on the economic and the cultural aspects of globalization because they constitute the most significant areas where the project of sustainable development departs from the current model of development. I also find the two concepts of the state's declining sovereignty and emergence of global society very pertinent to the evolution of sustainable development. For example, while the notion of the weakening of the nation-state's sovereignty caused by globalization raises challenges to the implementation of sustainable development, the notion of forging a global society offers, on the other hand, new room for activists to rally what has come to be known as "the global citizens" around new sustainability ethics.

To allow for a thoroughly informed analysis, it is essential to start this discussion with considering some of the most zealous views that advocate globalization and celebrate its benefits. Despite the worldwide criticism aimed at globalization, many zealous proponents of this phenomenon strongly argue that the whole world has benefited from it and particularly from global trade and capital flow. Neo-liberal theorists and economists such as Jagdish Bhagwati, (2007), Johan Norberg (2003/2007), Paul

Krugman and Anthony Venables (1995) defend globalization as the "engine of wealth creation" that will ultimately benefit all segments of society in both developed and developing countries thanks to what is commonly referred to as "trickle-down economics." Boosting the growth agenda, reducing trade tariffs, disseminating modern telecommunication technologies, and promoting more freedom of movement and communication are some of the principal concepts the advocates of globalization share and defend. In his book, *In Defense of Global Capitalism*, economist Johan Norberg, for example, argues that capitalism and economic globalization offer unlimited opportunities for the development and well-being of humankind: "At its core, belief in capitalism is belief in mankind. [. . .] In the cultural arena, that means freedom of expression and the freedom of the press. In politics, it means democracy and the rule of law. In social life, it means the right to live according to one's own values and to choose one's own company. And in the economy, it means capitalism and free markets" (2003/2007, pp. 266–267).

One major argument of the pro-globalization discourse is that globalization empowers both the poor and the rich nations alike to transcend geographical, political, ideological, and cultural barriers and open up on a wider world full of opportunities to improve living standards and great opportunities for sound development. According to its advocates, globalization has numerous benefits such as entailing more freedom and more options for the working class to seek out alternative opportunities and throw off local constraints. They also claim that these opportunities will ultimately lead to the "liberation" of our thinking as borders vanish and the world becomes more interconnected (Norberg, 2003/2007). Proponents of globalization dispute many anti-globalization arguments, pointing out that critics' attack on "hypercapitalism" is actually the same old opposition to free market and free trade, typical of Third World regimes, conservative intellectuals, new left movements, and environmental movements, who are afraid of globalization's empowerment of the people at the expense of their political institutions (Norberg, 2003/2007, pp. 263–264). According to this view, having a global interconnected economic system with a free flow of capital and liberalized trade is not a curse, but a blessing. Johan Norberg concludes that globalization is portrayed to the world as an unfettered monster only because politicians cannot subject it to their authorities (2003/2007, pp. 263–264).

At the social level, proponents of globalization (e.g., Bhagwati, 2007) argue that the poor would see their living standards improve as a result of inexpensive goods being no longer excluded by tariff barriers, and that unemployment rates would significantly plummet because foreign investment in the South would create countless jobs for them. According to this view, the disadvantaged would also benefit enormously from the flow of information on a global scale, awakening them to their right to choose their political representatives and enjoy political freedom and social well-being. In addition, advocates of globalization rebut the idea that neo-liberal capitalists have secretly plotted for capitalism to attain world domination in a conspiracy to control the whole world: "Deregulation, privatization, and trade liberalization, however, were not invented by ultra-liberal ideologues," argues Norberg, "but the biggest reformers were communists in China and the Soviet Union, protectionists in Latin America, and nationalists in Asia. In many other European countries, the progress has been spurred by Social Democrats" (2003/2007, p. 265).

In response to critics of globalization who argue that open market economy and international economic globalization limit democracy, the advocates of globalization claim that the unprecedented intensifying spread of information, ideas, protests, criticisms, and political theories thanks to global instantaneous telecommunication systems is in fact promoting democracy and freedom worldwide (Bhagwati, 2007). Pro-globalization views maintain that never before in human history has democracy been as widespread as it is today. Globalization is also believed to have significantly promoted freedom of communication, speeded up people's movements, and facilitated global capital flow. Jagdish Bhagwati, for instance, contends that "globalization promotes democracy both directly and indirectly," asserting that "as with the thesis successfully linking globalization with reduced poverty, we now have another two-step argument: globalization leads to prosperity, and prosperity in turn leads to democratization of politics with the rise of the middle class" (2007, pp. 93–94).

For many of these liberal thinkers, citizens in the twenty-first century are no more affected by the geographical size of their country, nor constrained by its borders anymore, which is a remarkable stride toward global democracy. Unlike eighteenth and nineteenth centuries' empires which resorted to conquering other nations' lands to achieve prosperity, peoples in the age of globalization achieve prosperity without having to fight or conquer because capital, not being restricted to one territory or country, flows to all parts of the world (Norberg, 2003/2007; Krugman & Venables, 1995). Ultimately, advocates of globalization conclude that the more countries try to distance themselves from globalization, the weaker their economies become, and the farther they stray from democracy: "In 2002," argues Norberg, "there were 47 states that violated basic human rights. Worst among them were Burma, Cuba, Iraq, Libya, North Korea, Saudi Arabia, Sudan, Syria, and Turkmenistan—that is, the countries least affected by globalization and least oriented in favor of the market economy and liberalism" (2003/2007, p. 271).

The pro-globalization views also reject the criticism that globalization has engendered global inequality between the developed and underdeveloped countries and exacerbated poverty, hunger, ignorance, and conflicts in the South. Economist Jagdish Bhagwati, for instance, asserts that "globalization cannot be plausibly argued to have increased poverty in poor nations or to have widened world inequality," for "the evidence points in just the opposite direction" (2007, p. 67). According to this approach, it is quite logical that not everyone would equally benefit from globalization because countries are at different stages of development and are at different levels of interdependence within the global capitalist system. However, this does not matter, in their opinion, as long as everyone is becoming better off. Hence, the most important benefit is for everyone to be as well off as possible, not whether one group or nation is better off than another. Like Norberg (2003/2007), Bhagwati (2007), Krugman and Venables (1995), Bo Kjellén defends the many benefits of globalization, asserting that "the evolution of multilateral institutions serves to underline that globalization as we perceive it today, in terms of free movement of goods, capital and labour, is really the dream of a generation come true" (2008, p. 22). In brief, the common conclusion that these advocates of globalization draw is that this phenomenon is after all leading the whole world for better not for worse despite all the scathing criticism it has received.

Notwithstanding this celebration of the benefits of globalization and neoliberal capitalism, the prominence of the environmental issue since the 1970s onwards cast a shadow on the validity of this model of growth. With the advent of sustainable development and the intensification of the process of globalization by the turn of the century, many of the benefits of neo-liberal capitalism have been called into question. As the "limits-to-growth" thesis has increasingly become the subject of global debates, many of the merits of globalization are refuted or at least seriously called into question. Furthermore, the uneven patterns of growth generated by globalization make clear to what extent globalization in fact works to the disadvantage of the impoverished nations of the South. Counterbalancing the big zeal for globalization, however, some lingering doubts about the alleged benefits of this phenomenon were constantly raised. Critics of globalization (e.g., McMichael, 2017; Milanovic, 2016; Speth, 2003; Kütting, 2004; Khor, 2001a, b; Rena, 2008) point to the negative effects of many treaties, laws, and regulations imposed by the developed countries through international financial and regulatory bodies such as WTO, IMF, and the World Bank on the countries of the South. Globalization is also widely criticized by other critics (e.g., Mlambo & Pangeti, 2001) for entrapping the poor countries of the South in ready-made development strategies formulated and enforced by those powerful international organizations.

To begin with, many critics of globalization such as Branko Milanovic (2016), Philip McMichael (2017, 2007), Leslie Sklair (2007), James G. Speth (2008), Robert H. Wade (2007), Ravinder Rena (2008), Martin Khor (2001a) and Vandana Shiva (2003, 2008), among many others, have over the past decades contributed significantly to the creation and development of an anti-globalization discourse that aims mainly at exposing what they see as the excesses of this phenomenon and the resulting uneven distribution of wealth. Some of these critics (e.g., Milanovic, 2016; Wade, 2007; Blewitt, 2008; Dale, 2001) particularly denounce open market policies especially designed to allow industrialized countries' giant TNCs to enter and dominate developing countries' markets more easily, with minimal restrictions and obligations. According to anti-globalization views, the globalization of the open market often pressures developing countries into offering cheap labor and opening their markets to TNCs' products.[3] Bilateral and multilateral trade treaties such as the North American Free Trade Agreement (NAFTA) and WTO, for instance, are regarded by some of these critics (e.g., Kütting, 2004; Blewitt, 2008; Robbins, 2009; Wade, 2007) as organizations that deny developing countries any possibility of achieving the kind of economic growth and prosperity that has been achieved in the Western industrialized countries as well as in the newly developed countries of East Asia. According to this view, these organizations are a big obstacle that limits developing countries' export capabilities and jeopardizes their inner self-determination:

Some critics of globalization (e.g., Milanovic, 2016; McMichael, 2017; Stiglitz, 2007; Byrne & Glover, 2002) overtly accuse the international financial institutions of pushing "market fundamentalism," based on open market principles that do not hold for both developed and developing countries. Other scholars (e.g., Dale, 2001; Kütting, 2003; Blewitt, 2008; Mlambo & Pangeti, 2001) also argue that the IMF has imposed these economic policies on developing countries without taking into consideration the far-reaching harmful effects of these policies on societies and the environment in those countries. Criticizing the way globalization is managed by these international institutions, the Nobel Prize-winning economist Joseph E. Stiglitz contends that "globalization itself has been governed in ways that are undemocratic and have been disadvantageous to developing countries, especially the poor within those countries" (2007, p. 295). Still other views (e.g., Milanovic, 2016; Wright, 2000; Strange & Bayley, 2008; Salih, 2001) assert that many of the benefits brought about by globalization have remained "highly regional," thus bypassing peoples of sub-Saharan Africa and parts of Asia who still live in abject poverty.

As I see it, the anti-globalization discourse overlaps with the sustainability discourse in many areas related to development options and issues of economic dependency. To begin with, both discourses argue for the necessity of allowing poorer nations more freedom in choosing their model of development and denounce the North's hegemony over poor countries of the South.[4] In addition, the North's insistence that full engagement in the world economy by developing countries will result in their development and reduction of poverty among their peoples is seriously called into question in both discourses. Critics of globalization and the advocates of sustainable development also share similar views of how nations at different stages of development are handling or mishandling globalization. Moreover, both discourses tend to address the same segments in society—those left behind by globalization and whose environment has been abused by unsustainable models of economic growth. Hence, exposing the dire social and ecological costs of the process of globalization is a shared aim for both discourses. Ultimately, both discourses strongly criticize "the solidifying of a new set of class divisions—between those who prosper in the globalized economy and those who do not, between those who share its values and those who rather not, and between those who can diversify away its risks and those who cannot" (Rodrik, 2007a, p. 316).

The view that the problem is not with globalization per se, but rather with how globalization is managed by different countries has also recently been voiced in the anti-globalization and sustainability discourses. More and more scholars (e.g., Baldwin, 2016; Kjellén, 2008; Byrne & Glover, 2002; Stiglitz, 2007; French, 2000) of both discourses defend the idea that globalization forces can actually be harnessed to serve social and ecological ends. According to this approach, the countries that knew how to manage globalization wisely and to control how far they should be engaged in the global economy—like those in East Asia, namely Japan, South Korea, Singapore, Hong Kong, and Taiwan—did actually reap significant benefits from this global system. Economist Joseph E. Stiglitz points out, for instance, that "the countries that have, by and large, had globalization managed for them by the International Monetary Fund and other international economic institutions have not done so well," asserting that "the problem is thus not with globalization but with how it has been managed" (2007, p. 295). In fact, many researchers are now convinced that "globalisation, by delivering the 'development' side of the sustainable development equation, will solve the social problems that contribute to ecological degradation" (Carter, 2007, p. 273).

In the absence of effective tools for harnessing economic globalization to serve sustainability, this phenomenon still constitutes, in my opinion, a huge impediment to the emerging project of sustainable development. The effects of economic globalization today are not limited to consolidating class division in society or even widening the gap between the haves and the have-nots, but they affect the entire base of sustainability as an alternative paradigm of growth. As globalization has transformed the economic, social, and intellectual climate by the turn of the century, its effects on the project of sustainable development have become clearer than before. The context in which the project of sustainable development was launched was almost the same that witnessed the advent of globalization, which makes the interaction between the two projects inevitable.

GLOBALIZATION AND SUSTAINABILITY: ASPECTS OF AFFINITY AND INCOMPATIBILITY

Over the last few decades, globalization has brought about dramatic changes in the structure of the international economic system. These changes manifest themselves mainly in the increasingly important role played by the IMF, the World Bank, and WTO in the world economy as well as the growing power of TNCs. However, this very juncture that witnessed the inception and intensification of globalization also witnessed the birth of the project of sustainable development. Being two products of the same age, globalization and sustainable development share some important structural characteristics. Ideologically, globalization and sustainable development are informed by totally different sets of principles and values. The juxtaposition of these two phenomena shows that they overlap structurally but diverge ideologically on a number of economic, social, and ecological issues. By throwing more light on the overlap of their structures, and analyzing the contradictions in their theoretical underpinnings, a deeper insight can be reached as to whether there is any potential to make them mutually supportive rather than mutually exclusive. A closer look at these two phenomena provides an illuminating insight into the structural affinity between them. Hence, my aim in this section is to examine the aspects of affinity between these two projects and throw light on the nature of interaction between them. My main focus will be on investigating whether or not globalization is essentially compatible with the project of sustainable development.

Common Characteristics of Globalization and Sustainability

Historically, both globalization and sustainable development started to gain momentum at the turn of the century with seeds dating back to the period of economic prosperity following World War II. The intensification of the process of globalization began with the astounding technological breakthroughs in telecommunications in the last few decades of the twentieth century while agreements consolidating trade liberalization were being forged and put into practice. This period was also particularly important for the inception and evolution of the project of sustainable development based on some important global landmarks such as the Stockholm Conference in 1972, the publication of *The Brundtland Report* in 1987, and the Rio Earth Summit in 1992. For the most part, this period witnessed the popularization of both globalization and sustainable development, albeit with two different agendas. Shedding light on this coincidence, Bo Kjellén argues that although "the term 'globalization' only became well-known in the last decades of the twentieth century, it is interesting to note that it coincides in time with the realization that there were global threats to the world environment" (2008, p. 18). Sharing the same view, Jennifer A. Elliott further explains that "[while] the challenges and opportunities of sustainable development actions [we]re being debated, designed and carried out," the whole world was "characterised by unprecedented rates and degrees of economic, political and social change" by the end of the 1990s (2000, p. 32).

Not only did globalization and sustainable development appear in relatively the same period, but they also share some important features. Popular and widespread as they are, these two phenomena remain highly controversial concepts. As I mentioned in earlier sections, both concepts have been defined differently from diverse angles, with a high degree of vagueness and a susceptibility to different, sometimes conflicting, interpretations. This vagueness adds considerably to the complexity of not only how to define them but also to whether or not they are compatible. Moreover, this vagueness is mirrored in the different approaches in which these two concepts have been interpreted and used in the literature by different schools of thought. In his book, *Understanding Sustainable Development*, John Blewitt argues that "sustainable development is therefore multidimensional, encompassing social, ecological and economic goals and perspectives, and this breadth has led some critics to view the concept as vague, self-contradictory and incoherent, incapable of being put into practice" (2008, p. 23). The same criticism is also directed to globalization by many critics (e.g., Carter, 2007; Hettne, 2008; Parkins, 1996), who contend that this looseness in conceptualizing the two projects has also resulted in the proliferation of various approaches to globalization and sustainable development.

Globally, both globalization and sustainable development are regarded as important parts in the global governance system that is weakening the nation-state's sovereignty and taking over some roles that were exclusively performed by the national government in the past. The two projects are essentially global in character and no country can claim to be able to implement any of them singlehandedly given the transcendent nature of their strategies for development. However, globalization is mainly fostered by certain international financial institutions and an intensifying process of global economic expansion while sustainable development is motivated by ecological issues of a trans-boundary nature and inequality concerns of global scale.

On the whole, the nature of the discourse adopted by advocates of globalization and sustainability is also of a global scale, which reveals much of their structural resemblance. The unrelenting drive to include as many countries as possible under the banner of each one of these phenomena and their advocates' reliance on international organizations such as the United Nations, the World Bank, and the WTO rather than on governments to popularize and implement their agendas are typical tactics shared by both projects. Critic Susan Baker argues, for instance, that "the globalization of environmental governance [through sustainable development] has been accompanied by pressure to try new and innovative procedures, including expanding the range and role of the non-state actors involved" (2006, p. 9). One more common characteristic is that both projects claim to be addressing humanity as a whole with a global discourse directed essentially to the global citizen of a global society. "As states decentralize," contends McMichael, "the opportunity for local political renewal presents itself, often quite compellingly [. . .] [and] as global integration intensifies, the currents of multiculturalism swirl faster" (2007, p. 227). Ultimately, both globalization and sustainable discourses claim that their model of development cuts across social, ethnic, and gender boundaries,[5] which constitute another area of affinity between these two projects.

The distinctive transcendence that characterizes globalization and sustainable development reveals yet another common characteristic of these two models. In a "risk society," often associated with global threats ranging from ecological disasters to nuclear threats, both of these two phenomena have become high profile concerns in global politics. As a consequence, the discourse employed to address these dangers is often global in nature and is developed within the framework of global institutions rather than local or national ones. Globalization and sustainable development, therefore, share many features of this global discourse generated by the exigencies in the twenty-first century risk society. These features include the reliance on international institutions or organizations to popularize and disseminate their developmental strategies, their interest in transforming the production and consumption habits of post-industrial societies, and their heavy reliance on advanced technology.

On the whole, the distinctive features common to globalization and sustainable development reveal an intimate structural resemblance that might open the door for a potential harmonization between their activists in the future. This structural affinity, however, pales into insignificance in the presence of a huge ideological contradiction that characterizes the two concepts. As a matter of fact, juxtaposing the theoretical underpinnings of globalization and sustainable development exposes stark contrasts between the aims and plans of these two projects. These contradicting underpinnings and the concomitant clash they have engendered between globalization and sustainable development are going to be dealt with thoroughly in the next section.

Aspects of Incompatibility: Neo-Liberalism vs. Sustainability

Despite their common characteristics, globalization and sustainable development are based on different theoretical underpinnings. In fact, two opposing sets of ideologies and ethics are vying to determine the direction of the process of development in today's world. By comparing and contrasting the pillars of globalization and sustainable development, my primary aim is to investigate how compatible (or incompatible) these two projects are and bring into focus the set of issues over which these two discourses clash. This, in my opinion, will provide us with a deeper insight into the climate in which sustainable development emerged and evolved.

Due to its holistic nature, the concept of sustainability is built mainly on a consensus-building strategy that aims at including all nations regardless of their economic or political power (WCED, 1987, p. 44). As a consequence this project aims first and foremost to forge a global partnership in which the rich, developed nations help the poor, developing ones. The Earth Charter stresses this notion of partnership as follows:

> We urgently need a shared vision of basic values to provide an ethical foundation for the emerging world community. Therefore, together in hope we affirm the following interdependent principles for a sustainable way of life as a common standard by which the conduct of all individuals, organizations, businesses, governments, and transnational institutions is to be guided and assessed. (Earth Charter Commission, 2012)

This project also aims at integrating the environmental and developmental issues not only at the economic level, but also at the social and cultural levels (WCED, 1987, p. 65). More to the point, sustainable development "seeks to reconcile the ecological, social and economic dimensions of development, now and into the future, and adopts a global perspective in this task," thus aiming at "promoting a form of development that is contained within the ecological carrying capacity of the planet, which is socially just and economically inclusive" (Baker, 2006, p. 5).

To promote a holistic paradigm of growth, sustainability theorists call for the intervention of the state in the public interest to control market forces and avoid the drawbacks of the excessive material economic growth typical of the industrialized countries. "The implementation of sustainable development," argues Ann Dale "is the human imperative of the twenty-first century, requiring strong leadership by local, regional, and national governments, and that governments must move beyond simply being governments to governance, actively engaging all sectors of society in its implementation" (2001, p. x). Essentially, sustainable development fosters a sensible type of states' intervention that controls market forces in order to achieve greater social equity and promote more sustainable patterns of consumption and production (Kemp, Parto, & Gibson, 2005). The Rio Declaration, drafted in the 1992 Earth Summit in Rio de Janeiro, delineates the government's role as follows: "states should reduce and eliminate unsustainable patterns of production and consumption," "enact effective environmental legislation," and "co-operate to discourage or prevent the relocation and transfer to other states of any activities or substances that cause severe environmental degradation or harm to human health" (as cited in Elliott, 2000, p. 72).

Globalization, on the other hand, represents a very different approach. First, the process of globalization fosters trade liberalization and prioritizes a rapid, uncontrolled flow of capital that goes beyond national and regional barriers (Baldwin, 2016; Norberg, 2003/2007; Kroll & Robbins, 2009). In addition, the reduction or elimination of state regulations on the market as a prerequisite for growth is also emphasized by neoliberal economists (e.g., Lamy, 2005). With this reduction of state intervention and elimination of trade tariffs, globalization enables free market forces to reign, empowering large TNCs to dominate local, national, regional, and global markets alike. Spotlighting the neoliberal political ideology that underpins these transformations, Martin and Huckle argue that: "supranational institutional governance has gone hand in hand with revitalized neoliberal political ideology. Neoliberals consider that the free flow of capital, goods and services across the globe will bring sustained economic growth and sustained social progress" (2001, p. 155). Governments are, therefore, discouraged from imposing regulations that protect the environment in the belief that free market forces would ultimately foster economic growth and help protect the environment (Sagoff, 2000). Globalization, therefore, entails a reduction of governmental intervention in the sector of social services and the welfare system through deregulations and privatization of services such as health care.

As the process of economic globalization intensifies, the negative consequences of untrammelled free market forces are often overlooked by the advocates of globalization. For example, facts about social justice and negative effects of a free capitalist economy such as increasing poverty, social inequity, and threats to indigenous cultures are usually dismissed as "exaggerations" and sometimes as "fallacies" (Bhagwati, 2007). The uneven type of development engendered by economic globalization is most often left to market forces to correct on the grounds that any intervention from the state would hinder the growth process. Accordingly, the poor, the ethnic minorities, and women are all better off because of the unprecedented changes brought about by this phenomenon (Norberg, 2003/2007).

By encouraging the elimination of trade barriers and the reduction of tariffs protecting national economies, economic globalization makes it easier for powerful corporations to freely invest and sell in countries whose economic options are significantly compromised by these TNCs. From an environmentalist point of view, however, this neo-liberal economic approach raises many obstacles to the implementation of sustainable development. Michael Redclift points out, for example, that "the triumph of global capitalism also marks challenges for sustainable development," asserting that "the emphasis on market convergence should not be allowed to obscure the importance of other economic dimensions—

such as scarcity and need—in addressing problems of sustainability" (2000, p. 100). According to other views (e.g., Milanovic, 2016; Elliott, 2000; Shiva, 2003; Wade, 2007), the neoliberal approach has for the most part resulted in social ills at the national level and more debts and backwardness for the poor countries at the international level. The dilemma that globalization has widely engendered, therefore, is that it "simultaneously increases the demand for social insurance while decreasing the capacity to provide it" (Ikeme, 2000).

Unlike economic globalization, sustainable development aims at consolidating the state's efforts to meet the needs of its citizens at the local and regional levels. Through its bottom-up strategy, the sustainable development project is based on a broad citizen participation in the decision-making process which would in turn result in more adequate attention to their needs and rights (WCED, 1987). John Blewitt highlights this sustainability concept, stressing the idea that "'localization,' smaller-scale production with local producers meeting local needs, and the 'deconstruction' of the present system of global economic governance, including the World Trade Organization, the International Monetary Fund and the World Bank, is the only true path of sustainable development" (2008, p. 134). Thus, while globalization consolidates the hegemony of the big business elite through placing decision-making in the hands of a small group of gigantic corporations, sustainable development stresses the necessity of building a wide bottom-up decision-making system that caters for the needs of local groups and indigenous cultures. These two conflicting drives in globalization and sustainable development will in fact be echoed repeatedly in many other areas over which a clash between the two projects occurs.

The current global mobilization of capital also exemplifies one of the main clashes between sustainable development and globalization, for it exposes the conflicting theoretical philosophies underpinning the two rival paradigms of development. For example, the intensifying mobilization of capital and the concomitant worldwide competition among TNCs tend to steer massive investment into countries with the most lax environmental standards (Baldwin, 2016; French, 1993). This, in turn, results in dire environmental degradation in these countries, thus erecting more obstacles to the achievement of a sustainable model of development (Mol, 2003). Academic studies (e.g., Ellis, 1996; French, 1993) indicate that this process contributes a great deal in creating what came to be known as "pollution havens" or "maquiladoras"—two terms referring to the mushrooming factories located in many developing countries (e.g., Mexico) with lax environmental laws that do not impose a strict scrutiny on the implementation of standard environmental regulations. For some scholars (e.g., Kates, 2003; Mander, 2003), the mobilization of capital in a globalized world economy can also be considered a major obstacle to the sustainable development strategy to achieve social equity, for it usually leads to investment in areas with lax child-labor laws, the least organized labor unions, and worst work and safety regulations.

Socially, the process of trade liberalization is seen by many critics as benefiting the affluent nations more than the poor ones while the overwhelming process of globalization contributes a great deal to erasing the indigenous cultural landscapes worldwide.[6] Jerry Mander, for instance, spotlights some aspects of what he calls "global monoculture" disseminated by globalization with "the most fundamental redesign of the planet's social, economic, and political arrangements at least since the Industrial Revolution" (2003, p. 111). From an environmentalist point of view, capital mobilization contributes to the TNCs' exploitation of the poor workers, and indirectly coerces the latter into abusing their local environment to survive. Ultimately, this process thwarts sustainable development strategies aimed at securing healthier working conditions for labor and encouraging more sustainable use of natural resources.

Preserving local cultures and indigenous knowledge, especially in developing countries, is yet another battlefield on which the two paradigms of globalization and sustainable development clash. Many critics (e.g., Mander, 2003; Radermacher, 2004; Kelbessa, 2001; Hart, 2009) argue that globalization helps popularize a homogenous, "global monoculture" which seriously endangers indigenous cultures of local communities, and undermines all efforts to preserve the richness of these cultures though acknowledging their autonomous identities. Because the promotion of such a global monoculture and the spread of global capital are mutually supportive, opting out of this predominant culture proved rather difficult (Mulinge & Munyae, 2001). Elmar Altvater points out, for instance, that "capital accumulation, global expansion, the subjection or extinction of other cultures and the exercise of political hegemony were thus mutually contingent processes. What distinguishes the new world system from older 'world empires' is the globality of the order" (1998, p. 25). This homogenization of culture, therefore, constitutes another impediment to the implementation of sustainable development, given that achieving sustainability principally entails preserving local cultures and indigenous knowledge. In his article "Local Knowledge and Sustainable Development in Developing Countries," Roy Ellen spotlights the importance of the notion of local knowledge in the project of sustainable development, stressing that "local knowledge has actively promoted biodiversity, ecological richness, and healthy living, and that cultural diversity and biological diversity are mutually reinforcing" (2000, p. 179).

Enhancing social equity through inclusive bottom-up mainstream participation in planning and decision-making both locally and nationally also constitutes one of the main tenets of sustainability. These efforts to engage ordinary citizens in local and national decision-making are once again reversed by an overwhelming process of "time-space distanciation" brought about by globalization "in which the decisions that affect people's lives become increasingly distanced from them" (Martin & Huckle, 2001, p. 156). Fomented by the unprecedented expansion of communication technologies, TNCs' global investments, trade liberalization, this process of time-space distanciation has increasingly become an unmistakable feature of globalization. As a consequence, the objective of sustainable development to give marginalized workers a say in the process of decision-making seems to be out of sync with an economic globalization which has placed decision making ever more in the hands of global financial institutions and multinational corporations. According to observers (e.g., Milanovic, 2016; Dale, 2001; Hart, 2009; Speth, 2008), globalization denies local communities opportunities to partake in decisions that directly affect their livelihoods. "Globalization, with its new configurations of time and space," argue Martin and Huckle, "has involved the pulling away of power from the local, disempowering individuals and communities and constraining their ability to manage local environments" (2001, p. 157).

The divergence of the ideologies underpinning globalization and sustainability on the economic, social, and cultural fronts indicates clearly that these two projects are on a collision course. Despite the structural affinity between them, these two projects have mutually exclusive objectives as reflected in their contradictory development agendas. The dissemination of a global monoculture has, for instance, had pernicious effects on sustainability goals aiming at localization and the preservation of indigenous cultures. With an unprecedented intensification of the globalization process widely popularizing consumer culture, the aims of sustainable development to raise consciousness about preserving local ways of living and indigenous cultures worldwide become very hard to achieve. The incompatibility between sustainable development and globalization, therefore, manifests itself in many areas; all the more so because these two projects are based on two conflicting theories—"ecologism"[7] and neo-liberalism. By and large, the major tenets of neo-liberalism as such seem to be at odds with the aims and strategies of sustainable development.

Neo-liberalism, based on principles of free market, minimal state intervention, and free capital flow, constitutes today the driving force of economic globalization. These principles, however, seem to be at odds with the discourse of sustainability today, which is based on another set of principles. According to this view, the great emphasis on the protection of private property and the accumulation of capital at the expense of other principles such as social equity is one of the major causes rendering the neoliberal free market today highly at odds with sustainability. Gabriela Kütting (2004) and Neil Carter (2007) point out, for instance, that the subordination of other liberal principles to this predominant objective of the creation of wealth has made the current form of neo-liberalism highly incompatible with the project of sustainable development. Economically, trade liberalization constitutes one of the most important tenets of this post-World War II neo-liberalism (Mlambo & Pangeti, 2001). Although there were periods of trade liberalization in the past, notably in the nineteenth century, the intensification of trade liberalization that the world witnessed at the turn of the century is no doubt unprecedented. This intensification has been channelled through an overwhelming process of institutionalization of global trade that began with the GATT in 1945, replaced by WTO in 1994, which has altered the landscape of international trade. This process of trade liberalization is based on a few neo-liberal principles that the WTO strives to maintain, one being the reduction of trade barriers.

The wide-ranging debate about the effects of global trade on the environment is unrelenting. Some views (e.g., Mander, 2003; Sampson, 2005; Jahiel, 2009) contend that trade barriers are sometimes erected intentionally to protect social and human rights or to safeguard the environment against an overwhelming process of industrialization that causes huge environmental abuse and overexploitation of natural resources. In fact, this prioritization of the free flow of capital and the liberalization of trade has alerted critics to the effects inflicted on the environment and on society as a whole. John Blewitt, for example, argues that "the activities of international financial and trading organizations like the International Monetary Fund, World Bank and World Trade Organization, together with the developed world as a whole, are often held responsible for the global inequalities, economic distortions and social dislocations accompanying globalization" (2008, p. 95).

Another aspect of the mismatch between globalization and sustainable development is the way the power of TNCs is perceived within these two paradigms. According to many scholars (e.g., Sakamoto, 1994; Hettne, 1994; Held & McGrew, 1994), economic globalization has made free market forces so powerful that they have started to erode the power of the state and handed some of this power to non-elected economic organizations such as TNCs. Environmentalists also point out that this empowerment of free market forces is particularly detrimental to the project of sustainable development for a number of reasons. For example, there is an issue of the legitimacy and the credibility of these TNCs in the global governance system. Although TNCs have come to enjoy huge economic and sometimes political power that many sovereign states cannot achieve, a closer look at the structure of these TNCs reveals that the boards governing their policies are not openly elected (Bakan, 2004). Unlike states, these TNCs are governed by executives with little regard for issues such as the environmental degradation, social equity, or the increasing poverty among the peoples of other countries (Sydee & Beder, 2009).

In the environment-trade relationship debate, criticism of TNCs seems to be one the recurrent themes. Very much empowered by a global neoliberal economic system, the TNCs are accountable to none but their shareholders, whose ultimate goal is to maximize their profits and consolidate their position in the global economy (Bakan, 2004; Ikerd, 2005). In essence, these TNCs are profit-oriented with little ethical responsibility toward people or the environment. Statistics (e.g., in Mander, 2003, p. 126) show, for instance, that despite the fact that the two hundred largest corporations in the world now account for about 30 percent of the global economic activity, they employ less than 0.5 percent of the global workforce. These TNCs, therefore, enjoy a power that equals or even exceeds the power of a state without assuming any of the state's social duties.[8] The huge power in the hands of TNCs constitutes another potential obstacle for the project of sustainable development which prioritizes mainstream participation in decision-making and development strategies. John Blewit contends that "a great deal of the anti-globalization market is also anti-corporate, and those who campaign for deglobalization, localization and eco-localism frequently argue that the corporation, far from being a potential vehicle for sustainable development, is irredeemably a barrier" (2008, p. 133). By the same token, Colin Hines asserts that "TNCs and international capital have become the *de facto* new world government" (2000, p. 16).

Another example of the incompatibility between sustainability and neo-liberalism is how the role of modern state is perceived in each approach. In fact there is a huge divergence between these two approaches given that "the state [is] becom[ing] a representative of the economic actors rather than social interests, marginalizing citizens and reducing them to economic actors rather than to private citizens" (Kütting, 2004, p. 14). Due to the growing neo-liberal market forces, the state has become much more interested in consolidating its economic position in the global economy than in the well-being of its citizens and the protection of the environment. Although liberalism has been always unmistakably supportive of principles such as private property, wealth creation, and trade liberalization, the state until recently was regarded as the "guardian" of this process, with an eye on other concomitant social problems such as social inequality and welfare issues (Kütting, 2004).

With the advent of neo-liberalism and the intensification of the process of globalization, the state has gradually given up its classical role as a guardian of its citizens' welfare, only to assume the new role of strengthening its position in an increasingly competitive world economy (Robbins, 2009; Sydee & Beder, 2009). This change, in my opinion, is particularly problematic for the project of sustainable development, which relies considerably on a strong state with "a political system that secures effective citizen participation in decision-making" (WCED, 1987, p. 65). The intensification of trade liberalization and the reduction or elimination of non-tariff trade barriers have crippled the state's ability to introduce or uphold some vital social and environmental standards which could be regarded as an unnecessary barrier to free trade. "In order to participate in the global markets," argues Gabriela Kütting, "states are compelled to comply with the rules set by the WTO. This affects and erodes their sovereign right to self-determination in terms of national legislation" (2004, p. 14). In fact, the state's sovereignty is not limited by law but is rather impeded in practice by a global economic system that makes it practically impossible for a state to opt out.

Although some views (e.g., Baker, 2006; Elliott, 2000) contend that the concept of state sovereignty is still intact because states are still the major actors in the international governance system, others (Sakamoto, 1994; Hettne, 1994; Held & McGrew, 1994; Kütting, 2004) point out that the process of economic globalization has consistently undermined this sovereignty over the past few decades. According to Stuart Hart (2009), Richard Robbins (2009), and Jasmin Sydee and Sharon Beder (2009), for instance, the creation of a massively interconnected world economy and the unrelenting process of trade liberalization have also caused the state to lose much of its sovereignty to more powerful institutions such as the WTOs, the World Bank, the IMF, and the TNCs. As a result of its shrinking role, "the Northern or Western state has increasingly given up on its social welfare role and become a representative or guardian of the interests of global markets and therefore 'the police officer role' previously fulfilled by states has been increasingly taken over by non-state actors" (Kütting, 2004, p. 38). Thus, while neo-liberalism tends to disconnect the drive of capital accumulation from any moral or ethical considerations toward nature, the environment, and society as a whole, the sustainability discourse stresses the vital role of the state as a guardian of the citizens' welfare and the environment.

Above all, the neo-liberal instrumental approach to nature and its sacrifice of ecological issues for the sake of maintaining high economic competitiveness particularly reflects the stark incongruity between neo-liberalism and the sustainability discourse. In my view, the prevalent neoliberal principles tend to ignore the serious link between wealth creation and environmental degradation, thus overlooking the dire effects of economic growth on the environment. The neo-liberal discourse, therefore, contradicts the sustainability discourse with regard to two main issues: First, neo-liberalism overtly encourages untrammelled economic growth and consumption at the expense of the carrying capacity of the ecosystem; and second, the neo-liberal cost-benefit approach to the environmental issue starkly overlooks the magnitude of the increasing social and ecological problems affecting societies nowadays. This discrepancy in approaches to the environment reveals much of the ideological incompatibility between the two conflicting paradigms of growth, which is going to be echoed in several other important issues such as the society-nature relationship, overconsumption issues, and social equity concerns.

With such contradictory ideologies, the rift between globalization and sustainable development makes of them two irreconcilable paradigms of growth as they stand today. Above all, the neo-liberal principles underpinning globalization have permeated present-day economic systems and societies so deeply that initiating any new alternative paradigm of growth raises huge challenges. As a consequence, the ideological differences between these two projects have almost made them mutually exclusive. Notwithstanding this ideological contradiction, bridging the gap between these two paradigms has been the objective of many scholars in the last few decades. Their efforts culminated in a new development project that was meant to be an alternative that maintains the benefits of neo-liberalism while at the same time aims at achieving sustainability. Dubbed "Ecological Modernization," this new project is no less controversial than globalization and sustainable development.

ECONOMIC GROWTH AND SUSTAINABILITY: BRIDGING THE GAP

Over the recent years, the new project of Ecological Modernization, has come to the fore as a solution to the ecological problems at the turn of the century. Aiming at bridging the gap between protecting the environment and fostering economic growth, this project has been advocated as a feasible alternative for the current model of development. My primary objective in this section is to discuss to what degree the new project of Ecological Modernization has departed from the neo-liberal capitalist paradigm of development and examine how compatible it is with the original sustainability discourse. I am going to start with examining some of the views defending this theory and then discuss its main criticisms and examine to what extent this theory has consolidated the position of sustainable development in its battle with unfettered economic growth.

The Inception and Popularization of Ecological Modernization

The term "Ecological Modernization" entered the literature of development studies in the 1980s originally to describe attempts to harness technological advances to serve environmental causes. However, the concept underwent some drastic changes which caused some critics to denounce it as yet another discourse to improve business competitiveness rather than articulating genuine changes in economic or political approaches to the environment. Like sustainable development, Ecological Modernization has become a highly controversial concept that is open to different interpretations. Consequently, strong and weak versions of Ecological Modernization have been used in defending this project that is meant to be a reconciliation between the capitalist system of development and environmental exigencies.

Originally conceived by German sociologists Joseph Huber, Martin Jänicke, and Udo E. Simonis within a group of scholars at Free University and the Social Science Research Centre in Berlin in the mid-1980s, the concept of Ecological Modernization came as a reconciliation between the growth agenda and environmental exigencies. The main proposition of this project is that economic growth can be adapted to meet environmental goals and that technological and scientific progress can remedy and reverse environmental degradation caused by economic growth (Redclift, 2000). Shedding more light on this project, Maurie J. Cohen explains that "Ecological Modernization provides a theoretical framework for situating the emergence of new technology-intensive modes of environmental reform such as industrial ecology, environmentally conscious manufacturing, and ecological design" (2006, p. 528). In essence, this new initiative aims at achieving a harmony between economic growth and environmental protection instead of the lingering conflict that characterizes the growth-environment relationship.

Although the difference between the "weak" and the "strong" versions of Ecological Modernization has been accentuated in a few studies (e.g., Blewitt, 2008; Christoff, 1996), the version that has been popularized in the literature is the one defending a strong harmony between economic growth and environmental protection without challenging the existent paradigm of growth. Regardless of the differences between the two versions of Ecological Modernization, this theory has succeeded in placing the environment as a high profile issue in the political and economic agendas of governments, global forums, and NGOs. Researcher Marteen Hajer points out that "at its [i.e., Ecological Modernization] centre stands the politico-administrative response to the latest manifestation of the ecological dilemma. Global ecological threats such as ozone layer depletion and global warming are met by a regulatory approach that starts from the assumption that economic growth and the resolution of ecological problems, in principle, can be reconciled" (1996, pp. 248–49).

On the whole, defenders of Ecological Modernization reject many environmentalists' claims—that the North consumes too much, that this theory is biased against the South, that the carrying capacity of the planet limits economic growth, and that increased consumption would inevitably result in the depletion of natural resources—which are often denounced as "misconceptions" (Sagoff 2000). In fact, views in defense of Ecological Modernization based much of their criticism on some inaccurate predictions made by scientists such as biologist Paul R. Ehrlich (1986), who warned that global shortages of natural resources would soon cause prices for food, fresh water, energy, and other material to soar and that humankind would suffer from an age of scarcity by the end of the twentieth century. Critics point out that all these apprehensions proved unfounded as the 1990s prices for food had plummeted and raw materials—including energy resources—were abundant and even less expensive than before (Sagoff, 2000). These views assert that new technologies have made more efficient use of natural resources possible and have come up with new alternatives to substitute for the depleted resources.

By and large, Ecological Modernization's major argument centers around one main belief that the only reasonable limits to growth are the limits of human knowledge. According to this approach, the elimination of hunger and poverty is constrained less by scarcity of natural resources than by trade barriers, misdistribution of wealth, corruption, and economic policies' inefficiency (Hayden, 2014). Explaining this point, Sagoff stresses that "it is simply wrong to believe that nature sets physical limits to economic growth—that is, to prosperity and the production and consumption of goods and services on which it is based. The idea that increasing consumption will inevitably lead to depletion and scarcity, as plausible as it may seem, is mistaken both in principle and in fact" (2000, p. 117). Ultimately, the whole limit-to-growth thesis is completely refuted, which calls into question the overall theories underpinning sustainability. Proponents of Ecological Modernization also draw on the no-limits-to-growth thesis to expose what they see as "the fallacy of energy shortage" that the world is going to suffer from in the near future. Sagoff argues, for instance, that new pollution-free energy is available in amounts that exceed our needs, and that all humans have to do is to focus on how to use this energy and combat whatever barriers show up in the path of green technology (2000, p. 124). Above all, advocates of Ecological Modernization decry the many obstacles erected in the way of green technology transfer from the North to South because of intricate issues such as property rights and trade regulations. In his book *Cool Energy: Renewable Solutions to Environmental Problems,* Michael Brower (1992) admits that any energy shortage that is likely to happen will be caused not by scarcity of natural resources, but rather by a vast array of barriers to trade and energy subsidies that tend to favor the same old inefficient and polluting energy uses.

The claim that the North exploits the South is also seen as a big misconception in Ecological Modernization theory. According to this view, the real problem is that the North imports too little from the South, and demands fewer of the South's exports now than in the past (Sagoff, 2000). This view is actually based on reports from the World Resources Institute showing that with a few exceptions—such as petroleum—most of the natural resources consumed in the United States are from domestic resources and that in the closing decades of the twentieth century the USA and Canada were in fact the world's leading exporters of raw materials. This approach, however, is at odds with the sustainability discourse based on the necessity of avoiding the current unsustainable Western economic model. Hence, by absolving the North of any historical responsibility for environmental degradation and exploitation in the South, Ecological Modernization seems to rebut the claims about the North's ecological debt[9] to the South in the sustainability discourse.

Everything considered, Ecological Modernization is widely celebrated as a promising project that not only marries economic growth to the environment, but also ensures better chances for sustainability thanks to technological innovations and scientific progress. By combining the generosity of nature and the ingenuity of humankind, Ecological Modernization theorists promise the world a model of development that offers the benefits of both economic growth and sustainability. The unmistakable primacy given to economic growth, nevertheless, underlies much of the criticism directed at the theory of Ecological Modernization. Critics from different schools of thought have called this theory everything from just another disguised discourse of neo-liberalism to a Northern attempt to deny the South its right to a sound economic growth.

Ecological Modernization and Sustainable Development: Allies or Enemies?

The theory of Ecological Modernization has been criticized because of what many critics consider as shortcomings in its theoretical underpinnings. In approaching this theory, some of these views reflect a rather Southern perspective, pointing to the "pro-Western" framework of thought that Ecological Modernization is based on. Critics scathingly decry the prioritization of economic growth as well as the spiritless version of sustainability this theory advocates. As I examine some of the main criticisms that the theory of Ecological Modernization faces, my aim in this section will be primarily to reveal to what extent this theory has helped or hindered the popularization and evolution of sustainable development, and how compatible this theory is with this project.

Critics of Ecological Modernization often point to a number of misperceptions they see as intrinsic to the basic tenets of this theory. First of all, Ecological Modernization is often denounced as legitimizing the very free market economic system and capitalist model of development that have engendered the current levels of environmental degradation. "Despite its name," argues Neil Carter "ecological modernisation is only superficially ecological because it largely ignores the integrity of ecosystems and the cumulative impact of industrialisation on them" (2007, p. 231). Likewise, Michael Redclift criticizes the idea that when it comes to economic growth, "it is assumed that advanced industrial societies can shift their technologies and patterns of production while leaving the structures of private capital accumulation fundamentally intact" (2000, p. 103). According to these views, the thinly disguised "growth agenda" that marks Ecological Modernization has overshadowed many of the strengths of this theory when it comes to serving sustainability. Hence, the argument that no major changes are needed in the capitalist economic system to achieve sustainability is denounced as a new form of "green capitalism" (Connelly & Smith, 1999).

While celebrating the benefits of economic growth, Ecological Modernization has, in fact, had rather insignificant influence on the patterns of production and consumption characterizing the global economy to date. Studies (e.g., Hayden, 2014; Carter, 2007; York & Rosa, 2003) point out that this project has failed to modify the dominant economic structures in both the developed and developing countries, denouncing "ecological modernisation as a facet of business development, rather than a means of raising environmental standards" (Redclift, 2000, p. 104). This failure seems to have cost sustainable development dearly in its clash with globalization. In intentionally eschewing any fundamental changes in the neoliberal capitalist model of growth, Ecological Modernization also makes it rather difficult to initiate the essential economic and societal preconditions to achieve sustainability within an environment-friendly "economic system that is able to generate surpluses and technical knowledge on a self-reliant and sustained basis" (WCED, 1987, p. 65). Thus, the undisguised alignment of Ecological Modernization with neo-liberalism and its celebration of the primacy of economic growth raise numerous challenges to the implementation of sustainable development.

Ecological Modernization also faces the criticism that it is not global in scope. Critics (e.g., Mol, 2003) point out that this project was designed and has been promoted by theorists in developed countries, who have concentrated their efforts on achieving some degree of sustainability by ensuring the protection of the environment without sacrificing continued economic growth and high consumption patterns. Other views contend that, because it has failed to grow into a global project, "the discourse of Ecological Modernization is often charged with being a discourse that supports the interests of political and economic elites in both the North and the South, with little regard for other communities" (Connelly & Smith, 1999, p. 185). Through Ecological Modernization, the industrialized counties have been trying to internalize environmental protection costs in the process of economic growth while adhering to the same principles of free trade and continuous economic and industrial growth, thus maintaining what is referred to as the "Business-As-Usual" (BAU) paradigm (Hayden, 2014). Critics (e.g., Porter & Brown, 1996; Baker, 2006; Tarnoff, 1992), however, point out that developing countries rank environmental concerns differently on their developmental agendas. In fact, concern with environmental problems in the South usually takes on a different dimension, in that more priority is given to problems of desertification, fresh water scarcity, and soil erosion than to global environmental problems like ozone layer depletion, global warming, and biodiversity loss (Baker, 2006).

According to another view, one more sign of the failure of Ecological Modernization is the fact that nearly two decades after the 1992 Rio Summit, global commitment to readjusting economic structures to internalize environmental concerns is still weak and the implementation of the Rio agreements is rather shaky (Khor, 1995). In sidelining the South's environmental concerns, Ecological Modernization has deepened even more the lingering North-South divide, thus making it harder for sustainable development to achieve the necessary global consensus on environmental exigencies in both developed and developing countries. Martin Khor (1995) contends that Ecological Modernization has also exacerbated the rift between the North and the South regarding options of development and environmental protection at a time when sustainable development is in urgent need of new efforts aimed at strengthening its consensus-building strategies.

Despite the multiple strengths of Ecological Modernization, what makes this project rather incompatible with sustainable development, in my view, is that the former adopts and advocates a rather distorted version of sustainability, thus undermining much of the hard-won public support for sustainable development as an alternative paradigm of growth. The dissemination of a rather weak version of sustainability through Ecological Modernization has also caused public zeal for this project to falter in many parts of the world when activists started to notice that no real changes were introduced. The theory of Ecological Modernization has, therefore, done more harm than good to sustainable development when it aligned itself with neoliberal capitalism at the expense of achieving sustainability. By and large, Ecological Modernization has failed to reflect a sound version of sustainable development that is sensitive to cultural differences, social values, and the indigenous local knowledge. It has also failed to cater to all those marginalized by the predominant socio-economic model of development based fundamentally on economic growth. Clearly, Ecological Modernization falls short of representing a radical move to change the patterns of production and consumption that have brought about the current plight of unsustainability in modern society.

CONCLUSION

As products of the same era, globalization and sustainable development share some interesting structural characteristics and exhibit a notable affinity in many respects. As such, these two projects reflect some concepts typical of the post-industrial societies in which they have been conceived and popularized. This structural affinity implies a potential for a harmonization between activists on both parts if it receives enough academic attention. An exploration of the classical theories of economic growth, however, shows that a harmonization between globalization and sustainability is extremely difficult to achieve today due to the significant incompatibilities in their theoretical underpinnings. A close look at the tenets of sustainability and those of neo-liberalism, for instance, exposes the yawning gap between the necessary conditions for economic globalization on the one hand, and the requirements of establishing a sustainable development paradigm, on the other. With its multiple economic, social, and cultural repercussions, globalization has created a rather unfavorable context for the project of sustainable development in its early years.

Based on conflicting theories and aiming at widely different goals, globalization and sustainable development seem to be on a collision course today. As a matter of fact, these two paradigms of development diverge on a number of contemporary issues. Empowered by mammoth TNCs, globalization has gained the upper hand in its battle with sustainable development, thus nullifying many of the new strategies for a sustainable way of growth. As a consequence, the seeds of sustainability seem to have fallen on rather barren soil as the process of globalization intensified and the globalized economy made it almost impossible for any country to opt out of the neo-liberal capitalist model of growth. The new sustainable strategies of development have also been met with obstruction, as many tenets of sustainability have been weakened by the neo-liberal strategies of exponential economic growth that far exceeded the ecological capacity of the planet.

The attempt to marry sustainability to neoliberal capitalism under the name of Ecological Modernization has also proven controversial and disappointing. Celebrating many of the blessings of today's globalized economy and modern technology, adherents of Ecological Modernization align themselves with neo-liberalism and thinly concealed their commitment to exponential economic growth, which, they contend, would ultimately help take care of the environment and achieve sustainability. Nevertheless, this marriage between sustainable development and neo-liberalism has been rather detrimental to the former, and its outcome—Ecological Modernization—has been disowned by many environmentalists for sacrificing sustainability for economic growth. On the whole, Ecological Modernization proved more of an enemy than an ally to the project of sustainable development. Hence, with public opinion divided between weak and strong versions of sustainable development, sustainability seems to be losing ground to the current capitalist paradigm of growth. Ultimately, it has become clear that sustainable development as a whole does not fit into the capitalist system, which intrinsically excludes any constraints to economic growth. The different aspects and repercussions of this emerging project's battle with the predominant socio-economic paradigm will be the subject of the next chapter.

NOTES

1. See Kelbessa, 2001, pp. 283–286; McLaren, 2003, pp. 32–35; Dale, 2001, p. 87; Mulinge & Munyae, 2001, pp. 104–10; Kütting, 2004, p. 55; Shiva, 2003, pp. 142–144; and Blewitt, 2008, p. 18.

2. See McMichael, 2017; Kelbessa, 2001; Mulinge & Munyae, 2001; McLaren, 2003; Dale, 2001; Shiva, 2003; and Blewitt, 2008.

3. For a thorough discussion of this issue, see McLaren, 2003, pp. 32–35; Khor, 2001a, p. 209; Wade, 2007, pp. 277–283; Blewitt, 2008, p. 4–9; and Dale, 2001, p. 87.

4. This affinity can be sensed in the points of view expressed by Rodrik, 2007b, pp. 308–310; Blewitt, 2008, p. 9; Carter, 2007, p. 9; WCED, 1987, p. 65; and Earth Charter, 2012.

5. See McAdams, 1996, pp. 57–63; Norberg 2003/2007, pp. 270–274; Dale, 2001, p. 132; Carter, 2007, 55; WCED, 1987, pp. 5–6, 65–66; and Earth Charter, 2012.

6. For a thorough discussion of this issue, see McLaren, 2003, pp. 32–35; Dale, 2001, p. 87; Kütting, 2004, p. 55; Shiva, 2003, pp. 142–144; Sydee & Beder, 2009, pp. 255–256; and Blewitt, 2008, p. 18.

7. This term is often used in the literature to refer to "a distinctive green political ideology encompassing those perspectives that hold that a sustainable society requires radical change in our relationship with the non-human natural world and our mode of economic, social and political life" (Carter, 2007, p. 6).

8. Statistics show, for example, that of the largest one hundred economies in the world, fifty-two are now corporations: Mitsubishi (the 22nd largest economy), General Motors (the 26th largest economy), and Ford (the 31st largest economy) are all larger than the economies of many countries such as Denmark, Turkey, South Africa, Saudi Arabia, Malaysia, or New Zealand, among others (Mander, 2003, p. 126). For a lengthy discussion of the real power of today's TNCs, see Rushkoff (2011).

9. The notion of ecological debt is based on the view that economies of the rich industrialized countries have been built on natural resources such as timber, minerals, oil, etc., from poor Third World countries, hence these developed countries' responsibility to limit their consumption and seek ways to curb and reverse ecological damage that industrialization has brought about ever since the Industrial Revolution (McLaren, 2003, p. 30).

THREE

Extrinsic and Intrinsic Impediments to Sustainability

Just before the debate on globalization came into vogue in the closing decades of the twentieth century, politicians, scientists, and the mainstream public realized that environmental problems were transcending boundaries ever more and indeed reaching global proportions. The globalization of the environmental issue triggered the first attempts of global environmental governance to contain the new trans-boundary threats. A wide array of ideas, theories, and principles were conceived to accommodate the new environmental exigencies, initiating what is now referred to as "global environmental politics." Over the last few decades, the rise of global environmental politics has also led to a widespread re-examination of established assumptions, interpretations, and beliefs about contemporary political theories and practices. Recognized ideologies such as liberalism, conservatism, socialism, and feminism have had to respond to this emerging environmental discourse, thus giving rise to several hybrid concepts and theories such as "eco-socialism" and "eco-feminism," among other derivations. Nonetheless, core political principles and theories did inform the underpinnings of environmental politics, as concepts such as justice, democracy, and equity are now central to "green politics."

Against such a backdrop, the new project of sustainable development came as a challenge to the current socio-economic paradigm of growth. Essentially, this new sustainability discourse preaches a new vision of how political, economic, social, and environmental factors ought to be combined in the light of new ecological challenges. In doing so, the new project of sustainable development departs significantly from the 1970s environmental movement's narrow focus on single issues of pollution, diversity loss, and other forms of the abuse of Nature. The most distinctive feature of this new paradigm, therefore, is that it not only questions the long-standing assumption of the inevitable trade-offs between the environment and economic growth, but that it also places environmental issues in a broader social, economic, and political context. Globally, North-South politics has failed thus far to capture the complexity of contemporary environmental issues, which has had significant implications for the integrity and popularity of the project of sustainable development.

EXTRINSIC IMPEDIMENTS TO SUSTAINABILITY

The worldwide celebration of sustainability as a concept belies deep conflict over its meaning and its implementation at the global scale. Within the contemporary socio-economic paradigm of growth, a combination of different political and economic factors has contributed to the weakening of sustainable development. Hence, my aim in the first section of this chapter is essentially to spotlight the obstacles facing this new project, which are of two types: extrinsic and intrinsic. The first category of these obstacles relates typically to the unpropitious climate of neoliberal capitalism in which sustainable development appeared and the unresponsive global governance system. On the other hand, the second category relates basically to the very theoretical conceptualization of this project and to the resultant incoherence of the various forms it has taken. Hence, I start this chapter with an examination of the obstacles facing sustainability in a context of a neoliberal capitalist paradigm of growth, and then I proceed to those obstacles rising from within this new paradigm itself. On the whole, my chief aim is to examine to what degree these extrinsic and intrinsic obstacles have crippled the evolution and implementation of sustainable development and what have come out of this project in the light of all these hardships.

Sustainability and the Rise of Modern Capitalism: A Disturbed Society-Environment Relationship

The rise of modern capitalism, based largely on Enlightenment thinking and the primacy of economic growth, has usually been considered as the starting point of environmental degradation. The rise of capitalism has also been characterized by a disturbed environment-society relationship that manifests itself in the prevailing instrumental view of Nature and the phenomenon of consumerism that has marked modern societies. Within this framework, I want first to examine the idea of whether the relationship between the environment and globalization dealt with in the previous chapter is but an extension of a broader relationship between capitalism and Nature as such. Secondly, I want to discuss whether or not the disturbed environment-society relationship is wholly at odds with the holistic view of Nature in the sustainability discourse.

Over decades, the principles of capitalism were upheld by theorists, economists, and politicians who asserted that free trade, more capital flow, and state non-intervention policies would lead to more economic growth, more wealth creation, and ultimately more well-being for the whole society. Neoliberal economists (e.g., Bhagwati, 2007; Norberg, 2003/2007; Sagoff, 2000) also argue that more consumption means more growth whereas less consumption can lead to slackening in growth and less well-being for the society. However, throughout this process of wealth creation, Nature, as an independent entity, has been almost excluded from this equation and existed only as a source of raw material or a recipient of industrial and chemical waste. More and more critics, however, consider the rise of modern capitalism as the main cause of why societies have become alienated from their physical environment, which has been conducive to a rather disturbed society-environment relationship. "The rise of modern capitalism, enlightenment, Newtonian science, and the industrial revolution," these critics argue, "acted in concert to bring about a change in society-environment relations as humans in the core economies saw themselves as increasingly mastering Nature rather than being dependent and dominated by it" (Kütting, 2004, p. 25).

Although some forms of environmental degradation with limited regional impact did exist in pre-industrial societies, many studies (e.g., Sachs, 2015; Goldemberg, 2003; Altvater, 1998; Dresner, 2002; Kütting, 2004) assert that the global features of environmental degradation have generally been associated with the Industrial Revolution and the process of economic growth taking place mainly in industrialized countries ever since. What is more, this relationship between environmental degradation and today's socio-economic model of growth was often regarded as part of the modernity project. For neoliberal economists, the "environmental problems, rather than being caused by economic growth as measured by GDP, can be solved by growth" (Robbins, 2009, p. 5). However, for scholars like Ann Dale (2001), Stuart Hart (2009), and Andres R. Edwards (2008), the subordination of the environment to economic growth marked a serious turning point in the society-environment relationship, ushering in a new phase of alienation between Man and Nature. Indeed, this growing estrangement between Man and Nature constitutes one of the main obstacles facing sustainable development which advocates a totally different conception of society-environment relationship.

One of the milestones in the ongoing debate on society-environment relationship was the publication of *The Limits to Growth* by Donella H. Meadows, Dennis L. Meadows, Jørgen Randers, and William W. Behrens III in 1974. As the environmental issue was gaining momentum in the 1970s, this document triggered a heated debate about the existence of ecological limits to economic and population growth. Using state-of-the-art computer modeling techniques at that time, the authors came to the conclusion that if existing growth rates continued, "the limits to growth on this planet will be reached sometime within the next one hundred years" (Meadows et al., 1974, p. 23). With all its alarming findings, this report acquired a substantial significance in boosting the cause of the environmental movement in the 1970s and in drawing public attention to the rising environmental concerns.

In addition to making the environment a high-profile issue on the political agenda of the time, *The Limits to Growth* informed green ideology or "ecologism" in various ways. As a matter of fact, this report gave the project of sustainable development a strong and solid *raison d'être* which thoroughly informed its discourse and articulated its approach to economy, society, and Nature. Neil Carter pointedly argues, for instance, that "the concept of finitude underpinning the 'limits to growth' thesis is unique to 'ecologism'; it implies that any future sustainable world will be characterised by material scarcity rather than abundance" (2007, p. 43). This document has also been an important eye-opener for the American public regarding the intricate interdependence between Nature and Man. Thus, in the wake of *The Limits to Growth* thesis, the prevailing environment-society relationship characterizing the current socio-economic paradigm of growth has been widely called into question.

As I see it, the contemporary society-environment relationship constitutes a salient feature of the incompatibility between the current socio-economic paradigm of growth and sustainability. While the overall message of *The Limits to Growth* is that environmental degradation is inextricably linked to the capitalist economic, social, and political systems, neoliberal economists (e.g., Bhagwati, 2007; Norberg, 2003/2007) still insist that the solutions for these environmental problems necessitate more economic growth. Therefore, a real shift in the society-environment relationship is still not on their agenda and radical changes in the capitalist modes of production and consumption are often dismissed. From an environmentalist point of view, the whole capitalist drive for continuous exponential economic growth simply contradicts the limits-to-growth principle and the need to live within the ecological carrying capacities of the planet Earth (Sachs, 2015; Dale, 2001; Speth, 2008). Achieving sustainability, therefore, requires fundamental transformations in the current approaches to growth, consumption, production, and above all, in society's relationship with the environment.

Over the process of industrialization, modern capitalism has also caused society to become more alienated from its natural environment. In fact, critics like Ann Dale (2001) and Stuart Hart (2009) believe that the more societies become industrialized, the more this alienation intensifies. Armed with modern science and technology, capitalist industrial societies developed a solid conviction that they have become the absolute masters of Nature rather than being an integral part of it. Critics of the capitalist system, on the other hand, argue that "by controlling public awareness of environmental issues, the media, corporations, and governments, and often religious institutions help foster the ideology that human beings were put on earth to dominate Nature," upholding a "patriarchal capitalism that equates the domination of Nature with the domination of women" (Robbins, 2009, p. 14). Thus, the unrelenting attempts to master Nature and harness its resources to achieve more material well-being, more capital accumulation, and further economic growth causes people to become more estranged from Nature, especially when their understanding of ecological limits of the planet is still limited.

Historically, the dichotomy between Man's mastery of Nature and Man's subservience to Nature dates back long before the inception of the project of sustainable development. In the literature, this notion has also been referred to as "mechanism-organism" dichotomy—between a machine-based approach to development, usually with a merely instrumental use of Nature, and a holistic view of development that caters for humans as an integral part of Nature (Kütting, 2004, p. 31). Gabriela Kütting claims that the current mechanical approach to Nature based on the notion "that Nature/environment can be neatly compartmentalized into constituent parts and that these parts are not interdependent" constitutes yet another impediment in front of achieving sustainability (2004, p. 31). Consequently, by dissecting Nature into independent parts, this view contradicts and reverses the holistic approach to Nature embraced in the sustainability discourse.

To my mind, the predominant "instrumental" approach to Nature seems to perpetuate a disturbed society-environment relationship in modern societies as it downplays the seriousness and urgency of the ecological problems caused by the prevalent unsustainable patterns of economic growth. It does so by trying to fix any environmental problem independently from other issues while claiming that it has little connection with other social and ecological issues. By thwarting the holistic view of Nature, modern capitalism also reduces Nature to simple compartmentalized parts that can be dealt with independently, thus weakening the main sustainability drive that is based on a totally different kind of society-environment relationship. As a consequence, "the anthropocentric view that Nature belongs to us rather than we to Nature," concludes Speth, "eases the exploitation of the natural world. The habit of focusing on the present and discounting the future leads away from a thoughtful appraisal of long-term consequences and the world we are making" (2008, p. 62).

Undoubtedly, the society-environment relationship varies according to the degree of industrialization and wealth of nations, the predominant culture in society, and the type of livelihood that the citizens have within this society. In modern societies, however, the alienation that characterized Man's relationship with Nature is exacerbated by higher rates of mass production and consumption nurtured by the principles of neoliberal capitalism. Indeed, the whole socio-economic paradigm of growth prevalent today systematically weakens efforts to raise the citizens' awareness of ecological problems and reverse the estrangement between society and the environment. As such, the instrumental approach to Nature in contemporary neoliberal capitalism jeopardizes strategies for a sustainable mode of development when it places Man as the master of his environment and downplays the intrinsic value of Nature. As this top-down society-environment relationship prevails, citizens become increasingly estranged from Nature, which limits their consciousness of their harmful abuses of the environment. This alienation intensifies even more when the process of globalization further obscures current environmental degradation by disconnecting people from the dire effects of their abuses of Nature.

Closely linked to the disturbed environment-society relationship that has marked current post-industrial societies, time-space distanciation is another feature of globalization that makes it highly incompatible with sustainability. One important aspect of this phenomenon is that the mass production and consumption processes typical of industrialized societies usually take place far away from the resource extraction process located in remote places, thus obscuring the concomitant environmental abuse and further degrading the environment-society relationship. Observers (e.g., Dale, 2001) note, for instance, that as a result of this distanciation, citizens of the post-industrial societies become gradually estranged from their environment and almost blinded by a false sense of well-being created by modern capitalism to the actual degree of environmental degradation.

To start with, I find it essential to spotlight the historical context in which the phenomenon of time-space distanciation came to the fore as one of the main aspects of globalization. There is now a widely held belief that the advent of globalization, with all its overwhelming and unrelenting economic, social, technological, and cultural processes, has made of the world a global village. Thanks to technological telecommunication breakthroughs, remote parts of the world have become unprecedentedly interconnected to a high degree. Many observers (e.g., Blewitt, 2008; Chasek, Downie, & Brown, 2010; Choudhary, 2004) today talk about how the local has become closely connected to the global not only economically, but also politically and culturally. As such, the phenomenon of globalization also ushered in a new concept of time-space distanciation defined by Gabriela Kütting as follows:

> The basic idea behind this concept is that under globalization social relations are spatially removed, creating global-local linkages through economic and cultural practices. At the same time social relations are also temporally removed in two ways: first of all, events can be experi-

> enced simultaneously in different places through sophisticated technology and, second, the consequences of an action or policy may not be felt in a different place until sometime after actual events (temporal distanciation). So, time-space distanciation is mostly about global-local linkages. (Kütting 2004, p. 33)

As I see it, the phenomenon of time-space distanciation reflects much of the incompatibility between sustainable development and the current model of growth. By disconnecting societies' economic activities from their particular social and environmental consequences, this phenomenon obscures causal links between industrialization and its negative effects on the ecology and on society. Pamela S. Chasek, David L. Downie, and Janet Welsh Brown explain that time-space distanciation "stretches the chains of production and consumption over great distances and across many locations, which increases the separation between sources of environmental problems and their impact" (2010, p. 367). This distanciation, therefore, raises a huge challenge for sustainable development as to how to make people conscious of the environmental damage caused by their consumption patterns if they cannot see this damage in their daily life.

The negative effects of time-space distanciation on sustainable development are best exemplified in two particular phenomena, namely ozone layer depletion and the growing of "cash crops" in the developing countries. Recent scientific studies have adequately demonstrated that the current ozone hole over Antarctica, Latin America, and Australia is caused primarily by the CFC (chlorofluorocarbons) gases and other Ozone Depleting Substances (ODS) released into the atmosphere during decades of mass production, mass consumption, and relentless fossil-fuel economic growth, mainly in the industrialized countries. What is more, the growing consequences of this global environmental problem strike first in small islands and some developing countries, which are poorly equipped to deal with such predicaments (Leichenko & O'Brien, 2008). Because wealthy industrialized societies can hardly feel the consequences of their daily abuses of Nature in concrete examples that touch their lives, their consciousness of their abuses of Nature grows weaker over time. Looking at the big picture, this type of time-space distanciation clearly works against efforts to forge a consensus on sustainability.

The second example of time-space distanciation relates essentially to what is referred to as cash crops[1] grown in the developing countries just to satisfy the consumers' demand in the global market usually at the expense of covering local food shortages in developing countries. According to John Blewitt, "poor nations are [usually] forced to grow cash crops and export raw materials to the affluent developed nations, who then 'add value' through production processes and refinement, while externalizing any environmental costs to the country of origin" (2008, pp.

12–13). Other views (e.g., Kütting, 2004; Maxwell & Fernando, 1989) point out that because these cash crops are grown in regions so remote from developed countries, the societies in these industrialized countries usually have a faint idea about what environmental damages these cash crops cause. Again, this type of time-space distanciation nurtured by the contemporary paradigm of growth engenders obstacles to building a worldwide ecological consciousness that sustainability is based upon. The consequences of this phenomenon are, therefore, detrimental to the strategies of sustainable development, for they insidiously corrode one of the chief foundations of this project—public consciousness of environmental exigencies and sustainable growth.

Revolutionary as it might be in other fields, the phenomenon of time-space distanciation, has proven alarmingly detrimental to sustainable development. By creating and popularizing an unrealistic society-environment relationship, time-space distanciation makes it difficult for society to spot the causal link between the accumulation of capital and the resultant environmental degradation as well as social dislocations. In addition, the supremacy of individual property rights and the intense pursuit of materialistic lifestyles prevalent in the post-industrial consumer society contradict the supremacy of preserving Nature and collective efforts to safeguard the environment in ecologism. This reduces even more the chances for survival of this new project in a hostile environment created by neo-liberal capitalism and perpetuated by a worldwide zeal for global consumerism.

Global Consumer Culture vs. the Limits to Growth and Social Equity

With the rise of neoliberal capitalism and the onset of the globalization process, human production and consumption volume has increased exponentially over the past century.[2] This explosion in production and consumption patterns has had profound economic, political, and cultural ramifications worldwide. The fervent quest for material well-being, the voracious accumulation of wealth, and the insatiable desire for further consumption in industrialized societies have all grown into a fast-growing phenomenon dubbed "global consumer culture." The global economic changes of the last quarter of the twentieth century and the early twenty-first century have also brought about numerous fundamental changes in the consumer ethics prevalent in these post-industrial societies. Due to the process of globalization, this consumer culture has been widely exported to the rest of the world, and non-Western societies have adopted and identified themselves with the Western lifestyle (Sydee & Beder, 2009, p. 255; Kütting, 2004). In the light of these changes, my focus in this section is going to be on the negative effects that global consumer culture has had on the emerging project of sustainable development. More specifically, I am going to spotlight the dramatic societal and cultural changes that hinder the progress of this new project in a context of neoliberal capitalism. Understanding the far-reaching effects of these economic and cultural changes, in my view, is essential to discerning the nature and the scope of the mismatch between the current paradigm of growth and sustainability.

Although culture is generally an elusive concept to define, I am going to consider the sum of the predominant social practices and beliefs underpinning the prevailing economic, political, and religious systems as the culture of today's post-industrial societies. In modern times, society-environment relationship has become both blurred and unrealistic, for it does not reflect the real magnitude of environmental degradation, with a concomitant sense of alienation and estrangement between society and its environment. This estrangement from Nature has contributed considerably to the surge of mass consumption especially in wealthy societies. Thus, consumerism has become not only a "pillar of modern capitalism," but also "an approach to life and social well-being that elevates the material conditions of life over the spiritual and social dimensions" (Speth, 2008, p. 147).

Globally, TNCs have played an important role in the popularization of the consumer culture in their quest for new markets and to keep the economy booming. "Such corporate dominance," contends Stuart L. Hart, "is leading to a worldwide commercial monoculture based upon the values of Western consumerism and bringing with it the decline of local cultures, products, and traditions" (2009, p. xxxvii). Cultural globalization—also referred to as Westernization—has contributed to the spread of standardized mass consumption patterns that have, in turn, led to the creation of what came to be known as "a global consumer." The phenomenon of cultural globalization has also been criticized for failing to produce a new form of a global culture as such, but rather aiming at "artificially creating a transnational cultural type that is predominantly characterized by the consumption of global brand names and a particular form of news and entertainment" (Kütting, 2004, p. 45). What is heralded as a global culture, other critics note, is but the spread of Western consumption patterns, which is closer to an economic phenomenon than to a new form of culture (Sydee & Beder, 2009). More important than these definitional problems, in my view, is the damage that this consumer culture or global consumerism causes to the project of sustainable development.

In the literature of development and environmental studies, the argument that excessive consumption of the earth's natural resources results in environmental degradation is not a new argument and dates back to the beginning of the environmental movement in the early 1970s. Reports such as *The Limits to Growth* by the Club of Rome had a wide-ranging influence on environmentalists and other activists who questioned the prevailing culture of consumerism and condemned its unprecedented consequences of environmental abuse. Being another distinctive feature of neoliberal capitalism, the issue of overconsumption represents one of the biggest obstacles to sustainability. Hence, the challenge facing this new paradigm is twofold: first, most attempts to implement sustainable development strategies take place in a very unpropitious context that is based on unsustainable fossil-fuel modes of economic growth with little consideration for ecological limits. Secondly, this new paradigm aims at establishing a broad type of "ecological consciousness" in post-industrial societies where consumer ethics are still deeply entrenched.

For the most part, many of the obstacles facing sustainability today are closely related to contemporary developmental options. Many studies[3] show, for instance, that excessive consumption of the planet's renewable and non-renewable resources has caused increasingly irreversible environmental degradation that grew from local to global by the turn of the twenty-first century. Nevertheless, the neoliberal capitalist approach that currently prevails in global economic, trade, and developmental institutions is based on the assumption that the high standards of living currently enjoyed by the richest 20 percent of the world's population can be extended to the rest of the world if they follow the same path of economic growth (Rostow, 1991). In fact, the affluent Western lifestyles with their high consumption rates make the present capitalist model of growth much more appealing to developing countries than the rather austere sustainable development paradigm. Besides, the powerful TNCs and relentless worldwide media propaganda popularizing global consumerism and exporting consumer ethics are insidiously dwarfing any efforts to popularize sustainability both locally and globally. All of these factors coalesce into economic and cultural impediments to sustainable development, which seeks to change the consumption patterns of society and its relationship with Nature as a whole.

As with production, consumption reflects yet another feature of the dichotomy between sustainability and neoliberal capitalism. Given their conflicting theoretical underpinnings, the neoliberal capitalist discourse and the sustainable development discourse have two contradictory visions of consumption. Neoliberal economists (e.g., Sagoff, 2000; Krugman & Venables, 1995; Bhagwati, 2007), for example, consider growth and consumption as an essential tenet of the current development model that can be extended indefinitely. Accordingly, consumption is thought of as the very engine of this model of growth in today's society "that considers trade and consumption the source of all well-being [. . .] built on the foundation of perpetual economic growth, in which we are required to produce and buy more this year than last year and more next year than this year in perpetuity" (Robbins, 2009, p. 1). In fact, this neoliberal capitalist approach considers consumption as the last stage in the production-consumption cycle, which means that once a product is consumed, more products must be manufactured to satisfy more demands and make more profits. Ultimately, this approach poses a big challenge to sustainable development because it fails to take on board issues like the carrying capacity of the planet and the necessity of recycling.

Counterbalancing this zeal for global consumption comes sustainable development's rallying cry for sagacious patterns of consumption within the carrying eco-systems of the planet. From an environmentalist point of view, consumption is but a stage that has to be interconnected with other stages such as environment-friendly production, preserving the common goods, and the process of recycling to alleviate the pressure on renewable and non-renewable natural resources. The limits to growth principle, therefore, plays an important role in sensitizing the public to the required rates and scopes of consumption within the project of sustainable development. "A green economy [that] would be based on production primarily for use rather than profit, and would thereby rule out such frivolous consumption" has, therefore, become one of the major objectives of this project, argues Neil Carter (2007, p. 48). However, this new conception is still evidently incongruous in a context of neoliberal capitalism that prioritizes economic growth and ever-increasing consumption at the expense of sustainability.

Another important feature of this dichotomy is also revealed by the issue of waste and recycling after consumption. On the one hand, the capitalist approach considers consumption as the last stage in the production-consumption process, and thus does not take into account the way the consumer disposes of the goods consumed. This neglect of the recycling process, critics argue, further alienates society from its environment and disconnects these consumers from their social and environmental responsibilities (Kütting, 2004). Environmentalists, on the other hand, consider that the disposal of the product consumed as waste is the last stage in the production-consumption-disposal cycle. However, only under huge pressure from environmentalists did governments in industrialized countries, international economic organizations, and TNCs start to pay attention to the issue of waste disposal (Chasek, Downie, & Brown, 2010, pp. 141–145). In fact, the way these governments and organizations dealt with this issue has raised a lot of apprehensions mainly because "corporations only take account of costs that are integral to their own functioning" and "wherever possible, the consequences of production are externalized, from waste products to the need to care for old or sick workers" (Mellor, 2000, p. 157).

Whereas most problems associated with excessive consumption can be related to the predominant consumer society ethic and the neoliberal capitalist model of growth in general, sustainable development does not absolve the consumers from their responsibilities in this process. Unlike the current socio-economic paradigm of development, the sustainability discourse does not consider consumption as the last stage of production and attaches great importance to recycling, the use of environment-friendly "green" technologies, and less energy-intensive growth. In essence, the perception of the consumer in the capitalist paradigm of development is radically different from the one held in the sustainable development paradigm, hence the discrepancy in the consumer ethics in the two discourses. While consumers, viewed as passive elements, are often targeted by the huge power of advertisement and the allure of modern lifestyle in neoliberal capitalism, they are held accountable for their choices and patterns of consumption in the sustainability discourse. This juxtaposition is, in my opinion, another illuminating insight into how divergent the two paradigms are and how difficult it is to establish new consumer ethics in this context.

On the whole, the current capitalist paradigm tends to thwart efforts to raise ecological consciousness when it absolves the consumers of their responsibilities on the grounds that they are constrained in their actions and choices by the market mechanisms of supply and demand. Critics (e.g., Kütting, 2004) point to the huge pressure from advertising to "keep up with the Joneses" and the prevalent ethic of the consumer society as a major impediment to effecting a social change with regards to consumption. Though it admits the heavy pressure of all these materialistic ethics of modern lifestyles, the sustainability discourse, nonetheless, places a lot of emphasis on the will of consumers as conscious citizens, and seeks to maximize their awareness regarding the need to consume sustainably in documents such as the *Brundtland Report*, the Earth Charter, and *Agenda 21*. For adherents of the sustainability agenda, "it is not convincing to take the consumer out of the equation by arguing that they are the unwitting victims of the production process or victims of the capitalist ethic of consumption" (Kütting, 2004, pp. 59–60). Hence, the contrast between these two different visions of the responsibility and awareness of consumers in society reveals that the incompatibility between sustainable development and the current paradigm of growth is not limited to economic features but extended to cultural and social aspects.

This discrepancy between the current socio-economic model of growth and sustainability is also reinforced by the prevalent unequal distribution of wealth[4] and its concomitant consequences on both society and the environment. Though consumption itself is one of the integral pillars of capitalism, the scale and nature of consumption nurtured by modern capitalism goes far beyond the natural human needs of food and shelter. Given this overwhelming drive in modern societies, it has become clear that "the most characteristic feature of modern capitalism is its insatiability" (Campbell, 1987, p. 37). What is more alarming, nonetheless, is that not only do modern consumer societies insatiably consume much more than what they need, but they also expect that increasing consumption rates guarantee more welfare, in an illogical defiance of the finiteness of the earth's natural resources. Critics such as Speth (2008), Hart (2009), Edwards (2008), Hawken (1997), and Dale (2001), among others, argue that if contemporary industrialized society is to survive this ecological crisis, it has to change from a *consumer* society to a *conserver* society. In such a conserver society, Neil Carter asserts, "any quantitative reduction in the overall material standard of life in the sustainable economy will be more than compensated for by the resulting benefits, both material, such as improved craftsmanship, healthier food and safer communities, and 'spiritual' in terms of happiness, individual fulfillment and a more co-operative society" (2007, p. 49).

The huge emphasis on the production-consumption processes, the dissemination of materialist ethics, and the neglect of environmental exigencies have all contributed a great deal to papering over social inequality in modern societies and to perpetuating patterns of environmental degradation. Looking at the big picture, this rather linear expectation of progress advocated in neoliberal capitalism is one of the major obstacles to the project of sustainable development, which strives to awaken consumers to the drawbacks of the consumer culture. These drawbacks become even more evident as this project diverges from neoliberal capitalism over the issue of social equity.

The yawning rift between neoliberal capitalism and sustainability is constantly echoed in the divergent economic and social approaches in these two models of development. According to the sustainability discourse, the challenges of changing deeply entrenched perceptions of the mastery of Nature, ongoing economic growth, and overconsumption are inextricably interconnected with another important issue, namely social equity. Indeed, the challenge of achieving intergenerational and intragenerational social equity is one of the most essential themes in the 1987 *Brundtland Report* (WCED, 1987). Nevertheless, social equity is often given much lower priority than ongoing economic growth, free capital flow, liberalized trade, and more wealth creation within a free market system. The mere juxtaposition of the two conflicting perceptions of social equity in the two discourses, in my view, bespeaks stark incompatibility and deep divergence of views. Given the predominance of the neoliberal capitalist economic system today, achieving the sustainable development version of social equity would be yet another cumbersome burden.

Many neoliberal economists and thinkers (e.g., Bhagwati, 2007; Norberg, 2003/2007; Krugman & Venables, 1995) claim that although rising rates of global inequality marked the late 1980s and early 1990s, global inequality decreased substantially during the first decade of the twenty-first century. Economist Jagdish Bhagwati firmly concludes, for instance, that "globalization cannot be plausibly argued to have increased poverty in the poor nations or to have widened world inequality. The evidence points in just the opposite direction" (2007, p. 67). Mark Sagoff (2000) shares the same view about the recent, noticeable improvement in living standards worldwide, pointing out that in 1960 nearly 70 percent of the world population lived at or below subsistence level whereas less than 30 percent of this population do now. Nevertheless, he admits that "what is worsening is the discrepancy in income between the wealthy and the poor" (2000, p. 131). According to this view, there is no harm in inequality as long as all people are becoming better off than before. "Surely the important thing is for everyone to be as well off as possible, not whether one group is better off than another," explains Johan Norberg (2003/2007, p. 272).

Counterbalancing the previous viewpoint is the stance of other critics (e.g., Hart, 2009; Kroll & Robbins, 2009; Mander, 2003) who claim that the very structure of the global economic system and free trade organizations aims not at achieving high standards of living for all peoples of the world, but more precisely at guaranteeing a constant inflow of consumer goods to the consuming elites mainly in affluent societies. John Blewitt further contends that "organizations like the World Trade Organization (WTO) were established specifically to serve global corporate interests, even if these run contrary to the policies and needs of democratically elected governments and their people" (2008, p. 134). This global economic system is also accused of serving primarily the interests of affluent industrialized countries at the expense of impoverished developing countries: "Many traditionally subsistence-based communities," critics argue, "have lost power and control over their lands and their practices, including women's knowledge and farming capacities, due to their interaction with capitalist economics and the dominant Western worldview" (Sydee & Beder, 2009, p. 255).

Using this analysis framework, I believe that the issue of equity reveals a profound contradiction between the neoliberal discourse and the sustainability discourse. On the one hand, the neoliberal economic policies of the industrialized countries today seemingly include the notion of poverty alleviation and achieving social equity albeit with a solid belief that this should be done without fundamental structural changes in the capitalist economic model of growth. On the other hand, the sustainability approach stresses the necessity of profound structural changes to the current model of growth in order to gear it to sustainable development goals including social equity and environmental protection.

The current divergence of views is further aggravated by the intensification of economic globalization which has made any fundamental economic structural changes extremely difficult, for they will not affect one country or economy but a whole network of inextricably interconnected economies. In fact, "expressed or tacit acceptance of being encompassed in globalization," critics point out, "entails a lessening, or in some cases a negating, of the quantum of political control exercised by the encompassed, especially in the least powerful and poorest zones of the global political economy" (Mittelman, 2000, p. 5). Thus, while the sustainablility discourse deems it vital to implement structural changes to the economic, political, and social system to counterbalance the widening social inequalities, globalization renders these changes highly unfeasible.

One clear example of how the current global economic system is rather inauspicious for achieving social equality is the cotton industry. Globally, cotton and the garment industry constitutes one of the largest industries with over twenty million jobs depending on it both in developed and developing countries (Kütting, 2004). Because cotton does not grow in Western Europe, major industrialized countries have been particularly concerned about their imports of the raw material coming from developing countries. As a consequence, this sector has always had a very special importance in the relationship between the North and the South due to the fact that "the cotton textile industry was a central consumer production sector in all of the European nations that scrambled to control African territories in the late nineteenth century" (Issacman & Roberts, 1995, p. 1). In fact, cotton is the most important export raw material for African countries such as Chad, Burkina Faso, and Mali, representing more than 40 percent of their export earnings (Kütting, 2003).

Globally, major financial institutions such as the World Bank and IMF policies have, over decades, been encouraging the growing of cash crops such as cotton for export to the global market in the hope that these policies would help the developing countries alleviate the debt crisis that has exacerbated over recent decades (Maxwell & Fernando, 1989). Some scholars (e.g., Robbins, 2009; Blewitt, 2008; Dale, 2001) also claim that these financial institutions, together with major trade organizations such as the WTO, have given the developing countries little choice but to abide by their planned policies. Knowing that the textile sector provides a comparative advantage to southern producers, developed countries, therefore, constantly encourage developing countries to grow cheap cash crops, and erect different types of trade barriers to processed cotton products exported from the South. Textile industry is still one of the most heavily regulated trade sectors in WTO, which imposes hefty trade restrictions on developing countries' textile exports. In fact, many critics (e.g., Blewitt, 2008; Carter, 2007; Kütting, 2004) denounce these cash crops as a short-sighted economic strategy that harms local economy and increases social inequity. Likewise, Vandana Shiva points out, for example, that "cash crop exports have been tried elsewhere and are a proven way to get trapped in food scarcity and spiraling debt burdens. Africa's food crisis and hunger and famine are linked directly to the underdevelopment of Africa's food production by cash crops leading to a decline in food production" (2009, p. 150).

Ever since the 1960s, the industrialized countries have witnessed a surge in the demand for cotton in a period that has also witnessed an equally massive surge in fashion and trendiness as a very important component of the modern Western lifestyle. This has led to waves of mass consumption of cotton products in the Northern countries and increasingly huge demands of cotton cash crops in the South. Meanwhile, however, Western consumers have become further alienated from the process of production of the garments they wear, which takes place far from them, and know very little about the products manufactured by a cheap labor force in outsourced factories and sweatshops in countries such as India, Bangladesh, Pakistan, and Thailand, among others (Kütting, 2004). Jasmin Sydee and Sharon Beder (2009) also point an accusing finger at the forces of the global market as the main culprits behind this exploitation because they "destroy work as a satisfying, meaningful activity for millions of people by fragmenting it and reducing some jobs to activities better suited for animals or machines" (2009, p. 263). As such, this kind of exploitation is difficult to combat because there is a huge global system administering it systematically. At the global level, fashion is not only created in the industrialized countries, but it is also popularized and exported to the rest of the world. As a consequence, this phenomenon has had symbolic effects on social equity at the global level. Western fashion is, for example, usually widely promoted in developing countries at the expense of national or local dress in these societies, which constitutes a cultural threat to the traditional heritage of these peoples. The promotion of Western fashion also contributes to the demise of local textile industries which are undermined by the popularity and price competitiveness of the Western products (Kütting, 2004).

Even what is left of the local textile industry in the developing countries is seriously threatened by the widening second-hand clothing market that further alienates the consumers in the South from their local textile products, thus contributing even more to stifling this vital sector. In fact, the second-hand clothing sector best exemplifies the peak of global social inequity between the North and the South. Observers (e.g., Maxwell & Fernando, 1989; Shiva, 2009) note that, by focusing on cotton cash crops to supply raw material and cheap labor for outsourced TNCs, developing countries are indeed damaging their long-term economic strategies. Thanks to these cash crops, the North can afford to consume more and at a lower price, and then disposes of the used products in the South. The discarded garments are then bought in developing countries' second-hand clothing market, which undermines local textile industries and jeopardizes their economic growth. At the end of the day, the North comes out with new low-priced products thanks to cheap labour and abundant raw material from the South while the South is left with an ailing local textile industry, very fragile exports, deteriorating work conditions, and lower wages for its labor force. This "race to the bottom," Kütting (2004) points out, clearly traps the South in a closed cycle that not only serves many of the North's interests, but also keeps the developing countries' position in the global economic system shaky and their citizens poorer.

The main conclusion that can be drawn from the case of the textile industry is that the neoliberal capitalist economic system and the current process of globalization do not serve all people equally, thus relegating the issue of social equity to a rather peripheral position. More importantly, this system clearly works against sustainability, which stresses a bottom-up economic and social growth that depends primarily on consolidating local industries, implementing indigenous knowledge, and preserving local culture, traditions, and identity. According to the sustainability discourse, sound human development can only be implemented if the local industries, identity, and indigenous knowledge are not subjugated to the global political and economic system, but rather constitute an integral part of it.

Even democratically elected Western governments, which have been entrusted by their citizens with making the right choices to safeguard the environment and achieve social equity, have increasingly become the "custodian" of neoliberal ideology and free market powers. This shift in the traditional role of government has raised major ethical problems as the standards of safeguarding the public interests and common goods have considerably changed in the last few decades. As the issues of protecting the environment are gradually left to the private sector and to free market forces, the overall sustainability strategies for achieving social equity become harder to implement. At the environmental level, for instance, some studies (e.g., Baker, 2006; Elliott, 2000) have shown that it is especially the poor who are often exposed to environmental degradation and suffer the most from the resulting health and poverty problems. "Left to the market," contends Robbins "the world would be divided into those who can afford a clean environment and those who can't. In fact, that is the situation that we are approaching, as poor nations and areas are exposed to far greater environmental hazards than are rich ones" (2009, p. 8). It is not a coincidence, therefore, that poor residential areas and slums are often situated in the most polluted parts of town, which has created the misconception that poverty causes pollution.

The current socio-economic paradigm of development is also at odds with the concepts of intra-generational and inter-generational equity advocated as pillars of sustainable development (WCED, 1987). According to the sustainability discourse, today's generation is actually borrowing "the environmental capital" from next generation and unfairly depleting their "environmental share." Achieving exponential economic growth, however, necessitates an extensive use of renewable and nonrenewable natural resources that makes intra-generational and inter-generational equity even harder to achieve. Commenting on this discrepancy, James Gustave Speth puts it as follows: "there are fundamental biases in capitalism that favour the present over the future and the private over the public. Future generations cannot participate in capitalism's markets. From an environmental perspective, that is a huge flaw because the essence of sustainable development is equity toward future generations" (2008, p. 61).

Overall, many aspects of the current socio-economic paradigm of development such as today's rates of economic growth, soaring energy use, and increasing environmental degradation all stand as impediments to achieving intergenerational equity. Some views (e.g., Hart, 2009; Kates, 2003; Blewitt, 2008; Kroll & Robbins, 2009) argue that the manipulation of world trade regulations on the part of the developed countries has had a negative impact not only on the national economies of the developing countries, but more importantly on the daily livelihoods of millions of poor citizens in these countries. For example, this manipulation has had a negative bearing on these nations' purchasing power and standards of living.[5] Some of the causes behind this situation, therefore, can be directly attributed to a widening global economic system that turns the countries of the periphery into sources of cheap raw material and underpaid labor. Ultimately, achieving social equity as envisioned in the discourse of sustainable development is still an unrealistic goal in the current global context for two main reasons: First, the uneven patterns of wealth distribution in the neoliberal capitalist economic system are a big hurdle in achieving social equity; and secondly, the weakening of the welfare system renders achieving social equity even more challenging.

Despite the prevalent rhetoric of caring for the environment, the neoliberal discourse is still holding to market efficiency as the predominant gauge for every issue related to the free market economy; hence, it starkly fails to take on board other equally important issues such as social equity, sustainable consumption, and equal distribution of wealth. This approach, I believe, leads to some serious consequences such as the alienation of the consumer from the production and consumption processes, and the separation of the environmental policy from other social and economic policies, which ultimately would result in the marginalization of environmental concerns. This chain of policies and the consequences thereof are in fact but another impediment to the bottom-up developmental strategies of sustainable development, which denounce the practice of gauging environmental, social, and cultural issues solely in terms of economic efficiency. In fact, this discrepancy embodies many of the conflicting sets of values and priorities in neoliberal capitalism and sustainable development. Globally, this contradiction is also echoed in some other areas such as the global governance system, the global trade system, and North-South politics.

Sustainability in a Global Context: Global Governance System, Global Trade, and the North-South Divide

The evolution of sustainable development cannot be thoroughly understood outside the context of three main spheres—global governance network, the North-South divide, and global trade liberalization. As the boundaries of these three spheres get more and more blurred in a context of an intensifying globalization, the project of sustainable development is very often faced with obstacles that set back its evolution and might very well bring it to a halt. Above all, sustainable development is now caught in the crossfire between the push for exponential economic growth and trade liberalization on the one hand, and a compelling need to reverse catastrophic ecological threats and social exigencies especially in the developing countries, on the other. Internationally, the current structure and scope of global governance in general, and environmental global governance in particular, constitutes more of a challenge than a help for the emerging sustainability paradigm. Against such a backdrop, my aim in this section is to pinpoint the different challenges to the implementation of sustainable development in the field of global governance, and discuss to what extent these challenges are closely related to the structure and scope of this dominant system. In the second part of this section, I want to examine the evolution of this new paradigm within two other important spheres, namely global trade and the North-South politics.

The last few decades have definitely been marked by an unprecedented outburst in international negotiations on global environmental issues and the signing of a big number of bilateral and multilateral international environmental treaties.[6] This proliferation in international environmental agreements, however, has not guaranteed more environmental protection on the ground. On the contrary, recent environmental studies (e.g., Goldemberg, 2003; Kates, 2003) point to alarming rates of ecological degradation that led to global problems such as global warming, ozone layer depletion, and biodiversity loss, among others. Despite the burgeoning number of environmental treaties, global environmental politics has been plagued with an unmistakable ineffectiveness.

Before I elaborate on the global governance's ineffectiveness and the resultant impediments to sustainability, I would like first to define global governance and throw some light on its structure. In contemporary literature, global governance is often used as an umbrella term that refers to rules, regulations, and decisions concluded by a whole network of international governmental institutions, NGOs, and other global financial bodies (Chasek, Downie, & Brown, 2010; Kahler, 2003). Within this realm, numerous actors with different structures and conflicting approaches interact to formulate political, economic, or environmental regulations that can be either binding or non-binding on the countries that have agreed upon them. Pamela Chasek, David Downie, and Janet Brown point out that "global governance, in essence, can be described as the political interaction of states, international organizations, and other transnational actors aimed at solving problems that affect more than one state or region" (2010, p. 370). Some of the most prominent actors in global governance today include the UN organizations such as UNDP, UNEP, UNICEF, and UNESCO. In addition, there exist other international institutions such as the WTO, IMF, GEF, and the World Bank, which also have a big say in developmental, economic, and even environmental global policies. Consequently, "there has been a shift," argue David Held and Anthony McGrew, "from government to global governance, from the modern state to a multilayered system of power and authority, from relatively discrete national communication and economic systems to their more complex and diverse enmeshment at regional and global levels" (2002/2007, p. 361).

The current sustainability demise is also precipitated by the clash between the global governance major actors' agendas and the long-term goals and plans of sustainable development. Observers note, for example, that, within the current global governance system, "whenever economic growth clashes with environmental concerns, economic growth almost always wins" (Robbins, 2009, p. 12). In essence, this predominance of the "growth agenda" raises huge challenges to sustainability especially in a context of neoliberal capitalism, which is fundamentally hostile to any form of curbing economic growth or meddling with market forces. As a consequence, "global economic and political governance, which structurally determines environmental governance, leads to the sidelining of ecological considerations and a disregard of environment-society relations," concludes Gabriela Kütting (2004, p. 36).

The proliferation of actors within the global governance system such as the NGOs, the TNCs, the different UN bodies, the World Bank, the IMF, and the WTO, among others, also adds a further complication to the sustainability impasse today. In fact, this proliferation of participants in negotiating and concluding environmental regimes reduces possible chances of reaching common grounds and shared visions of development. Given that "an increase in the number of actors often causes more heterogeneity of interests and perceptions as well as more uncertainty within each actor as to the preferences of others," argue Chasek, Downie, and Brown, 2010, "the search for solutions to an environmental problem becomes more difficult as the number of parties increases" (2010, p. 285). Environmental priorities and sustainability plans are also believed to be marginalized in any large-scale developmental and economic plans endorsed by these institutions. Critics (e.g., Dresner, 2002; Mlambo & Pangeti, 2001; Kütting, 2004) point out, for instance, that the "structural adjustments" policies of the World Bank and the IMF have relegated environmental consideration to a very peripheral position, usually as an externalized issue.

Effective environmental treaties would undoubtedly have a strong bearing on the economic, political, and social activities that have to be altered for these treaties to be implemented properly, hence the difficulty of finding a common ground among different parts. Thus, another example of the conflict between the different stakeholders' interests is that the transition from fossil fuel-driven economic growth to sustainable, clean economic growth can be very disadvantageous to the oil-exporting countries that rely heavily on the petroleum exports for boosting their economic growth and development in general.[7] Negotiations over environmental issues, therefore, intersect and overlap, to a large degree, with other political and economic interests with wide social and ecological ramifications.

Despite NGOs' proliferation, their role in the global governance system has rather been limited to mere advisory role in the formulation and negotiation of developmental and environmental agreements. Although these NGOs have been accorded a certain presence in big influential organizations such as the UN, the World Bank, and even the WTO, for instance, they do not really have any significant influence on the process of decision-making (Thomas, 1992). And even the NGOs that have made it into the corridors of these strong international organizations are generally reformist rather than radical organizations. Gabriela Kütting points out, for instance, that the "radical organizations do not participate in shaping global governance because they believe that there are fundamental systematic shortcomings and that these cannot be addressed through a reform of existing forms of global governance" (2004, p. 38).

By and large, opening the door to NGOs in the global governance system seems to be empty rhetoric. Critics (e.g., Stiglitz, 2007; Thomas, 1992) point out that environmental NGOs are often sidelined by the predominant corporations and global financial organizations which still have the final say in this global governance system. Likewise, John Blewitt argues that "through their creation of think-tanks and business associations, the big corporations have intentionally shaped the global economic agenda to meet their own specific commercial ends at the cost of both the environment and the democratic process" (2008, p. 134). For these critics, the seemingly pluralistic global governance system contributes in many ways to thwarting the rise of sustainable development as a new paradigm of growth when this system excludes any real sustainability agenda.

Another major defect in the global governance system is what has come to be known as "the lowest-common-denominator" principle. This kind of procedural problem occurs especially when active participation by many countries is required to address a global environmental problem but not enough countries are interested. The countries most interested in concluding this global environmental treaty, therefore, often need the support of countries which are less interested to join this treaty. As a consequence, "an environmental treaty can be only as strong as its least cooperative state allows it to be," which results in the regime's overall effectiveness being undermined by the compromises made in persuading these states to endorse this treaty (Chasek, Downie, & Brown, 2010, p.

279). Observers (e.g., Barnett, 2008) also note that the lowest-common-denominator principle has severely limited the strength of many environmental treaties such as climate change treaties and protocols on reducing CFC emissions, among many others. This kind of shortcoming in the global governance system in general, and in the global environmental governance system in particular, has crippled many interesting environmental treaties that could have boosted the project of sustainable development further up the global political agenda.

Being another feature of global governance, the current "anarchical structure" of international politics seems to jeopardize the sustainability process at a global scale. Theoretically, the anarchical features of contemporary states are reflected by the absence of a global government or any type of hierarchy that can effectively implement all the agreements and maintain order among nations. Within such global political anarchy, states tend to follow their own interests and prefer independence over interdependence. The result is usually a huge mistrust among strong and weak states, which makes achieving effective international cooperation rather difficult (Carter, 2007). Given the trans-boundary nature of ecological problems, the current political system is relatively incapable of effectively responding to the environmental exigencies as global cooperation necessitates collective commitment to stop and reverse environmental damage. This mismatch between the anarchical global political system and the gravity of ecological and social issues today makes sustainable development's implementation rather unfeasible. Even within such an anarchical global political system, there are still some other types of difficulties that relate directly to the nature of lengthy procedures that negotiating, agreeing upon, and ratifying an environmental agreement entail. Indeed, creating and implementing a strong global environmental policy involves many lengthy and thorny processes. Each of these steps can be time-consuming and problematic in itself. This tedious process results usually in procrastination and lethargy in forging and implementing environmental treaties.

Another example of the international lethargy and procrastination in forging and implementing environmental treaties is the slow reaction to global phenomena such as global warming and the ozone layer depletion. In fact, the discovery of the greenhouse gases' effects on the environment goes back more than 180 years when the French physicist Baron Jean Fourier discovered that these gases could increase the surface temperature of the earth. Then, in 1896, the Swedish scientist Svante Arrhenius warned that temperatures would rise 5° degrees Celsius if CO_2 levels in the atmosphere doubled. And even when scientists discovered the threat to the ozone layer in 1974, negotiations on this issue did not start until 1982 and the first binding controls took six further years to come into being in 1988 (Thomas, 1992). "It is now an understatement to say we are running out of time," argues James G. Speth, "for such crucial issues as climate change, deforestation, and loss of biodiversity, we ran out of time quite a while ago. Appropriate action is long overdue" (2008, p. 19). This lethargy in adopting efficient policies is also due to scientific uncertainty and research complexity about the environmental issues, which, in turn, hinders forging and implementing sustainable development strategies.

The interconnectedness of environmental, economic, and even political issues has also resulted in more challenges to sustainable development in global politics arena. For the most part, these challenges are closely related to the question of whether or not there is a genuine political will to face up to the overwhelming power of corporations and a whole global economy and put sustainable development into practice. Against this backdrop, many critics maintain today that "the biggest obstacle in changing the current system of global governance in general and global environmental governance in particular is political will" (Chasek, Downie, & Brown, 2010, p. 371). Generally, most politicians show unwillingness to endorse policies which are likely to be unpopular among the business elite and corporate sector.

The lack of political will and governments' reluctance to endorse sustainability can also be associated with the lengthy procedures of reaching agreements on ecological issues. One of the most articulate comments on this point was made by UNEP former executive director, Mostafa Tolba, who succinctly observed that "the difficulties in negotiating the Montreal Protocol had nothing to do with whether the environment was damaged or not. It was all about who was going to get the edge over whom" (as cited in Nadeau, 2006, p. 39). Thus, while sustainable development plans usually take several years to be concluded and an even longer time to be implemented, the political system of governments today usually operates in far shorter terms dictated by elections and terms of political office. Put differently, politicians usually focus on short-term plans to satisfy voters and tax-payers while corporations are mainly interested in short-term plans that pay off within a reasonable timeframe.

Judging by all the characteristic features of this global governance system, it is clear that sustainability comes way behind numerous other issues such as trade liberalization, avoiding economic recessions, and fighting terrorism. The procedures and mechanisms used when negotiating and concluding environmental treaties are, in my view, not responsive enough to today's ecological exigencies. Politically, hindrance to sustainability stems mainly from the discrepancy between the short-lived governmental and corporate interests and the long-term sustainability strategies to be implemented. As such, the whole global governance system is still highly unresponsive to the prerequisites of sustainable development.

The second sphere that entails numerous extrinsic obstacles to sustainability is global trade. Over the last few decades, the unprecedented degree of trade liberalization has often been considered as the most iconic sign of a globalized economy. Above all, the current rates of trade institutionalization are also regarded as one of the most powerful engines of this global economic system. However, many observers such as Gabriela Kütting (2004), John Blewitt, (2008), John Khor (2001a, 2001b), Vandana Shiva (2003, 2005, 2008), Gary Sampson (2005), and James Speth (2008), among others, claim that this ever-increasing trade liberalization has had very dire environmental consequences, especially as it became increasingly associated with unsustainable practices worldwide. According to this view, global trade liberalization has become one of the main adversaries of sustainable development. Hence, my aim in this section is chiefly to investigate whether global trade liberalization has been favorable or unfavorable to the project of sustainable development and shed light on the effects of this phenomenon on sustainability.

Before probing into the relationship between global trade and sustainability, I would like to shed more light on the historical context in which today's global trade institutions were established in order to gain an insight into these institutions' role in global governance. The major supervisory body of free trade today is the World Trade Organization (WTO), whose foundation dates back to 1944 when U.S. President Franklin D. Roosevelt convened a meeting of the leaders of forty-four nations in Bretton Woods, New Hampshire. The outcome of the meeting was a plan to establish the International Bank for Reconstruction and Development (also known as the World Bank), the International Monetary Fund (IMF) to control currency exchange, and the General Agreement on Tariffs and Trade (GATT) established in 1948 to regulate trade between member countries. With many new member countries joining it, the GATT was significantly enlarged in 1995 and was renamed the World Trade Organization. As they expanded over time, these Bretton Woods institutions have become very important actors in shaping the structure and the scope of global governance system through global financial treaties and policies, thus impacting considerably on all nations' development options. This notable impact, nevertheless, has increasingly been called into question as the effects of global trade on the environment became the subject of a heated debate.

To begin with, the question of whether or not trade liberalization and sustainability are compatible is highly problematic as academic studies and analyses of the relationship between trade and the environment have led to different, and often conflicting, results. Many economists and thinkers (e.g., Antweiler, Copeland, & Taylor, 2001; Lamy, 2005; Bhagwati, 2007; Norberg, 2003/2007), for instance, claim that, in most cases, free trade can actually lead to environmental improvement if ecological considerations are taken seriously in global trade policies. They assert that free trade helps create more wealth necessary for safeguarding the environment and making people better off. Others (e.g., French, 1999; Shiva,

2003; Sampson, 2005; Wade, 2003/2007), on the other hand, argue that trade liberalization and sustainable development have mutually exclusive goals. They particularly point to the inherent incompatibility between trade liberalization and sustainability, arguing that "whereas the GATT [now the WTO] aims at deregulation of international trade, national environmental policies use instruments that regulate trade, such as licenses, product standards, levies and subsidies" (Hemmer, 1992, p. 19).

On a theoretical level, neoliberal economists (e.g., Bhagwati, 2007; Sagoff, 2000) often contend that global free trade and global free capital not only stimulate economic growth and help alleviate poverty, but also make a significant contribution to curbing and reversing environmental degradation. Their main argument is that the process of capital flow and trade liberalization leads to economic prosperity within member countries and therefore provides the community with enough money to clean up pollution and engage in an environment-friendly lifestyle (Lamy, 2005). The ministers of trade at the 2001 WTO meeting in Doha, Qatar, for example, confirmed their commitment to sustainability, putting it as follows: "We strongly reaffirm our commitment to the objective of sustainable development. We are convinced that the aims of upholding and safeguarding an open and non-discriminatory multilateral trading system, and acting for the protection of the environment and the promotion of sustainable development can and must be mutually supportive" (WTO, para.6).

As a response to the neoliberal economists' claims, more and more voices have decried the dire effects of liberalized trade on the environment in the last few decades, arguing that economic growth has exacerbated rather than alleviated ecological crisis. Gabriela Kütting, for instance, argues that "this liberalization and its supporting institutional framework have led to a new form of ecological imperialism that subjugates resource extraction and production to market ideology" (2004, p. 42). Likewise, John Cavanagh, Jerry Mander, and the other authors of *Alternatives to Economic Globalization: A Better World Is Possible* sum up global trade effects on the environment as follows:

> Economic globalization is intrinsically harmful to the environment because it is based on ever-increasing consumption, exploitation of resources, and waste disposal problems. One of its primary features, export-oriented production, is especially damaging because it is responsible for increasing global transport activity [. . .] while requiring very costly and ecologically damaging new infrastructures such as ports, airports, dams, canals, and so on. (Cavanagh and Mander 2002, p. 61)

The first issue that proponents of sustainable development and those of free globalized trade disagree about is whether tariffs between countries are even justified and whether the environmental standards are accepted as legitimate regulations on global trade. This issue becomes more complicated as the notion that liberalized trade is the equivalent of free trade is called into question (Buttel, 1995). "It should not be forgotten," contends Gabriela Kütting, "that although we live in an age of trade liberalization, world trade is far from free" given that the agricultural market is still heavily regulated by countries of the North to eliminate potential competition from countries of the South (2004, p. 40). Other critics (e.g., Sampson, 2005) argue that it is not trade per se that is destructive to the environment and detrimental to the strategies of sustainable development but rather excessive trade liberalization that is really harmful. This controversy raises the issue of when trade liberalization is to be considered excessive and who can judge it to be so. All these factors, in my view, contribute significantly to the complexity of the trade-sustainable development relationship.

Despite the intricacy of this issue, there is still significant evidence that although natural resource exploitation has always been an important feature of the capitalist model of growth, there is definitely a new element to it in the contemporary context of global trade liberalization. Many scientific studies (e.g., Elliott, 2000; Goldemberg, 2003; Mander, 2003), for instance, show that the world has witnessed a huge shift from the use of renewable energy to non-renewable types of energy just to feed the ever-growing fossil fuel-based economy and trade liberalization, resulting in unprecedented rates of environmental degradation locally and globally as well. This shift has laid bare some features of the incompatibility between global trade and sustainable development. John Cavanagh and his colleagues explain, for instance, that "to achieve hypergrowth, the emphasis is on the ideological heart of the [neoliberal] model—free trade—accompanied by deregulation of corporate activity. The idea is to remove as many impediments as possible to expand corporate activity" (2002, p. 20).

To my way of thinking, prioritizing free trade and free capital flow over the protection of the environment constitutes the root cause of the incompatibility between global liberalized trade and sustainability. This incompatibility is precipitated by the unmistakable powerful influence of the Bretton Woods institutions over national governments and the global governance system as a whole, thus isolating sustainable development even further. As local authority and state's sovereignty are continuously on the wane due to the overwhelmingly powerful effect of globalization, calls for more sustainable ways of production and consumptions have remained sheer slogans. This atrophy of the the state's sovereignty in the age of a globalized economy and ongoing trade liberalization has further hindered the implementation of sustainability strategies.

Although the WTO does have a provision in Article 20 ensuring that nothing in any agreement between member countries should hamper the conservation of exhaustible natural resources, critics (e.g., Mander, 2003; Buttel, 1995) point out that the WTO dispute panel has ruled in favor of trade and against environment every time an environmental regulation has been challenged as a trade barrier.[8] "The economic growth paradigm of the WTO," concludes Abigail Jahiel, "has encouraged its members to support a greening of WTO rules only partially and only where it furthers their own interests, with continued adverse effects on the environment" (2009, p. 242). As a consequence, WTO's blocking of environmental regulations significantly cripples the establishment of a legal and public foundation for the project of sustainable development.

As such, the effects of trade liberalization on the environment and the concomitant difficulties for implementing sustainable development are issues that go far beyond the scope of this section. Therefore, my aim here is to particularly focus on a few significant WTO rules that best exemplify the challenges that the current global trade system poses for sustainable development. Within this framework, I want to pinpoint the extent to which the recent WTO agreements on intellectual property, investment, and trade in services hamper developing countries' potential for sustainable growth. The first WTO agreement that I focus on in this respect is the Agreement on Trade-Related Aspects of Intellectual Property Rights (TRIPS), which was forged in the course of the Uruguay Round (1986—1994) and entered into operation in 1994. This agreement seemingly obliges WTO members to enact precise standards for intellectual property such as copyrights and patents, thus protecting it against any unauthorized use or theft. However, recent studies show that the implementation of TRIPS has caused scientific research to be both more often privatized and more costly, which, in turn, "widen[s] the North/South gap in access to scientific knowledge" (Wade, 2003/2007, p. 279) and discourages researchers from doing any research on problem areas of primary interest to populations in the developing countries. By rendering both scientific research and the mastery of technology prohibitively expensive for the developing countries, the WTO's TRIPS regulation denies these countries one of the essential pillars of sustainability, namely transfer of "green technology."

Whether developed countries themselves complied with such strict intellectual property rights when they were developing is also called into question by Robert Wade (2003/2007), who maintains that many of these countries such as the United States, Japan, Taiwan, and South Korea were infamous for being "the counterfeit capitals" of "pirating" scientific and technological patents during the stages of their development. Other observers (e.g., Roberts & Parks, 2007) also note that putting a price tag on intellectual properties through TRIPS has, for instance, denied many poor regions and countries their right to an alternative environment-friendly technology. Robert Wade concludes that "TRIPS raises significant development obstacles for many [developing] countries that the earlier developers did not face" (2003/2007, p. 281). Ultimately, these WTO regulations hinder green technologies transfer on which almost all the sustainability strategies for development rely. When denied access to green technologies, poor people in developing countries are actually deprived of a good chance to follow a sustainable mode of development rather than replicating the Western model of growth. With respect to this issue, Jasmin Sydee and Sharon Beder denounce the fact that "the commodification of culture and resources to integrate it into the global marketplace overrides other social values leaving economic value as the global value" (2009, p. 256). As the WTO turns a blind eye to complicated social issues such as poverty and inequity, it is impacting on the resilience of sustainable development, which seeks to balance the economic, social, and ecological imperatives in the process of growth.

The second example pertinent to the discussion of the incompatibility between WTO policies and sustainability is related to what it referred to as the Agreement on Trade-related Investment Measures (TRIMS). Another product of the WTO Uruguay Round, TRIMS prohibits governments from giving any special differential facilities to local manufacturers at the expense of foreign investors who are most of the time giant TNCs with which local manufacturers can hardly compete (Wade, 2003/2007). With restricted minimal governmental aid, local investors would undoubtedly be no match for the giant TNCs, which results in the whole process of local economic growth being jeopardized. By putting pressure on local governments to include TNCs as a major player in their economic policy, TRIMS impedes attempts to initiate the bottom-up sustainable development strategies to build "an economic system that is able to generate surpluses and technical knowledge on a self-reliant and sustained basis" (WCED, 1987, p. 65).

Through measures such as TRIPS and TRIMS, the WTO imposes a top-down economic growth model that systematically reverses the bottom-up sustainability strategies. Commenting on these far-reaching repercussions of WTO measures, Stuart L. Hart points out that "indigenous cultures, once able to live in a self-sufficient manner based upon the principles of community, frugality, and sufficiency, have been irreversibly changed by the introduction of cash and wage employment," arguing that "structural adjustment, privatization, and free trade have accelerated this trend over the past two decades" (2009, p. 36). At the Doha Ministerial meeting of WTO, both the United States and the EU wanted to modify the current TRIMS agreements to become even tougher in the enforcement of those regulations in the developing countries, taking any country that disobeys the TRIMS to the Dispute Settlement Mechanism. Yet, India and Brazil resisted such modification, which led the developed countries to drop it from their agenda (Wade, 2003/2007). This kind of global trade measure has been harshly criticized by many observers who denounce the WTO as the custodian of corporate interests at the expense of the local communities. John Blewitt contends, for instance, that "organizations like the World Trade Organization (WTO) were established specifically to serve global corporate interests, even if these run contrary to the policies and needs of democratically elected governments and their people" (2008, p. 134).

The third blow that the WTO directs at an effective implementation of sustainable development is the General Agreement on Trade in Services (GATS), which entered into force in January 1995. Another product of the Uruguay Round, this measure represents an extension of WTO rules from trade in products to trade in services such as banking, health care, education, tourism and so on (Sampson, 2005). The main goal of GATS, as with other WTO agreements, is to promote market and trade liberalization, hence its insistence on the non-interference policy that national governments should abide by. According to this policy, national governments must not interfere in the privatization of the market and liberalization of trade, and therefore, must not place any barriers in the way of services and trade between different countries, nor must they regulate the activities of TNCs operating in their territories. Critics (e.g., Sampson, 2005), however, denounce GATS as impinging even further on developing countries' domestic policies and further limiting their development options. For example, GATS is criticized for requiring all WTO countries to treat local and foreign firms equally regardless of the differences in capital and market competitiveness among them. Robert H. Wade further argues that this measure "makes it next to impossible for developing country governments to protect their own service industries from competition from well-established foreign firms, in the way that virtually all the successful developers have done in the past" (2003/2007, p. 278).

By and large, GATS cripples plans to encourage and consolidate local economies and preserve indigenous ways of life. GATS requires, for instance, that both foreign and local companies should be given exactly the same degree of access to the nation's market, and stipulates that foreign firms should not be obliged to use local products or hire local staff unless local firms are obliged to follow suit. This agreement is not only undermining the local economies which cannot compete with TNCs, but also eroding social stability by excluding local communities from taking part in their economic growth. Against such a backdrop of corporate hegemony, it is essential to invoke once again the issue of alienation within local communities whose members feel excluded from active participation in deciding on their own development options. As a consequence, the affinity that sustainable development seeks to create between local communities and their environment is actually being undermined by these hegemonic top-down corporate development policies.

Looking at the big picture, one feature that WTO provisions (i.e., TRIPS, TRIMS, and GATS) have in common is the intense degree of restrictions they tend to impose on the developing countries' potential to opt for a sound local economic growth. To varying degrees, these agreements also erect different obstacles to policies that promote sustainability and encourage domestic industries and services. WTO member countries that do not abide by these regulations, for example, would face serious punitive provisions that can legally deny them access to other countries' markets (French, 1999). These trade measures have essentially been widely criticized for being "vague at points where vagueness benefits the developed countries, and precise at points where precision works against developing countries" (Wade, 2003/2007, p. 284). Other observers (e.g., Dale, 2001; Blewitt, 2008) see in the different regulations imposed by the WTO but another way of keeping these weak nations under hegemony after the decolonization period, drawing on various tools to implement their hidden agenda in international organizations such as IMF, WTO, the World Bank, and sometimes the United Nations programs. Given all these restraints, the requirements for entry into the world economy not only reflect little awareness of sound development prerequisites, but also constitute serious obstacles in the path of developing countries' sustainable growth.

Concerning issues of social equity, critics (e.g., McLaren, 2003; Chasek, Downie, & Brown, 2010) point out that global trade has steadily widened the gap between the rich and the poor. In fact, by standardizing norms for manufactured goods worldwide, WTO rules have unleashed fierce competition between countries at different stages of development. Other studies (e.g., French, 1993; Radermacher, 2004; Kütting, 2004) assert that this global competition—critically referred to as the "race to the bottom"—results mostly in hideous social ills like child labor, the inhumane exploitation of labor resulting from TNCs outsourcing, and environmental disasters in developing countries where regulations are lax or not properly enforced. This race to the bottom is, in my view, the very antithesis of sustainability strategies to achieve more social equity, safeguard the environment, and consolidate local economy. Thus, the aptitude of institutions such as WTO and IMF to accommodate today's global environmental exigencies must be seriously rethought and reassessed.

As part and parcel of the global governance system, the WTO has proven out of sync with efforts to achieve sustainability and new aspiration for an alternative to neoliberal capitalist paradigm of growth. Despite some efforts to integrate the environmental concerns in its governing policy, promoting sustainable development remains a low-profile issue for WTO. The cases that I discussed clearly show that the trade policies of the WTO erect serious obstacles to any efforts to pursue a sustainable mode of development. The main cause for this antagonism toward sustainability, in my view, is that the WTO is an integral part of a global economic system that was established with little consideration for the environment. As a whole, the global governance system has been rather unpropitious to the project of sustainable development. Many of the sustainability basic tenets such as growing within the limits of ecosystems, fostering a bottom-up model of development, and encouraging sustainable local economies are still marginalized in this system to date. What is more, much of the incompatibility between sustainable development and the global trade system is due to the fact that the major actors in this global governance system were established when the environment was not a high profile issue. As a result, the very objectives of these organizations such as the WTO, the World Bank, and the IMF do not include sustainability in their policies. However, the struggle to follow a sustainable path of development goes far beyond the WTO policies with the North-South divide casting a strong bearing on attempts to achieve sustainability.

In such a global context, the trade-sustainability rift also takes on many features of the longstanding North-South divide, which is the third sphere, generating extrinsic obstacles to sustainability. More to the point, the drawbacks of enforcing the WTO measures in the South have not only crippled developing countries' economic growth, but also exacerbated even more the capital flow from North to South. These consequences exemplify, in my opinion, one of the several ways neoliberal capitalism in general, and trade liberalization in particular, thwart strategies designed to promote sustainability in the developing countries. Moreover, the current widespread approach to globalization which emphasizes the benefits of trade liberalization and the free capital flow tends to overlook the concomitant tensions of social injustice. This view has recently been called into question by many critics who argue that "the Bretton Woods Institutions, designed after the Second World War to manage the international financial system, no longer appear to be up to the task" (Hart, 2009, p. xxxiv).

Ever since the era of colonization in the eighteenth and early nineteenth centuries, there has been a growing conviction among most developing countries that global economic relations are inequitable (Petesh, 1992). Recently, this shared conviction has often been reflected in the developing countries' responses to global environmental issues, including their conception of sustainable development as a new paradigm of growth. As the North-South divide has been significantly shaping global environmental politics, developing countries have become more and more wary of the essence of sustainable development. Hence, many calls have denounced this new project as just another disguised attempt of the North to curb developing countries' economic growth and exploit their cheap raw material (Chasek, Downie, & Brown, 2010; Petesh, 1992). The North, however, has been adamant that all countries should adhere to the environmental treaties that have been agreed upon. In fact, over the last few decades, the global environmental issues have increasingly been perceived as an important concern in the North-South politics at many global environmental conferences from the 1972 Stockholm Conference onwards. Throughout these decades, many developing countries have kept a wary eye on the growing influence of global environmental treaties for fear that they could be another disguised attempt to sabotage their aspirations for development (Baker, 2006; Schrijver, 2008). These apprehensions were voiced as early as 1971 in what is referred to as the *Founex Report*, produced by a group of Southern intellectuals in preparation for the 1972 Stockholm Conference on the Human Development.

Before dealing with the implications of the North-South divide on sustainable development, let me first give a brief historical background of this divide. During the last few decades of the twentieth century, many economists, thinkers, and politicians (e.g., Rostow, 1991; Huntington, 1971/2007; Yeh, 1989; Norberg, 2003/2007) argued that developing countries could achieve the industrialized countries' economic growth by simply following their path of development. Southern countries were urged, for instance, to adopt development options endorsed by international financial institutions such as the World Bank and the IMF so as to reach the "take-off" phase of overall development. Some of these views (e.g., Rostow, 1991; Sagoff, 2000) contend that the benefits of development and advantages of modernization would inevitably flow from the North to the South if the latter embraced open market policies and abided by the World Bank and IMF's "structural adjustments." In his article "Globalization: Myths and Realities," Philip McMichael sheds more light on this project:

> Developmentalism was, indeed, a project originating in the stabilization of world capitalism after the inter-war crisis and in the context of the Cold War [. . .] In this respect, not only would each state replicate the modernity of the First World (with the US at the apex), but there were expectations that the development gap between First and Third Worlds would be progressively closed. (McMichael 2007, p. 220)

Some other views (e.g., Fotopoulos, 1997; Mlambo & Pangeti, 2001) note, however, that as the decades of the 1970s and 1980s brought even worse levels of inequality among and within the developing countries, the result of following open market economic policies was far from rewarding. Though many of these countries had achieved some kind of economic growth as measured by Gross National Product (GNP), this development was not shared equally among the populations of these countries. Statistics show, for instance, that 66.7 percent of the total national income in Brazil ended up in the hands of only the richest 20 percent of the population, while the poorest 40 percent of this population shared only 6.5 of total national income (Elliott, 2000, pp. 10–11). This and other similar cases in developing countries caused the South's dreams of development to shatter on the rock of reality. The 1970s were a sobering decade for many southern scholars who started to have second thoughts about this ready-made Western model of development. As a matter of fact, Dependency Theory scholars (e.g., Andre Gunder Frank, Fernando Henrique Cardoso, Paul Baran, and Theotonio Dos Santos) argue that development strategies have to emanate from the very conditions existing in the South and have to be closely related to the particular economic, social, and cultural circumstances of these developing nations. "Development has, in fact," argues German scholar Wolfgang Sachs, "deepened the crisis of injustice between the North and South, just as it has provoked a manifold crisis of Nature which undercuts its prospects for the future. It has revealed itself to be finite in (global) space as well as in time" (1997, p. 71).

The North-South divide has also been increasingly deepened by Southern accusations that the South's contemporary developmental plight is actually an outcome of the early heavy industrialization in the North, which exploited its colonies for decades. In fact, many Southern thinkers claim that the North's development and their underdevelopment are actually two sides of the same coin. Inspired by Dependency theory, some of these scholars (e.g., Shiva, 2009; Blewitt, 2008; Möller, 2004) contend that their countries have been entangled in an overwhelming globalized economy based on unequal distribution of benefits, which went exclusively to the industrialized countries—"the core"—at the expense of the developing countries, which constituted the periphery. Due to developing countries' chronic development problems, some scholars recurrently voiced their apprehensions that the further these countries become involved in such a globalized economic system, the further they find themselves from development and opportunities for real progress. "The global agenda did not spring bottom-up from actual impacts on people," confirms James G. Speth, "it was forged top-down at the international level by science, often disputed science; by NGOs, often with circumscribed credibility; and by a tiny U.N. agency—the UNEP—tucked away in Nairobi" (2003, p. 8). By the same token, Neil Carter further argues that "economic inequality between North and South is underpinned by an international trading system that encourages less developed countries to produce cash crops for Northern consumption (rather than developing self-sufficient economy), primarily to pay off debts to those same countries [in the North] and their financial institutions" (2007, pp. 62–63).

From a Southern perspective, the contemporary Western development model that the North is trying to export to the South is an attempt to obstruct the South's own process of growth, hence "the [western] discourse on sustainable development is seen to share characteristics of colonizing discourse" (Baker, 2006, p. 160). Indeed, many views (e.g., Shiva, 2008; McMichael, 2007; Blewitt, 2008; Strong, 2003; Fotopoulos, 1997) strongly denounce the one-size-fits-all Western model that perpetuates the North's supremacy and exacerbates social inequalities and ecological problems in the South. This criticism is mainly backed up by many studies substantiating the high economic, social, environmental, and cultural prices that developing countries pay for adopting neoliberal capitalist policies of economic growth. That global financial institutions are used as tools to pressure the South into adopting this Western development model is also another concern for many observers. "Global institutions such as the Global Environment Facility, the World Bank and the World Trade Organization (WTO)," contends Susan Baker, "form an important way of institutionalizing the relationships of imperialism and colonialism," when allowing "colonial relations to be played out in trade conflict between the industrialized countries and the Third World" (2006, p. 159). This poisoned atmosphere in global environmental politics has, in my opinion, negatively impacted on the readiness of the South to embrace the project of sustainability. Accordingly, the lingering mistrust between the North and the South has significantly colored the developing countries' conception of sustainability, thus weakening the global consensus that this project is based on.

Being part and parcel of the North-South politics, sustainable development has been received with suspicions and apprehensions especially in the South. From a Southern perspective, today's global environmental politics is barely responsive to their environmental and developmental priorities. Some developing countries,[9] for instance, denounced a number of the global environmental regimes such the Montreal Protocol as disguised attempts to maintain the North's economic and political supremacy and control over resources and markets in the South (Baker, 2006). "Not surprisingly," observers note, "this environmental movement found little support in the developing nations. Many developing nations had only just gained independence and were skeptical regarding the motives behind proposals which seemed to limit their development objectives and remove sovereign control over resources" (Elliott, 2000, p. 22).

In most global debates on the environment, developing countries were adamant that industrialized countries are historically responsible for most of these global environmental problems such as ozone layer depletion, global warming, hazardous toxic wastes, and acid rain, among many others. More to the point, activists in the South claim that the North's reliance on unsustainable patterns of fossil fuel-based growth and encouragement of unrestrained mass consumption has brought about the ecological disasters that the South has to face today. Jennifer A. Elliott points out, for example, that "these underdeveloped nations saw their development problems as being linked to too little industry rather than too much and contrasted this with the position of the developed countries which used the bulk of resources and contributed most to the resulting industrial pollution" (2000, p. 22).

When it comes to implementing the sustainability agenda, the North-South divide similarly arouses suspicions and disagreements between developed and developing countries. Most developing countries stress, for instance, the North's historical responsibilities of causing global ecological problems, arguing that it is the industrialized countries' duty to reverse this damage and compensate the South for exploiting their natural resources. Consequently, the North is asked to bear the financial burden of implementing strategies to reverse the ecological damage done (Shiva, 2008). This mistrust grows stronger as the North and the South further disagree about the amount and aim of aid given to the South to combat these environmental hazards: "developing countries were concerned," observers note, "that instead of raising new funds for dealing with global environmental issues, the North and international finance institutions would simply divert resources previously targeted for development toward the environment" (Chasek, Downie, & Brown, 2010, p. 325). From a Southern point of view, it is still unfair to be asked to allocate scarce financial resources to dealing with environmental problems at the expense of their pressing developmental exigencies like economic growth, combating poverty, and curbing overpopulation. This attitude, however, is met with Northern suspicions that the South is using the sustainability agenda to squeeze more aid from the North without being genuinely committed to the sustainability agenda (Baker, 2006).

Caught in the crossfire between the South and the North, the project of sustainable development has to face rising suspicions that significantly undermine its popularity, especially in developing countries. By linking aid to these countries' acceptance of the North's environmental agenda, the North has tarnished the global image of sustainable development in the South, which has interpreted this pressure as one more aspect of the longstanding North-South divide. Seen as another tool in the hands of the North to curb Southern development, sustainable development has, therefore, lost much of its popularity in southern countries. The southern suspicion of sustainable development has also been deepened by the developing countries' growing dissatisfaction with what they consider unfair governing structures of international organizations such as the World Bank, IMF, and WTO. Many economists, thinkers, and activists, (e.g., Carter, 2007; Blewitt, 2008; Payne, 1998), especially from developing countries, claim that the structures of these institutions perpetuate Northern supremacy through devious, undemocratic processes. These critics point an accusing finger at the current structure of the World Bank and IMF, which, they argue, is dominated by Northern corporate interests that can outvote the rest of the countries in the decision-making process (Gupta, 2006). As a consequence, the Southern countries insist that the World Bank's decisions on financial aid for environmental problems should be made through democratic governing bodies in which each country is represented equally as "such 'Green conditionality' may well reflect Northern priorities and perceptions and be supervised by global financial institutions in which the south has little faith" (Baker, 2006, p. 162). The industrialized countries, on the other hand, insist that, being the major donors, they have the right to have a final say in the World Bank decisions and policies (Payne, 1998).

Against a backdrop of North-South mutual mistrust, the developing countries' attitude toward sustainable development remains a mixture of apprehensions and expectations. Some views (e.g., Chasek, Downie, & Brown, 2010) contend that developing countries are mostly apprehensive of being asked to sacrifice their right for economic growth and denied their "environmental space" while having to bear the worst of environmental and social costs of the Northern long exploitation of Nature. Others (e.g., Gupta, 2006; Roberts & Parks, 2007; Baker, 2006) argue that the South is also wary of the North's manipulation of environmental concerns and the sustainability agenda to impose new conditions on overseas development aid—dubbed "green conditionality"—administered usually by global financial institutions in which the South has little faith. What is certain, however, is that this fear not only deepens the Southern mistrust of the North, but it also weakens their readiness to embrace sustainability for fear it would be "another example of Western arrogance towards the Third World" (Baker, 2006, p. 192).

At numerous conferences on development (e.g., 1992 Rio Conference, the 2002 WSSD Conference in Johannesburg, and 2012 Rio+20 Conference in New York), delegates from developing countries have made it clear that they will not be able to gear their developmental policies toward a more sustainable mode unless the North takes Southern demands much more seriously. These delegates also defended the developing countries' right to feasible solutions for problems of increased debt, low export competitiveness, ailing economic growth, and insufficient technology transfer. To my way of thinking, this willingness on the part of the South to cooperate with the North on environmental and developmental issues can at times be part of the solution and at times part of the problem. It is part of the solution when both parts agree on one approach to implementing sustainable development and harmonize their visions of issues such as aid, trade policies, and technology transfer. On the other hand, this willingness might very well be part of the problem when the North and the South stick to their conflicting agendas as has more often been the case.

Facing different economic and social problems, most of the southern countries agree on a set of priorities, which indeed mirrors their concerns, apprehensions, and aspirations for a better future. These priorities range from eradicating poverty and ensuring rapid economic growth at the economic level, to improving standards of living, education, and health care. They also raise problems of sanitation and housing at the social level while they insist on conserving their natural resources, combating deforestation and desertification, and protecting biological diversity at the ecological level. Many of these Southern development priorities, however, do not match the Northern ones. Developing countries insist in global conferences such as the 1992 Rio Conference, for example, that the promotion of sustainable development in the South hinges first and foremost on finding appropriate solutions to their intricate economic, social, and political problems, making it clear that any treaty that overlooks or excludes these complex issues would be resisted (Chasek, Downie & Brown, 2010; Baker, 2006; Dresner, 2002). Thus, from a Southern point of view, implementing sustainable development is inextricably linked to finding effective solutions to South's chronic economic and developmental problems. As justified as it may well be, this stance places a huge burden on the already struggling project of sustainable development, for it broadens its battle with neoliberal capitalism to include combating the South's longstanding problems such as poverty and population growth.

Although most of them admit they have a historical responsibility for the current rates of environmental degradation, developed countries still put a lot of emphasis on the common responsibility for solving current ecological problems when discussing environmental treaties in global summits such as the 1992 Rio Conference in Rio de Janeiro, the 2002 WSSD Conference in Johannesburg, and 2012 Rio+20 in New York. Politicians in the Western countries, for instance, warn that some of the developing countries such as China and India today are among the biggest contributors to some global environmental problems because of their heavy industrialization and their determination to duplicate the unsustainable Western mode of fossil fuel-based economic growth (Baker, 2006; Strange & Bayley, 2008). The North, therefore, insists that these emerging economies must be curbed if global environmental problems such as global warming or ozone layer depletion are to be reversed, making it clear in the 1992 Rio Summit that the South had to make many economic and social changes to earn sustainability (Baker, 2006).

In world politics, the problem of population growth stands out as a good example of the widening divide between the North and the South. On the one hand, the North considers it an obligation for the South to curb population growth and introduce more effective political reforms in order to minimize internal political unrest and better solve social problems. This demand, on the other hand, is usually faced with strong resistance on the part of the South, which sees it as a disguised type of encroachment on their sovereignty. Some observers (e.g., Elliott, 2000) point out, for instance, that control on population growth touches upon many political, cultural, and even religious considerations in these Southern countries. Others (e.g., Goldemberg, 2003; Ling, 2012; Strange & Bayley, 2008) argue, however, that the question here is not about population growth but rather about population impact, pointing out that while it is true that the South's population growth rates are higher than the North's rates, it is the population of the North that has had by far greater impact on the earth's finite natural resources and ecosystems. Susan Baker, for instance, asserts that "overconsumption in OECD countries contributes more to global unsustainable patterns of development than population growth in the low-income countries" (2006, p. 162).

Another challenge to the sought-after global consensus on sustainability also stems from the fact that the nations lumped together as developing countries are indeed not as homogenous as they seem to be. Despite having many characteristics in common such as overpopulation, heavy indebtedness, and ailing economic growth, the various Southern countries are actually at many different developmental stages. In fact, some development studies (e.g., Elliott, 2000; Kerbo, 2006) draw attention to significant differences in the levels of economic development as reflected by trade and export abilities, level of industrialization, GDP, and even degrees of political stability and accountability in the South. The United Nations Organization, along with many other international organizations, for instance, makes a distinction between the developing countries and the "least developed countries," which came to be known as LDCs. As a matter of fact, the LDCs are typically among the poorest and most vulnerable in the global economic system, which makes them the least capable to deal with the increasing ecological and social problems of this century.

The ailing economies of LDCs add to the challenges of sustainable development as how to meet their economic, social, and environmental needs and avoid abusing the environment. "Promoting sustainable development in LDCs is particularly problematic," argues Susan Baker, who explains that "they are among the most vulnerable in the international trading and economic system and have the least capacity to respond to global environmental change, including climate change, although these changes will have significant adverse effects for many of them" (2006, p. 163). In the absence of a solid infrastructure and democratic political systems, getting these countries to follow a sustainable mode of development has become a real challenge. Studies (e.g., Kerbo, 2006) also show that most of the sustainability strategies in these LDCs are likely to be thwarted by corrupt political and economic elites who monopolize wealth and power at the expense of their populations. This corruption, in turn, leaves millions of people living under the poverty line and struggling to eke out a living even at the expense of their environment. As I see it, this combination of corruption and abject poverty in the LDCs erects yet more hurdles in their path of development and further cripples the implementation of the project of sustainable development.

As with the global governance system, the current North-South relations constitute a rather unfavorable context for implementing sustainable development. Linked to green conditionality in the North, and looked at with suspicion in the South, this emerging project has been tarnished and chances for its implementation have diminished. Looking at the big picture, the current overlapping spheres of the global governance system, the global trading system, and the current North-South divide coalesce into a major hurdle in the path of sustainability. The incompatibility between the current global economic system and sustainability has also resulted in huge difficulties facing this new project. Notwithstanding, this hostile climate created by neoliberal capitalism, the global governance system, and globalization has not been the only cause of the stalemate of sustainable development today. Some inner conflicts and contradictions inside the paradigm of sustainable development itself can also be counted as elements precipitating this gridlock. These inner defects and contradictions are going to be thoroughly dealt with in the following section.

SUSTAINABILITY'S INNER CONFLICTS

Ever since its inception, sustainable development has constituted a challenge to many deeply entrenched political, economic, and social beliefs in post-industrial societies. Now matured, the project is on a collision course with the predominant neoliberal economic system, constitutes a nuisance to the structure of global governance, and is a remarkably controversial issue in North-South politics. However, the project itself was born out of a conflict between two opposing needs—the need for continuous economic growth and the need to protect the environment. Reconciling the needs for development with concerns for the environment has been a very intricate and thorny process, hence the controversy over its definition, aims, and feasibility. Within this framework, my aims are manifold: first, I want to shed light on these two conflicting debates that preceded the emergence of sustainable development, namely the debate on development and that of the environment; second, I want to focus on what is referred to as "the traditional environmental paradigm" of the 1970s and 1980s that focused primarily on single ecological issues and higlight its implications for sustainability. Ultimately, I would like to place a particular emphasis on "ecologism" as an ideology underpinning sustainable development and examine whether or not it has been coherent enough in framing a theoretically radical project that is applicable in the present time.

Growth or the Environment: Two Conflicting Agendas

Though human concern for development and economic growth dates back to the pre-Industrial Revolution era, patterns of industrialization and urbanization accelerated dramatically in the early twentieth century and reached unprecedented rates in the decades following World War II. This particular period was also associated with other important phenomena such as decolonization, nation-building, liberalization of the economy, and debates over a New International Economic Order (NIEO). About two decades later, the environment gradually emerged as a high-profile issue at international gatherings such as the Stockholm Conference in 1972 and the Rio Conference in Rio de Janeiro in 1992. However, midway between these two points in time, a fusion between the drive for economic growth and the concerns about the degraded environment took place. This fusion of these two concerns was widely popularized by documents such as the *Brundtland Report* in 1987 and the coinage of sustainable development as a concept that combines both economic growth and the protection of the environment.

At a global level, the debate about development has increasingly been marked by longstanding issues such as the North-South divide, the South's chronic development problems, and the recent process of globalization. Academically, the development debate often involved juxtaposition of conflicting concepts such as development and underdevelopment, affluence and impoverishment, and modernity and backwardness. Nonetheless, the prominence of the environment issue has introduced new elements to this debate, thus extending its scope with new concepts such as sustainability, green development, and environmental justice. Although touching upon some development concerns, the environmental debate is still essentially centered on ecological problems and ways to safeguard the environment. Overall, the predominant concern in this debate is not the North-South divide, but rather the Man-Nature divide. It also includes other juxtapositions such as that of sustainability and unsustainability, of common goods and personal benefits, and of global concerns and local issues. These stark differences in the essence of the two debates on development and the environment are, in my opinion, indicative of the difficulty to reconcile their conflicting discourses.

Given this divergence, the harmonization of the development and environment concerns has been slow and laborious, leading ultimately to "some interesting contradictions and realignments" (McNeill, 2000, p. 21). In this process, formulating a definition of sustainable development was shrouded in confusion and ambiguity, for balancing the conflicting imperatives of the North-South divide and the Man-Nature divide in one clear definition of sustainable development proved far from easy. Moreover, a conflict has also emerged between those in the North who prioritize the conservation of Nature over the alleviation of poverty, and those in the South who are primarily concerned with issues of combating poverty, famine, and underdevelopment. Finding the right order of priorities in conceptualizing a discourse that serves both the environment and development was the first big challenge that faced thinkers and activists when the concept of sustainable development was still in an embryonic state (Robertson, 2014). Hence, to use John Blewitt's words, "one of the main obstacles to developing a common conceptual framework incorporating social, economic, and ecological problems is the lack of genuine consensus among experts in each discipline as to how ecological, economic and social system relate to one another" (2008, p. 28).

As I have already dealt at length with the issue of vagueness about the definition and aims of sustainable development in previous chapters, I would like to focus particularly on the effects of this ambiguity on the solidness of this project's theoretical background rather than dwelling on its definitional problems. If it is to combine different aspects of the global environmental crisis and the current developmental challenges, however, this new project clearly requires a host of new intellectual tools and a broad, interdisciplinary vision. For this project to take on the features of a holistic development paradigm, this interdisciplinary vision must draw upon a full range of disciplines including social sciences, economics, politics, and cultural studies. Observers (e.g., Robertson, 2014; Leichenko & O'Brien, 2008; Axelrod et al., 2009; Dale, 2001) pointedly assert that today's classical academic approaches are incapable of dealing with new global projects such as sustainable development or globalization. In his preface to *World in Motion: The Globalization and the Environment Reader,* Richard Wilk asserts that "the academic disciplines invented in the nineteenth century which we have inherited are simply not up to the task" (2009, p. viii), pointing out that "it is important to remember that the whole concept of global environmentalism is in its infancy, [and that] we are really the pioneers at the very dawn of a new era" (2009, p. ix).

One of the main factors behind the vagueness in formulating a definition of sustainable development is the ongoing debate between the proponents of the "growth agenda" and those of the "environment agenda" within the environmental movement itself. "Sustainable development is therefore multidimensional," argues John Blewitt, "encompassing social, ecological and economic goals and perspectives, and this breadth has led some critics to view the concept as vague, self-contradictory and incoherent, incapable of being put into practice" (2008, p. 23). This struggle resulted in a great confusion as where to draw the demarcation line between the need for economic growth and the environmental exigencies in this discourse. As a consequence, the proponents of economic growth and those of the protection of the environment are now vying to impose their own interpretation of sustainability, which resulted in such uncertainty about what this new project is all about.

Because of the unmistakable vagueness that characterized the formulation of sustainable development, a wide array of criticism has been directed at the formal discourse of the project promoted by the United Nations agencies and international summits in the late twentieth century. Some views (e.g., Baker, 2006; Blewitt, 2008; Dresner, 2002) accuse this discourse of legitimizing the open market economic system's depletion of natural resources to achieve its goals, rather than reshaping and harnessing the market, processes of production and consumption as well as all other aspects of the neoliberal capitalist model of growth to protect Nature. Neil Carter argues that "the traditional policy paradigm, which emerged in the 1970s to deal with environmental problems, and which is still deeply entrenched among most policy elites, reflects the way power is distributed and exercised in all capitalist liberal democracies" (2007, p. 172). Hence, ever more often suspicions are being voiced as to whether sustainable development advocated by UNCED is promoting any kind of sustainability or calling for a radical re-conceptualization of the development discourse itself. Carter (2007) asserts that the merger of the development and the environment agendas in formulating sustainable development has been significantly skewed toward giving rise to what is referred to as "the traditional environmental policy paradigm" which largely reflects the hegemony of the growth agenda.

In the literature, this traditional environmental paradigm is defined as a paradigm in which "government policies were reactive, piecemeal and tactical" with "agencies [that] had few powers over decisions taken in other policy sectors and there was little policy co-ordination and considerable scope for problem displacement" (Carter, 2007, p. 181). Despite the idiosyncratic features and multi-dimensionality of the environmental issue, this traditional environmental paradigm has indiscriminately treated it just like any other policy area, thus conspicuously failing to recognize the interdependency of the relationships between the economic, social and ecological areas. Neil Carter refers to the prevailing approach to environmental problems as a "traditional policy paradigm" which "has been found wanting, unable to stem long-standing problems of pollution and resource depletion or to deal with the new tranche of global problems that have emerged in recent years" (2007, p. 174).

According to critics such as James Speth (2008), Ann Dale (2001), Pamela Chasek, David Downie, and Janet Brown (2010), most environment ministries in industrialized countries tend to rely on various unrelated sectors and agencies which usually decide on the environmental issues with little policy co-ordination among them. The result was that important decisions such as the US Clean Act in 1970 and the UK Control of Pollution Act in 1974 introduced strict controls on pollutants and toxic substances, but failed to meet many deadlines and missed many targets because of decision fragmentation (Carter, 2007). Other observers (e.g., Strange & Bayley, 2008) contend that most governments today rely on bureaucratic networks of offices that tend often to break problems down into small sub-issues to be treated separately by different governmental sectors. Criticizing this incapability to deal with the interdependent nature of ecological problems, James Speth argues that "global environmental problems have gone from bad to worse, governments are not yet prepared to deal with them, and at present, many governments [. . .] lack the leadership to get prepared" (2005, p. 97). Overall, this type of fragmentation stands in stark contradiction with the interdependence of economic and ecological factors that characterizes current environmental problems.

In my view, despite the ascendancy of the environmental issue and the rise of sustainable development, the fragmented issue-specific approach to the environmental challenges has become more of a problem than a solution. Due to its restricted scope, this traditional environmental paradigm has grown increasingly incompatible with the holistic approach underpinning the sustainable development paradigm. Hence, this fragmented approach is clearly at odds with the nature of "many environmental problems [which] are cross-sectoral and require co-ordinated responses that transcend sectoral boundaries" (Carter, 2007, p. 180). Solutions for problems like climate change or global warming, for instance, need the involvement of the ministries responsible for transport, energy, industrial emissions, forestry, and natural resources, and other sectors. Observers point out that even "international environmental law is plagued by vague agreements, imprecise requirements, lax enforcement, and underfunded support" (Speth, 2003, p. 9). Eventually, the ambiguity that characterizes most environmental regulations and treaties further shatters the public consensus that the project of sustainable development seeks to achieve.

By and large, today's ministries and governmental institutions, mostly founded within the framework of the traditional paradigm, pursue narrow fragmented policies with little consideration for their overall environmental impact. These fragmented policies make current ministries and bureaucracies incapable of accommodating the necessary integration of overall environmental concerns in decision-making. In fact, this particular issue was raised in the *Brundtland Report*, stating that "the objective of sustainable development and the integrated nature of the global environment/development challenges pose problems for institutions [. . .] that were established on the basis of narrow preoccupations and compartmentalised concerns" (WCED, 1987, p. 9). Nonetheless, the same old fragmented procedures continue to characterize most national bureaucracies, which resist change, particularly when it comes to decision making. "This fragmentation of responsibility," argue critics, "is a major obstacle to sustainable development because environmental considerations need to be integrated into the formulation and implementation of policies in every sector" (Carter, 2007, p. 224).

Institutionally, planning and implementing sustainable development is believed to be mostly the job of the government in collaboration with NGOs and civil society groups (WCED, 1987). The government's responsibility to ensure continuity, harmony, and efficiency, therefore, is vital in this respect. On the ground, however, most of the governments today are faced with waves of privatization as corporate powers seem to be overtaking more and more governmental sectors every day. Critics (e.g., Dale, 2001; Speth, 2008; Robbins, 2009; Bakan, 2004) contend that private companies are more interested in quick profit-making than in ensuring continuity in dealing with different issues including the environment. Over the last few decades, corporations have exerted power they took over from the governments in profit-making policies, which resulted in further environmental degradation (Shiva, 2009). Some observers confirm that, "in practice, the environmental advantages of privatization are difficult to document" and that "privatization of state resources often produces new pollution-producing enterprises" (Robbins, 2009, p. 10). They particularly cite the example of privatizing the energy sector in which new environment-unfriendly techniques of mining, oil drilling, and lumbering have been used widely. "By opening Nature to corporate control," concludes Robbins, "we are allowing corporations to select those seeds and crops that create the most profit, rather than those that are most environmentally sound" (2009, p. 11).

The formulation of sustainable development in the *Brundtland Report* is also considered by many scholars (e.g., Lee, 2000; Dobson, 2000; Elliott, 2000) as an attempt to find a middle ground between the North and the South in a discourse that does not challenge the dominant neo-liberal ideology, while avoiding any calls for slowing down economic growth or fundamentally altering the capitalist economic system. This reformist aspect of the *Brundtland Report* is very much informed by the traditional environmental paradigm that has evolved since the 1970s. Although some views (e.g., Carter, 2007; Dresner, 2002) still believe that a potential for radicalism in the current discourse of sustainability is unmistakable, the prevalent inclination toward reform rather than radical change has created a widespread impression that the sustainability discourse has significantly been impacted by the process of economic globalization. Clearly, amid heated debates about whether sustainable development is radical or reformist, the project has lost much of its appeal. The overall integrity of this new project has been dramatically affected by many characteristics typical of the traditional approach to the environmental issue. By and large, this project's popularity is further undermined by the proliferation of "weak" and "strong" versions of sustainability which are sometimes conflicting and contradictory. The nature of this rift and its consequences are going to be the focus in the following section.

Green Ideology: Ecologism and the Anthropocentric-ecocentric Dichotomy

Ever since the 1972 Stockholm Conference, there has been a notable growth in the literature on the theoretical distinction between the reformist and radical approaches to sustainability. Generally, reformist approaches adopt a rather managerial approach to environmental problems, which can be solved without effecting fundamental changes in the current socio-economic paradigm of development whereas radical approaches insist that such radical changes are necessary if humans are to live within the ecological capacity of the planet. At the heart of environmental politics, therefore, lies this ongoing struggle between these two approaches, which has ultimately impacted on the potential of sustainable development.

Before delving into this discussion, I want first to shed more light on the ideological background underpinning sustainable development and examine its coherence in contemporary literature. For the most part, ecologists such as Andrew Dobson, Wolfgang Sachs, and Brian Baxter consistently emphasize the differences between ecologism and other ideologies, arguing that it stands alone as an independent ideology underpinning much of the current green activism. First published in 1991, Dobson's book, *Green Political Thought: An Introduction*, asserted that ecologism was "neither left nor right, but in front," proclaiming it as a fully-fledged ideology distinct from environmentalism as a mainstream movement. In his landmark book, Dobson contends that his principal aim "is to describe and assess that set of ideas regarding the environment which can properly be regarded as an ideology—the ideology of ecologism" (1995, p. 1). In a similar vein, Brian Baxter explains that ecologism, as an ideology, is "fundamentally a thesis about the moral considerability of other living creatures [. . .] [and] the human interconnectedness with the biosphere of this planet" (1999, pp. 5–6). Sharing the same view, Neil Carter characterizes this ideology in the following words: "Ecologism should be regarded as an ideology in its own right. It offers a persuasive critique of (capitalist) industrial society and the liberal democratic polity, holding them largely responsible for the current ecological crisis; it outlines a vision of an alternative sustainable society; and it suggests strategies of change that might achieve that utopian vision" (2007, p. 353).

By and large, ecologism as an ideology is based on two main tenets that differentiate it from other traditional ideologies: First, the need for a complete re-conceptualization of contemporary human-nature relationship that places Man as a master of Nature rather than being an integral part of it; and secondly, the need to abide by the principle of limits to growth in future development policies. According to ecologists (e.g., Dobson, 2000; Orton, 1994), the contemporary environmental crisis has for the most part been caused by human arrogance towards the natural environment, resulting in growing Nature abuse to satisfy human wants. Central to ecologism, therefore, is the principle that Man is not necessarily placed at the top of an ethical hierarchy (Carter, 2007). In essence, this principle radically opposes anthropocentrism, which attaches intrinsic value predominantly to humans as the center of the universe whereas non-human entities are only of instrumental value and have value only in so far as they serve human needs and enhance human well-being.

Counterbalancing this approach is a non-anthropocentric or an ecocentric approach that opposes what ecologists see as the "human chauvinism" of anthropocentrism and stresses the intrinsic value of non-human entities (Carter, 2007). According to this approach, non-human entities like animals, trees, plants and other species, and even inanimate objects like rivers and mountains have their own intrinsic value. Hence, ecologists such as the Norwegian philosopher Arne Næss, Bill Devall, and George Sessions reject the Enlightenment view that Man and Nature are separate entities, and they especially decry the principle that Man is seen as the master of Nature (Devall & Sessions, 2001). The concept of "ecological consciousness" that changes people's view of Nature is, therefore, highly celebrated in the writings of these ecologists. David Pepper (1996), for example, emphasizes the holistic aspect of ecologism and highlights the close interdependence of ecosystems, which underpins a whole reappraisal of the human-nature relationship and Man's ethical duties toward Nature.

On the whole, ecologism poses an ideological challenge to the Western predominant socio-economic paradigm of development at different levels of principles, developmental policies, and implementation. Based on ecologism, the sustainability discourse claims that it draws upon familiar concepts such as participatory democracy and social justice borrowed from other ideologies to ensure a sustainable human development. In the words of Neil Carter, "[g]reen politics has drawn on other political traditions, notably socialism, for its critique of capitalism, and from anarchism for its suspicion of the state" (2007, p. 354). These principles assume today a crucial role in raising ecological consciousness and fostering greener political and economic policies. The father of ecologism, Arne Næss, stresses the new vision in what he refers to as "deep ecology" or "ecologism," putting it as follows: "I believe that multifaceted, high-level self-realization is more easily reached through a lifestyle which is 'simple in means but rich in ends' rather than through the material standard of living of the average citizens of industrial states" (1995, p. 82).

When it comes to formulating and implementing sustainable development, ecologism, in my opinion, has contributed to the current impasse of this new project. The inherent anthropocentric-ecocentric dualism in ecologism has brought about different versions of sustainable development, thus undermining the public zeal for a new alternative model of development. As a matter of fact, this rupture has caused environmentalists to split into two different camps advocating two different, sometimes conflicting, versions of sustainability. Division has made impossible the consensus so urgently needed in the face of the many obstacles facing this new paradigm of development. As such, ecologism is also regarded with lingering suspicion that this ideology is coherent and exhaustive enough to give rise to a comprehensive and realistic model of political, economic, and social development. One formulation of this suspicion is that "ecologism is rather hazy about how the change to a sustainable society is to occur, and who will take the lead in bringing it about" (Carter, 2007, p. 71). This ideology is, therefore, criticized for setting forth a rather inchoate development paradigm that can hardly be applicable today. While it harshly criticizes the current neoliberal capitalist model of growth, ecologism fails to specify, for example, how exactly a society can opt out of the existing socio-economic paradigm and engage in the new alternative green lifestyles. Ecologism also claims to offer a new framework for activism within which participants such as local communities and NGOs can play a bigger role in building an "ecological consciousness," but it falls short of designing precise methods for putting this process into practice. As a consequence, some critics (e.g., Carter, 2007; Dale, 2001; Harrison, 2000) have started to reject these calls for fundamental change, denouncing them as utopian and impractical.

From a reformist point of view, environmental politics has significantly impacted on contemporary national and global politics, which is a very clear sign of its success (Connelly & Smith, 1999). What is more, this view celebrates green movements' success and popularity in some of the industrialized countries, which has "forced most parties to treat the environment more seriously, at least by developing a greener rhetoric and strengthening policy programmes" (Carter, 2007, p. 355). According to this view, the weak or reformist version of sustainable development can be more successful at achieving environmental protection and social equity by boosting economic growth and entrusting the business sector with this type of development. Proponents of this version of sustainability also believe that attaching a price tag to the environment is the best way to protect it: "The object of policies to promote weak sustainable development remains economic growth," argues Susan Baker, "but environmental costs are taken into consideration through, for example, accounting procedures" (2006, p. 33).

Critics of this reformist approach (e.g., York & Rosa, 2003; Blewitt, 2008; Dobson, 2000), on the other hand, attribute the failure of environmental politics in reshaping the established political and economic systems to the prominence of weaker versions of sustainability. According to this view, the prevalent zeal for reform has resulted in an ineffective version of sustainable development that has aligned itself with big business and governmental interests at the expense of real changes that would better serve the environment and society. Other critics, especially "deep ecologists," go as far as to denounce the current UN version of sustainable development as a "political fudge" that "seeks to bridge the unbridgeable divide between the anthropocentric and biocentric approaches to politics" (Richardson, 1997, p. 43).

The proliferation of different versions and interpretations of sustainable development has made it a highly debatable concept, which ultimately raises a fundamental question about the essence and integrity of sustainability as an alternative paradigm of growth. In the absence of a precise definition of sustainable development, many conflicting ideas or principles can be claimed as part of this project, thus emptying it of any coherent essence. "At the root of these conflicting interpretations," argues Baker, "lies deep conflict over whether sustainable development is a tool for the construction of radically different environmental futures or whether it should be rejected out of hand, as it represents little more than an anthropocentric management tool, useful to help capitalism to find a way out of its environmental crisis" (2006, p. 215). In a context of an overwhelming process of globalization, this project, in my opinion, can hardly afford to lose the public consensus that characterized its inception in the 1970s and 1980s and which is at stake now. Besides, the vagueness of what sustainable development is all about has not only emptied it of any meaning, but also seriously weakened it in front of strong overwhelming phenomena such as globalization and trade liberalization.

The vagueness of the concept of sustainable development, however, is regarded by many scholars (e.g., Dale, 2001; Robinson, 2004) as one of the main strengths of this concept. This view celebrates the open-endedness of concept as a positive asset that helps the message of sustainability to resonate worldwide. Marteen Hajer argues, for instance, that "the coalition for sustainable development can only be kept together by virtue of its rather vague story-lines at the same time as it asks for radical social change" (1995, p. 14). This "constructive ambiguity" and contestability of this concept, therefore, is regarded as a political strength when it promises every sector on the political and economic scenes a role to play, thus widening the coalition that endorses sustainable development nationally and globally (Dale, 2001).

While some of its aspects can be useful in finding a common ground among different actors, the vagueness that marks sustainability today has, on the whole, done more harm than good to the project of sustainable development. Most significantly, the internal divisions between radical and reformist ecologists and the ambiguity that shrouds sustainable development have shattered the public consensus about the essence and solidarity of this new project. Public opinion has become divided over which version of sustainable development to endorse while most politicians have allied themselves with big business and opted for the weakest version of sustainability. More importantly, this ambiguity has given politicians a chance to pledge their full support for sustainable development and at the same time maintained all aspects of a neoliberal capitalist economic growth. The popularization of a weak form of sustainability has also paved the way for the emergence of "ecological modernization" as a new approach to fix environmental problems. The bias of politicians and corporate elites in favor of unfettered economic growth has also found in the concept of ecological modernization a good opportunity to enjoy the public support for sustainability and boost their unsustainable economies even more. The effects of this new approach on sustainable development will be in focus in the following section.

Ecological Modernization and the Concept of "Green Capitalism"

Sustainability's controversial ideological underpinnings and the concomitant proliferation of different versions of this concept precipitated the emergence and popularization of what is referred to as ecological modernization. As I mentioned in the last section of chapter 2, this new approach ideologically departs from sustainable development by adopting much of the growth agenda dominating the current paradigm of growth today. In this section, however, I am not going to dwell on theoretical and definitional debates about ecological modernization again, but rather it is my aim here to investigate whether this new approach supports or hampers the project of sustainable development.

Although some views (e.g., Cohen, 2006; Mol, 2002) claim that ecological modernization aims principally at effecting important changes to the current socio-economic paradigm of growth, others (Hayden, 2014; Carter, 2007; Baker, 2006; York & Rosa, 2003) argue that this theory clearly distances itself from any calls for a fundamental restructuring of the neoliberal free economic system. Most of these views admit, however, that the concept of ecological modernization concedes that the contemporary ecological crisis is a product of the capitalist economic system. According to this theory, capitalism can be made more environmentally friendly if the right technology is used and the appropriate reforms are put in place, so that the conflicting goals of ongoing economic growth and the protection of the environment are reconciled (Hayden, 2014). In a similar vein, Richard York and Eugene Rosa point out that this project "argues for the potential of attaining sustainability from within—a greening of 'business as usual'—thereby avoiding such challenging alternatives as radical structural or value changes in society" (2003, p. 274).

Ecological modernization as a concept differs from sustainable development with respect to a few important points, the most important of which is its utilitarian approach of attaching a price tag to the environment through measures such as the "polluter pays principle." Put differently, this theory upholds the concept that "a clean environment [. . .] is a commodity, just like television sets, computers, or soap, and if people desire the commodity, the market will supply it" (Robbins, 2009, p. 7). Ecological modernization, therefore, places a lot of emphasis on the business sector that can make profits by protecting the environment and fostering green technology. As a consequence, costs can be reduced by enhancing the efficiency of environment-friendly production. Ecological modernization also fosters the concept of "green consumerism" which is based on the consumption of recyclable, environment-friendly products with minimal ecological damages.

While the principle of green consumerism is applicable in sustainability, the heavy reliance on the role of business and the absence of the limits to growth principles are highly incompatible with the project of sustainable development. This dichotomy has grown more conspicuous as most industrialized governments started to shift their attention from sustainability to ecological modernization on the grounds that the latter offers more practical cost-effective and business-friendly solutions. Studies show, for instance, that countries such as the Netherlands, Germany, Britain, and Japan have become leaders in applying ecological modernization strategies (Baker, 2006; Hayden, 2014). Ultimately, the prominence of ecological modernization at a time when sustainable development was still formulated further tilts the balance in favor of the reformist approach and weakens the consensus on this project.

Internal as it is, this discrepancy between ecological modernization and sustainable development is echoed in these two projects' agendas for development. With a huge emphasis on devising practical solutions to solve the current environmental problems, "ecological modernization also discards much of the political baggage of sustainable development, notably the 'development' agenda of North-South issues, inequalities, social justice and democracy, which can prove controversial and costly to implement" (Carter, 2007, p. 229). Thus, while sustainable development embraces a wider agenda of setting holistic goals and strategies for an environment-friendly development with more social equity, ecological modernization offers instead a set of practical techniques for fixing ecological problems in industrialized countries. As such, ecological modernization offers feasible technical solutions to contemporary environmental problems without theorizing about replacing the prevailing development paradigm. Some scholars (Baker, 2006; Connelly & Smith, 1999) point out that the focus on devising profit-oriented practical solutions to fix current ecological problems is clearly at odds with the deep concern with a wide array of social, economic, and cultural issues that characterizes the sustainability discourse.

By disregarding social issues such as poverty and inequality in modern consumer society, the discourse of ecological modernization, in my opinion, has made great concessions on the holistic agenda defended in sustainable development. Moreover, ecological modernization's neglect of political issues such as the North-South divide, global governance, and trade liberalization makes it much more appealing to politicians who want to enjoy the rhetoric of sustainability without enacting any radical political or economic changes. This ascendancy of ecological modernization as a practical solution to ecological ills has, therefore, significantly limited the chances of sustainable development to be adopted and defended by politicians given the hard choices entailed in this project vis-à-vis development.

All in all, the popularization of ecological modernization, especially in the Western countries, has been detrimental to sustainable development and contributed to the gridlock this project has reached. By and large, the prominence of ecological modernization has weakened the public consensus about the need for an alternative paradigm of growth that the discourse of sustainability is based upon. The success of ecological modernization in some industrialized countries has also dissuaded politicians and decision-makers from embracing the project of sustainable development, especially as they found in ecological modernization a quick solution to environmental problems without having to question the whole economic and political systems. In addition, ecological modernization seems to be at odds with the sustainable development strategies designed to curb and supervise TNCs' hegemony as it entrusts them with producing the green technology needed for solving environment problems. Ultimately, the holistic sustainability approach to tackling ecological, economic, and political problems has been marginalized by the focus on quick technical solutions to environmental problems that characterizes ecological modernization.

CONCLUSION

Today's wide celebration of sustainability in global summits belies deep conflict over the meaning and definition of sustainable development. Within an unfavorable context of neoliberal capitalism, a combination of different political, economic, and social factors erects numerous obstacles that have brought the evolution of sustainable development to a grinding halt. Because of its radical agenda, this new project has been confronted with many impediments mostly inherent in the current socio-economic paradigm of development. This project also faces many hurdles obstructing its progress within a globalized economy dominated by corporate power. Overall, all these obstacles reflect high levels of incompatibility between sustainable development and neoliberal capitalism.

One of the main features of the incompatibility between neoliberal capitalism and sustainable development is manifest in the current disturbed environment-society relationship, which is at odds with the holistic view of Nature in the sustainability discourse. This disturbed relationship, in turn, reflects the rather instrumental capitalist approach to Nature that reduces it to mere exploitable natural resources. This instrumental approach to Nature jeopardizes strategies for a sustainable model of development when it places Man as the master of his environment and downplays the intrinsic value of Nature. When disconnecting people from the dire effects of their abuses of their environment, this top-down view of the society-environment relationship also causes people to become further estranged from Nature and to lose sight of their abuse of the environment.

The overall context of the global governance system, the North-South divide, and the issue of global trade liberalization has also had a strong bearing on the evolution of sustainable development. The project of sustainable development faces today numerous impediments, setting back its evolution and minimizing its chances for a sound implementation. Closely linked to global trade and the North-South politics, the contemporary global governance system has become more of an obstruction than a solution for the stalemate of sustainability today. Heavily influenced by the Bretton Woods principles of free market and liberalized trade, the predominant actors in global governance have usually promoted their own agendas, which are incompatible with the long-term goals and plans of sustainability. For the most part, the current global governance system has crippled the project of sustainable development by targeting many of its basic tenets such as growing within the limits of ecosystems, fostering a bottom-up mode of development, and encouraging local sustainable economies.

Within a context of economic globalization, global trade liberalization has contributed to unsustainable practices among farmers and manufacturers worldwide, with scant regard for the dire environmental consequences. In doing so, global trade liberalization has become one of the main adversaries of sustainable development. In global politics, the plight of this new project takes on new dimensions as the environmental issues have increasingly been perceived as an important concern in the North-South politics. With the long-standing North-South divide unmistakably echoed in most of the global summits about sustainable development, reaching a common ground about sustainability has become even more challenging than before. The mutual mistrust between the North and the South has also created such a poisonous atmosphere that has negatively impacted on the prospects for sustainable development, not least in developing countries. Just like neoliberal capitalism and globalization, the North-South politics have proven to be a rather unfavorable context for the project of sustainable development to evolve in.

A closer look at the theoretical background of sustainable development reveals that the hostile climate created by neoliberal capitalism, the global governance system, and globalization has not been the only cause behind the plight of sustainability today. Some inner conflicts and contradictions inside the paradigm of sustainable development itself have also weakened this project and crippled its implementation. In addition to facing numerous external impediments, this new project encounters considerable hindrance from the different approaches to sustainability and growth within this paradigm itself. In essence, reconciling the needs for development with concerns for the environment has proven another big challenge that has a serious bearing on defining and formulating this project. It is precisely the clash between the growth agenda and the environment agenda that has resulted in a notable vagueness about the essence and aims of this project. This ambiguity, in turn, has further undermined the public consensus on sustainability.

What is referred to as "the traditional environmental policy paradigm" has also been at odds with the project of sustainable development as it focuses rather on single ecological issues at the expense of other aspects of human development such as social equity and sustainability. By and large, this traditional environmental paradigm fails to take on board the holistic approach connecting the social, the economic, and the ecological issues in the sustainability discourse. Sustainable development's popularity has also been undermined by the proliferation of numerous interpretations of what sustainability means, giving birth to several weak and strong versions of this project. Not only has internal division confused public opinion over which version of sustainable development to support, but it has also given politicians and corporate elites an opportunity to opt for the weakest one of those versions. More to the point, this ambiguity has given politicians an opportunity to publicly pledge their full support to sustainable development and at the same time to maintain the business-as-usual attitude toward the environment.

The political willingness to adopt a rather reformist approach to sustainability has also displaced the public consensus from endorsing sustainable development to celebrating the practicality of ecological modernization and the soundness of the neoliberal economic system. The holistic view combining the ecological, economic, and political issues in sustainability has also been marginalized by the focus on quick technical solutions to fix environmental problems that ecological modernization offers. Eventually, all these extrinsic and intrinsic impediments have contributed, to different degrees, to the current gridlock that sustainable development has reached.

NOTES

1. The term "cash crop" is defined differently in the literature, but the most commonly used definition refers to a crop exported and "grown specifically for sale or might be sold because production was surplus to 'domestic' demand" (Maxwell & Fernando, 1989, p. 1678).

2. Recent statistics show, for example, that over the twentieth century (from 1890s to 1990s): the overall world economy doubled up to 14-fold; world population doubled up to 4-fold; overall energy use doubled up to 16-fold; Carbon dioxide emissions doubled up to 35-fold; water use doubled up to 16-fold; and marine fish catch doubled up to 35-fold (Speth, 2008, p. 50).

3. See Goldemberg, 2003; Venetoulis & Talberth, 2009; Radermacher, 2004; Elliott, 2000; and WWF, 2012.

4. Recent statistics of the *Global Wealth Report 2010*, published by the Credit Suisse Research Institute, show, for instance, that 0.5 percent of global population (adults) share 35.6 percent of global wealth whereas 68.4 percent of global population (adults) share only 4.2 of global wealth (Pizzigati, 2010).

5. Elizabeth A. Ellis notes, for instance, that because of the unsustainable activities of TNCs in maquiladoras on the American-Mexican border, the pollution rates are soaring in the whole region, resulting in children's facial deformities and mental retardation as a result of prenatal exposure to toxic chemicals. Social consequences also

include overcrowded areas with people settling in slums which lack sewage systems and wastewater treatment, and where rates of toxic contamination are extremely high (1996, pp. 630–33).

6. Surveys indicate that over 319 multilateral and bilateral environmental agreements were completed in the 20 years from 1972 to the 1992 (with an average of 16 agreements per year), and 189 agreements completed from 1993 through 2002 with an average of 19 agreements per year (Mitchell, 2003, p. 438).

7. Observers decry, for instance, the obstructive role played by the Organization of Petroleum Exporting Countries (OPEC), which repeatedly blocked and delayed progress in the global climate regimes to keep high oil prices and avoid any reductions in the emissions of greenhouse gases from the burning of oil (Barnett, 2008, pp. 1–4). For a broader discussion of this issue, see Jon Barnett's article "The Worst of Friends: OPEC and G–77 in the Climate Regime."

8. For a detailed analysis of these cases, see Chasek, Downie, & Brown, 2010, pp. 347–352.

9. The Malaysian delegate to the second Meeting of the Parties to the Montreal Protocol in 1990 declared, for example, that for some industrialized countries the protocol was a "pretext to place new obstacles in the way of efforts by developing countries to develop their economies" (as cited in Chasek, Downie, & Brown, 2010, p. 324).

FOUR

Beyond Sustainability Gridlock

A New Approach to Sustainable Development

Despite the numerous, extrinsic obstacles it faces and the multiple, intrinsic contradictions from which it suffers, the project of sustainable development still poses a challenge to the fundamental tenets of the prevailing socio-economic paradigm of growth. The manifold incompatibilities between these two paradigms economically, socially, and ecologically are so deep that they have precipitated a daunting gridlock in the evolution of this new project. Evolving in a context of neoliberal capitalist model of growth, sustainable development has faced not only economic obstacles, but also social, cultural, and political ones. Despite clear evidence that ecological disasters and concomitant social dislocations are imminent, the dominant socio-economic paradigm of growth has systematically resisted the fundamental structural changes required for sustainability. Although still in an inchoate state, sustainable development has gradually become entangled in a stalemate that almost brought its evolution to a halt. Understanding the different features of this gridlock requires a thorough examination of the diverse factors that have perpetuated this status quo and blocked initiatives for change. My chief aim in the first section, therefore, is to spotlight the different factors that perpetuate the sustainability gridlock and that thwart attempts to bring about new structural changes to the current paradigm of growth. In doing so, I want also to highlight the interconnectedness between the economic, political, and social factors. However, my ultimate aim in the second section is to discuss the options that sustainable development still has at its disposal in its efforts to overcome the current stalemate in the political, economic, and social areas.

THE CURRENT SUSTAINABILITY GRIDLOCK: ROOT CAUSES AND MAIN FEATURES

Theoretically, the social and economic changes that sustainability entails would touch every aspect of the predominant socio-economic paradigm. Basically, these changes involve the adoption of a new society-environment relationship, of new lifestyles, of new patterns of production and consumption, and of new national and international governance systems. Notwithstanding, the efforts to effect these changes have encountered resistance on the part of the current paradigm of development. My aim in this section is twofold: First I want to shed more light on the main factors that have helped perpetuate this status quo and form the gridlock that sustainable development is trapped in. Second, I would like to examine the different repercussions of this impasse on prospects of the implementation of sustainable development.

Governmental Bureaucracies' Resistance to Change and Today's Institutional Incapacities

Despite the growing evidence of imminent ecological disasters (e.g., global warming, ozone layer depletion, and biodiversity loss, among others), the dominant socio-economic paradigm of growth has been resistant thus far to any fundamental structural changes to serve sustainability. On the contrary, there has been an intensifying resistance to emergent new concepts about society and the environment on the part of modern governments' bureaucracies and corporations. Many politicians and decision-makers are still unwilling to take any radical decisions in spite of the abundance of evidence that ecological and social capital is being eroded at alarming rates and indeed may have reached the point of no return. More seriously, resistance to change has permeated many governmental departments and other very influential institutions such as universities, research centers, and financial organizations.

A closer look at the structure of modern governments today reveals that bureaucracies, which function as disconnected sectors, would usually cripple attempts to effect radical changes with regard to implementing sustainable development. In the words of Ann Dale, "the forces against change appear to be much more systematic, pervasive, and multifaceted than is normally appreciated, and they operate at both the group and individual levels" (2001, p. 97). Governmental bureaucracies, for instance, exhibit a lot of inertia in responding to new issues such as ecological exigencies and social inequity problems. More often than not, these bureaucracies "seek to undermine those efforts [of change] and constrain them within narrow limits" (Speth, 2008, pp. 85–86). Inherent values and ideologies within these bureaucracies constitute, therefore, a growing force that blocks any new concepts or initiatives from coming to the fore.

Over decades, the values and ideologies celebrating exponential growth, supremacy of mankind, and consumerism have permeated large bureaucracies, financial institutions, and even universities but have rarely been questioned. In most contemporary governments in industrialized countries today, for instance, the current drawbacks of environmental abuse and social dislocations are still presented by economists (e.g., Sagoff, 2000; Norberg, 2003/2007; Bhagwati, 2007) as unavoidable but affordable costs of economic growth. Thus, the ecological costs of economic growth are downplayed and externalized as mere trade-offs in the continuous process of wealth creation.

On the whole, the prevalent "growth values" have crippled efforts to implement the sustainability agenda because they have contributed to the disconnection of the three main tenets of sustainable development, namely the ecological, the social, and the economic imperatives. Researchers (e.g., Holmberg & Samuelsson, 2006; Strange & Bayley, 2008) confirm that in most governments, economic and social organizations, and educational institutions, researching and deciding on economic issues is usually still done independently of the ecological and social side-effects of those development options. Similarly, researching and deciding on social ills and societal dislocations is very often done independently of the possible far-reaching repercussions of ecological crises and environmental abuses that have some integral connections with both the economic and social imperatives. Accordingly, hindrance to implementing sustainable development policies is caused essentially by widespread vision of economic, social, and ecological imperatives as unconnected issues, requiring different solutions.

In the absence of a clear political vision and solid public awareness of the integral interconnectedness of the ecological, social, and economic imperatives, the separation of these issues seems both rational and practical. Most of modern governments, for example, have a department or ministry for the environment that seeks to alleviate environmental degradation and encourage sustainable uses of energy and other departments or ministries for economy and trade that support more exploitation of natural resources. As such, the role of the economic departments is actually to boost economic growth with scant regard for the resultant ecological problems and social dislocations. These "sectoral divisions within the institutional structure of government," argues Neil Carter, "both reflect and reinforce a special-interest approach to public policy in which each ministry tends to act as a sponsor for the key producer or professional groups within its policy sphere" (2007, p. 182).

The fragmentation that plagued most governmental bureaucracies is highly at odds with the holistic approach to development in the sustainability discourse. This pervasive fragmentation often results in some contradictory economic, social, and environmental policies that not only work against one another, but also further confuse the public and thwart attempts to change to more sustainable modes of growth. Hence, this fragmented approach to development has led to contradictory development and environmental policies, resulting in the perpetuation of the sustainability impasse. The fragmented governmental policies are also highly indicative of how responsive today's governmental bureaucracies are to the exigencies of sustainability. Critics (e.g., Leach, Mehta, & Prabhakaran, 2016; Vig & Kraft, 1990; Dale, 2001) point out, for instance, that even the current governmental departmentalization, scientific analytical tools, and research methods at universities are often at odds with the interdisciplinary nature of the sustainability discourse. The fragmentation that characterizes most of today's bureaucracies is also a feature of most universities in both developed and developing countries.

Despite the remarkable development of research methodology in recent decades, many observers (e.g., Adam, 1998; Adams, 1990; Leichenko & O'Brien, 2008; van Dam-Mieras, 2006) argue today that researchers' strong adherence to a one-discipline perspective clearly impedes interdisciplinary research that is highly collaborative. An in-depth insight into the essence and potential of sustainable development, however, necessitates a strong and wide collaboration of researchers from different disciplines as well as a robust interdisciplinary approach that cuts cross major issue areas informing this new paradigm of growth (Robertson, 2014). Intrinsically holistic, sustainable development discourse draws upon diverse disciplines such as economics, political science, sociology, environmental studies, and geography among others. This debate, in my view, raises the important question of how responsive today's academic disciplines and research methodologies are to the intricacies and sophistication of a new holistic paradigm of growth.

Today's governmental and educational institutions' insensitivity to the intricacies of sustainability poses no less a challenge than other factors to the potential of this new project. The institutional incapacity to take on board the holistic approach to development has led to an incomplete, and even shallow, understanding of sustainable development in both governmental sectors and academia. Inadequate scientific and academic tools and approaches to deal with the intricacies of sustainable development has, for example, resulted in dissecting this project into independent areas in such a way that is fundamentally irresponsive to the current ecological, social, and economic challenges. Hence, "interdisciplinary and transdisciplinary, as well as integrated modes of inquiry, are required if we are to really understand sustainable development," argues Ann Dale (2001, p. 111). For a significantly radical paradigm of development that projects itself horizontally by mapping social, economic, and ecological issues and vertically by considering the needs of both present and future generations, conventional research tools and methods are certainly obsolete and inadequate.

More important than any other sector in shaping the success or failure of sustainable development today, in my view, are the government's bureaucracies, universities, and research centers. For the most part, however, these institutions were established before the issue of sustainability came to the fore as a high profile concern in global politics. What is alarming, however, is that most governmental departments, universities, and research centers still use the old linear policies and research methodologies and apply them to the new global exigencies with scant regard for their particular characteristics (Holmberg & Samuelsson, 2006). Although there are many universities and research centers that succeeded in revolutionizing their research methodologies so as to accommodate new issues like sustainable development and globalization,[1] many other institutions have not risen to the challenge yet. Many studies (e.g., Leach, Mehta, & Prabhakaran, 2016; Vig & Kraft, 1990; Axelrod et al., 2009; Dale, 2001) reveal that, instead of accommodating the emerging sustainability challenges, most educational institutions and research centers have clung to their old approaches, policies, and methodologies, thus failing to take on board the far-reaching dimensions of emerging issues such as sustainable development. Professor Ann Dale further contends that "it is particularly disturbing that the inherent structures of two institutions that need to provide leadership in the promulgation of knowledge about sustainable development and its implementation—universities and governments—work against this" (2001, p. 105). This institutional incapacity is particularly detrimental to sustainable development because many of these institutions claim to be endorsing sustainability while they still approach it with old, narrow methods that hamper innovative approaches to grow sustainably.

As I see it, the mismatch between the structures and policies of these institutions, on the one hand, and the new sustainability challenges that they are supposed to deal with, on the other, reflects a serious flaw in the current paradigm of development. Highly uncongenial to radical changes and new models of growth, the current socio-economic paradigm of development systematically produces institutions that contribute to the perpetuation of the status quo. For example, most of today's governmental departments are still committed to the drive for achieving more economic growth, implementing more efficient ways to master nature, and creating more ways for wealth-creation despite growing evidence of looming ecological disasters and concomitant social dislocations. Inherent in the current model of growth, this institutional incapability has triggered scathing criticism from many observers. Precisely, critics raise a serious question: "how can individuals, groups and businesses fashion and act on their ecological obligations when so much of our social and economic lives are structured unsustainably or offer so many contradictory and incompatible forms of satisfaction and rewards?" (Blewitt, 2008, p. 119).

With factors maintaining the status quo, the current socio-economic paradigm has become highly self-perpetuating. This feature creates what is referred to as a strong "dysfunctionality" that reinforces itself from within this dominant paradigm of growth itself. Considering an alternative model of development would certainly be incompatible with short-term interests of big business which seeks quick profits, politicians who seek re-election, and even universities which seek more funding and governmental support. What is more, some of these institutions tend to maintain the status quo by not only rejecting new alternatives of research, new modes of development, and new approaches to growth, but also by projecting only positive images of the current model of growth to the political leaders and decision-makers. Altogether, these institutions perpetuate the status quo by creating "a pervasive gridlock of resistance to all alternative paradigms and policy initiatives" (Dale, 2001, p. 108).

More than ever before, there is today an urgent need to recognize and address these underlying structural conflicts between the necessity to change and the push for maintaining the status quo within today's socio-economic paradigm of development. In the absence of any radical structural transformations in today's political, economic, and educational institutions, any attempt to popularize and implement sustainable development would have meager results. Unless they are transformed from within, these institutions will go on applying their disjointed approach that dissects the sustainability problem into sub-issues and deals with them one at a time. Plagued by this institutional incapacity, the current socio-economic paradigm of development will, therefore, continue to be blind to the interdependence of the ecological, social, and economic imperatives. Critics point out, for example, that instead of maintaining this status quo, "sustainable development involves a *process of change* in which core components of society—resource use, investment, technologies, institutions, consumption patterns—come to operate in greater harmony with ecosystems" (Carter, 2007, p. 212). Hence, bringing about the necessary changes and transforming these institutions from within must be at the top of the sustainability agenda if a sound implementation of this project is ever to take place.

The required transformations within today's model of growth will not be possible without a strong public consensus for the primacy of living within the planet's carrying capacity. A genuine political will together with a serious civic commitment to uphold the values of sustainability rather than those of consumerism are also badly needed to ease this transition. Hence, and in the words of Neil Carter, "the transition to a sustainable society involves more than institutional restructuring by governments and social learning by policy elites," arguing that "neither businesses nor governments are likely to change their behavior until they can be assured that consumers and citizens will support them" (2007, p. 359). For the time being, however, it is clear that such institutions are incapable of the effective holistic approach that contemporary environmental exigencies necessitate. This incapacity for change constitutes one reinforcing element in the current sustainability impasse.

By and large, the institutional resistance to change is but a reflection of the values and ethics associated with the current socio-economic paradigm of growth; hence most governmental institutions, universities, research centers, and companies are but a product of this paradigm. Government bureaucracies cannot approach sustainable development holistically while sustainability is researched within disconnected disciplines and with outmoded tools that are incapable of capturing the intricacies of this new project. Universities, in turn, cannot apply an effective interdisciplinary approach to this project if the whole society is still saturated with materialist ethics of growth, the supremacy of Man over Nature, and the infinity of natural bounties.

Corporate Domination and the Perpetuation of Consumer Culture

The modern corporation is a relatively recent phenomenon which dates to the mid-nineteenth century. Recent studies show that in 2002, over 61,000 TNCs, with over 900,000 foreign affiliates, were engaged in different projects around the world (Assadourian, 2005). Observers also note that TNCs have proliferated so rapidly that they now accounts for 80 percent of the world's output (Speth, 2008). The corporation as we know it today has certain defining characteristics that not only determine its policies, but also impact dramatically on important issues such as preserving the environment and achieving more social justice. Widely referred to as "corporatism," corporate policies tend to encourage high rates of consumption and disseminate a consumer ethic in both developed and developing countries through advertisement and other marketing strategies (Rushkoff, 2011). Although production patterns change constantly as technological breakthroughs help these corporations expand further and further, TNCs remain always guided by the same consumer ethic and growth agenda.

To begin with, I find it essential to shed light on some of the most common characteristics of modern corporations that impact on the resilience of any attempt to change to a more sustainable model of growth. Firstly, one of the salient characteristics of modern corporations is the separation of ownership from management which means that shareholders who own the corporation do not run it but instead assign executive managers to do this job (Rushkoff, 2011; Bakan, 2004; Ikerd, 2005). This principle is closely linked to another one called the "best interest of the corporation" principle, which simply means that the managers directing the corporation have an obligation under corporate regulations to act in the best interest of the corporation. This legal obligation of managers to maximize profits usually rules out the adoption of any holistic approach to growth that balances social, ecological, and economic concerns in development strategies. Clearly resonating with the fragmented approaches of governmental bureaucracies that sideline ecological issues, this corporate vision focused entirely on profits maximization also works to reinforce the predominant unsustainable paradigm of growth,.

The second characteristic of corporations that I want to highlight is the legal status of these corporations before the American law. In his book, *The Corporation: The Pathological Pursuit of Profit and Power*, Joel Bakan (2004) asserts that corporations enjoy the protection of constitutional provisions that were originally meant to protect the rights of the individuals, which gives these corporations many rights that only individuals must enjoy. Clearly, this advantage enables corporations to dodge responsibilities that harm the environment and have wide-ranging repercussions on livelihoods, local communities, and social ties. Corporations, for instance, are absolved of any accountability for the social dislocations that their policies of mass production and highly mobile capital result in. Bakan contends that "nothing in its [i.e., the corporation's] legal makeup limits what it can do to others in pursuit of its selfish ends, and it is compelled to cause harm when the benefits of doing so outweigh the costs" (2004, p. 60). This leniency in holding these corporations accountable for the ecological and social side-effects of their policies consolidates the corporate predominance in the current socio-economic development paradigm. Ultimately, absolving corporations of their responsibility toward society and the environment further perpetuates the fragmented approach to development and the environment, toughening even more the stalemate of sustainability.

The third issue related to corporatism that I want to highlight is the externalization of environmental costs that may affect the corporate profits. Studies (e.g., Rushkoff, 2011; Assadourian, 2005; Bakan, 2004; Mellor, 2000) clearly show that, in their fervent drive to maximize the profits of their shareholders, corporations tend to externalize any cost for wreaking social or environmental damages. In so far as these costs are externalized, the ecological issue is treated separately from any other economic and social concerns, thus consolidating even more the fragmented approach to growth. "Thus, corporate ownership frequently seeks to remove all social and ethical constraints on a company's pursuit of ever-greater profits and growth," maintains economist John Ikerd (2005, p. 17). Because of these self-interested policies and tendency to externalize any other issues that can be affected in their pursuit of more profits, the modern corporation, in my view, not only fits well in the fabric of the current socio-economic paradigm, but also constitutes another reinforcing element that maintains the status quo and blocks any genuine attempt at change.

Still, another prominent feature of corporations relevant to this discussion is the invisible corporate political influence on governments, decision-makers, and the media. Whether through lobbying, political campaigns funding, or numerous other ways, the corporate sector exerts huge pressure on politicians and decision-makers especially in Western industrialized countries. According to many critics (e.g., Rushkoff, 2011; Chasek, Downie, & Brown, 2010; Bakan, 2004; Ikerd, 2005), corporations can also affect, and even shape, public opinion through the ownership of the mass media, funding of research at universities, and think-tanks and foundations. This huge media power is consolidated by an ever-increasing economic power that corporations have at the national and global levels. Given the intense competition among developed and developing countries alike to attract as much foreign investment as possible, corporate economic and political power has notably increased in recent years. In his book, *Who Rules America?,* William Domhoff asserts that "this combination of economic power, policy expertise, and continuing political success makes the corporate owners and executives a dominant class, not in the sense of complete and absolute power, but in the sense that they have the power to shape the economic and political frameworks within which other groups and classes must operate" (2006, pp. xiii-xiv).

With the contemporary intensification of globalization, these corporations have grown into powerful giants. Of the hundred largest economies in the world, for instance, fifty-three are corporations, including Exxon, whose capital is larger than the revenue of economies of 180 different countries (Speth, 2008, p. 170). Often dodging ecological or social responsibilities, the huge power of the global corporations today constitutes a big hindrance to the implementation of sustainable development given the firm corporate grip on the world economy and resistance to following an alternative paradigm of development. What I deem more serious than the increasing corporate hegemony, however, is the fact that the current globalized economy structures are not only shaping the social, intellectual, and environmental conditions, but also are toughening the sustainability gridlock.

Corporations are also regarded as the main culprit behind the popularization of the consumer ethic at the expense of imminent ecological and social imperatives. While proponents of neo-liberalism (e.g., Norberg, 2003/2007) argue that in a consumer society, consumers are free to choose what and when to consume thanks to globalization, many critics (e.g., Kütting, 2004; Carter, 2007) denounce this freedom as a fallacy. Attempts to change these patterns, however, have been met with strong resistance from business elites who want to keep making the same profits from the high rates of consumptions that characterize the consumer society. Chasek, Downie, and Brown cite the example of the International Chamber of Shipping, which represents thirty national associations of ship owners, and the Oil Companies International Marine Forum, representing the interests of major oil companies, which "ensured that the convention [i.e., the International Convention for the Prevention of Pollution of the Sea by Oil] would be compatible with oil and shipping interests—and quite ineffective in preventing oil pollution of the oceans" (2010, p. 105). Other examples of corporate resistance to change especially in the auto, chemical, and manufacturing industries in developed countries such as the USA, Canada, and Western Europe indicate clearly that TNCs have crippled efforts to implement sustainable development (Chasek, Downie, & Brown, 2010, pp. 106–07).

Altogether, the governmental bureaucracies' fragmented policies, the relative institutional and academic incapacity to accommodate the highly interdependent imperatives of sustainability, and the increasing corporate hegemony over economy and society have constituted a huge obstacle to a sound implementation of sustainable development. In addition, the current socio-economic paradigm of growth is constantly reinforcing, and at the same time being reinforced by, the materialistic ethic that perpetuates this sustainability impasse. This ethic has, in my view, permeated every aspect of modern human life so deeply that any attempt to bring about change is fought by these predominant forces at the political, economic, and even intellectual levels. Above all, for sustainability to overcome its current gridlock, a whole economic, political, and intellectual system has to be called into question and radically altered.

BEYOND THE SUSTAINABILITY GRIDLOCK: RETHINKING GROWTH

Despite the predominance of the current socio-economic paradigm of development and the permeation of the growth-oriented values, the first decades of the twenty-first century have witnessed a surge in scholarly rethinking of sustainability and of the notion of development in general. The alarming impasse that this project has reached has constituted a strong eye-opener that sensitized many contemporary thinkers, economists, and activists to the need for reconsidering the meaning and implementation of sustainable development in the light of the hard choices that this project faces today. Within this context, my aim in this section is twofold: first, I want to shed light on the most prominent features of the new holistic approach to sustainability that claims to have benefited from the weaknesses of the previous approaches; and second, I want to assess how feasible this approach is in the face of the lingering plight of sustainability that has marked the new millennium.

A New Holistic Approach to Sustainability: From Fragmentation to Integration

Under huge pressure from the currently prevailing socio-economic paradigm, sustainable development has turned from a radical project into a distorted, ineffective version of its past self that bears little resemblance to the essence of sustainability. In an attempt to counterbalance the excesses of the current neo-liberal capitalist model of growth, however, some new scholarly approaches have been cautious not to adopt the same vision that contributed to sustainability's current plight. This new holistic vision of sustainability claims that the project of sustainable development has been dramatically derailed by some outmoded governmental and organizational sectors that worked toward the fragmentation rather than the integration of this project.

One of the main aspects of the fragmentation inflicted by the contemporary institutions and organizations is what is referred to as the traditional environmental paradigm that I discussed in an earlier section. The new holistic approach to sustainability claims to be the antithesis of this traditional paradigm that deals with environmental issues one at a time. There has been a growing conviction among thinkers and activists that tackling the ecological issues separately would only result in more confusion and inadequate understanding of what development means (Leach, Mehta, & Prabhakaran, 2016; Portney 2015; Dale, 2001). According to this holistic approach, these imperatives are to be addressed evenly because any attempt to prioritize one over the others would be counter-productive. Proponents of this approach confirm that these three imperatives are causally interdependent in that it is not possible to change one of them without affecting the other two. Basically, the interdependence of those three imperatives makes sustainable development fundamentally holistic in nature, and therefore any attempt to deal with any one issue independently might result in failure in the other two, particularly in the long term. Indeed, it is the context where sustainable development is to be implemented that dictates which imperative to accentuate, for "in some cases, there may well be greater emphasis on development than sustainability, whereas in others the reverse may be true" (Dale, 2001, p. 37). It follows that the emphasis on growth or sustainability would vary from nation to nation, and from region to region, for local factors such local economy, population, culture, and indigenous knowledge determine how sustainable development is implemented.

According to other observers (e.g., Portney 2015; Edwards, 2008), this holistic vision is already spelled out in many UN documents and therefore needs only to be activated to effect the required change in today's development paradigm. After the 1972 United Nations Conference on Human Environment in Stockholm took a first step toward sustainability, this concept was further consolidated by the 1984 Worldwatch Institute's first annual report *State of the World,* which stressed the interconnection of environmental, economic, and social issues. Three years later, this interconnection was further highlighted by the publication of the WCED's report, *Our Common Future,* in 1987, stating that "ecology and economy are becoming ever more interwoven—locally, regionally, nationally, and globally into a seamless net of causes and effects" (1987, p. 5). For Andreas Edwards, both the WCED's report and Agenda 21 "contained the first articulation of the key to contemporary sustainability—the importance of evaluating any proposed initiative with reference to the interaction of three fundamental criteria: ecology/environment, economy/employment and equity/equality, known today as the Three Es" (2008, p. 17).

Over the past decades, the complexity of the interdependence between the ecological, social, and economic imperatives in sustainable development has made it extremely difficult for researchers to predict with any precision the long-term consequences of the current situation. Michael Thompson argues, for instance, that "just as there is no single culture, there is no single meaning of sustainable development," illustrating that we "cannot homogenize development, unsustainable or otherwise, in the presence of what are multiple, distinctly heterogeneous cultures and actors" (1993, p. 55). However, other researchers (e.g., McMichael, 2017; Sachs, 2015; Dale, 2001; Edwards, 2008; Hart, 2009) are calling for an "integrative approach" based on reconciliation between these imperatives. Professor Ann Dale, for one, contends that "reconciliation of these three imperatives is the first step towards integration and it is a necessary condition for the implementation of sustainable development" (2001, p. 118). This reconciliation and integration of objectives and approaches has, in my view, a great potential for counterbalancing the fragmented governmental approach to sustainability, as only in this way can disconnected sectors in governments cease to be out of sync with one another. Awareness of the high level of interaction and interdependence between today's three sustainability imperatives is certainly a prerequisite for a clear insight into the essence of this project.

The new extended approach to sustainability has also boosted the formation of broader coalition for economic, societal, and political change at the local, regional, and global levels. In fact, the sustainability discourse is now offering a much wider context in which the legitimate interests of different parties in economy, politics, and social activism can be reconciled and harnessed to become mutually supportive. Within this new holistic approach, I find the "social equity" issue particularly important for a reshaping of sustainable development, for this dimension undoubtedly adds much richness and versatility to this paradigm. With more focus on the social equity issue, the sustainability discourse has more chances to gain the support of the poor and disadvantaged who feel more related to this paradigm that supports their rights for a decent life than to a paradigm that sidelines them.

The fundamental integration of ecological, social, and economic imperatives in one comprehensive model of development has been recently regarded by many critics[2] as an alternative to the current fragmented approach to development. Thanks to this integration, the economic, social, and ecological exigencies can change from competing interests to reconcilable, complementary issues. The aim of this new approach is also to eliminate any trade-offs between the three imperatives which do not have to exclude one another any more to receive enough attention from decision-makers. It is essential, therefore, to examine the different features of this new "reconciliation framework," and discuss to what extent it can right the wrongs in the project of sustainable development. In a context of globalization, the huge pressure of the growth agenda exerted by the current socio-economic paradigm of development has confined sustainability to an anthropocentric approach that has significantly limited its resilience and potential. This limitation has systematically impacted on the nature and scope of sustainable development and changed it from a radical to a reformist project. Being another feature of the contemporary sustainability gridlock, this limitation has hampered this project from transcending today's developmental impasse. On the other hand, observers note that "the present historical system is in fact in terminal crisis [. . .] [and that] the issue of ecological degradation [...] is a central locus of this debate" (Wallerstein, 1999, p. 85). In fact, the plight of today's model of growth has become the subject of a worldwide debate today.

The current challenges facing sustainability also render some of its loose definitions either incomplete or irrelevant. If the current sustainability impasse is to be overcome, a more exhaustive definition of sustainable development that stresses its holistic nature is definitely needed. In what she refers to as a reconciliation framework, Ann Dale maintains that "any workable framework must be holistic enough to transcend current sectoral and vested interests" (2001, p. 121). Ultimately, some critics (e.g., Axelrod et al., 2009; Portney 2015) also point out that there is an increasing need to make this framework both simple and applicable in diverse contexts, "transferable across space and time scales," and "regularly revisited, critically evaluated, and updated whenever appropriate" (Dale, 2001, p. 121). Optimistic and exhaustive as it claims to be, this new reconciliation framework is still in an embryonic stage. The challenges of integrating the economic, social, and ecological imperatives in one comprehensive approach must not be underestimated; all the more so because most economic and social forces in the current paradigm are self-perpetuating and highly resistant to change. The first step in this battle, therefore, would be to expose the "fallacy" of the notion of human affluence and well-being in the current socio-economic paradigm of growth. Taking this important step, however, necessitates replacing most of the conventional tools for gauging growth such as GDP with new ones that better reflect the interdependence of the ecological, social, and economic imperatives.

Rethinking Development Gauges

The new holistic approach to sustainability has raised a number of challenges for the political, economic, and social systems in the current socio-economic paradigm of growth. Changing the concept of growth, for instance, would be meaningless if economists continue to interpret the Gross Domestic Product (GDP) as the main indicator in the assessment of countries' development given that this tool of measurement does not include many important integral aspects of human development. Hence, my main aim in this section is to discuss how accurate indicators such as GDP are in reflecting the degree of development and examine some of the alternative development gauges that claim to be more exhaustive and responsive to the requirements of sustainability.

Although many economists, including William J. Baumol and Alan S. Blinder maintain that GDP is by no means "a suitable measure of the well-being of the nation" (2009, p. 103), this indicator has been widely considered a reliable and accurate measurement of growth for many decades. Economists define GDP as "the sum of the money values of all final goods and services produced in the domestic economy and sold on organized markets during a specified period, usually one year" (Baumol & Blinder, 2009, p. 88). In recent years, however, this measurement has been subject to heavy criticism from environmentalists and proponents of sustainable development. James Speth points out, for instance, some shortcomings of the GDP indicator, arguing that it takes into account "everything that can be sold or has monetary value, even if it adds nothing to human well-being or welfare" (2008, p. 138). In a similar vein, Ann Dale asserts that "the perversity is that this measurement, which is currently used to define 'progress,' is a more accurate indicator of social decay. Indeed, primary indicators of social decline—such as crime, violence, and mass-media addiction—actually increase the GDP. Divorce, for example, makes a significant contribution to GDP through legal bills" (2001, p. 61).

For the most part, GDP is criticized for neglecting to count many important welfare benefits generated by volunteer community work, household labor (Sachs, 2015; Strange & Bayley, 2008; Hart, 2009), and all forms of "unpaid human activities [. . .] that create *social capital,* the cement that keeps communities and societies functioning normally," (Agyeman, 2005, p. 57). By contrast, GDP includes revenues gained at the expense of the environment. A country, for instance, is free to exhaust its natural resources, pollute its environment, exploit its fisheries and wildlife to extinction, but still count the income derived toward GDP with no consideration of the environmental disasters that this overexploitation causes (Speth, 2008). "The result," explain economists Robert Repetto et al., "can be illusionary gains in income and permanent losses in wealth" (1989, p. 3).

How income is distributed in society and whether or not all layers of society share wealth evenly is also believed to be a missing variable in the GDP equation. Julian Agyeman, for instance, points out that "GDP provides no information on wealth distribution, on social development, or on externalities like oil spills or environmental injustices" (2005, p. 57). According to this view, this defect lays bare the failure of indicators such as GDP to take on board concerns for social equity and a fair distribution of income, which constitute fundamental tenets of sustainability. In fact, many critics denounce "the existing conceptions of 'development' and 'modernization' [which] reflect a Western cultural bias and a preoccupation with simply raising income and GDP per capita . . . [and] hinder efforts to imagine and build communities and markets at the base of the [social] pyramid" (Hart, 2009, p. 26). GDP measurements are, therefore, giving a false image of industrialized countries' development given that post-industrial societies have become worse off environmentally and socially. Indeed, these societies are being misled by all the GPD improvement indices, which urge for more growth at dramatically ever-increasing environmental and social costs. These misleading indices constitute some pervasive elements that deepen the alienation of societies from their environment and at the same time help perpetuate the current paradigm of growth.

The GDP measurement also fails to include many serious determinants of human well-being such as the ecological and social aspects of human life. As such, GDP is both a product of the capitalist paradigm, and a reinforcing element perpetuating it through reflecting a phony positive image of continuous growth and human well-being especially in industrialized countries. The reliance on GDP reinforces also the fragmented approach to development prevailing in governmental bureaucracies and the private sector, resulting in conspicuous discrepancies between "countries with similar levels of GDP per capita [that] can and do have very different levels of human development and welfare" (Speth, 2008, p. 139). This controversial vision has stimulated a proliferation of alternative measures and indicators seeking more exhaustive methods of gauging sound human development.

Creating comprehensive alternatives to GDP has been a concern for many researchers and economists in the last few decades. One of the most interesting new alternatives is what came to be known as the Index of Sustainable Economic Welfare (ISEW), which departs from GDP in adding "non-market" contributions to welfare, such as household, charity, volunteer work, and different forms of unpaid work. This measure also subtracts out "defensive expenditures" which do not add to ISEW, such as pollution control, police protection, and curbing social problems. Applying ISEW to gauge development in six major industrial economies, namely the USA, Germany, the UK, Austria, the Netherlands, and Sweden, shows some stark contrasts with GDP findings. A refined version of the ISEW, labeled the Genuine Progress Indicator (GPI), shows that the economic growth impact on the welfare of Americans since the early 1970s has been far less than indicated by GDP (Speth, 2008).

Other attempts to devise more comprehensive measures than GDP were carried out by some economists and social scientists like Daniel C. Esty and his colleagues, who developed a global Environmental Sustainability Index (ESI), which evaluates nations' environmental performance, not their economic growth. The *2005 Environmental Sustainability Index*, for instance, ranks the United States down the list at forty-fifth among 146 countries whereas Finland and Norway were ranked the first and the second respectively (Esty et al., 2005, p. 45). Richard Estes of the University of Pennsylvania has also developed a Weighted Index of Social Progress for 163 countries which focuses mainly on measuring the social and environmental conditions in these countries. Again, his raking puts the United States far down the list at the twenty-seventh place, indicating clearly that "America's affluence is thus not being translated into outstanding environmental *or* social performance" (Speth, 2008, p. 143). Still, another example is the Happy Planet Index (HPI), which basically measures human well-being by multiplying a country's life satisfaction score times its life expectancy, and then it divides this by the country's ecological footprint. The result gauges "how well a country converts the earth's finite resources into the well-being of citizens" (Speth, 2008, p. 143). Thus, the longer the people of a country live with minimal environmental impact, the higher the score can be. Again, the United States is relegated to near the bottom, below many nations of Western Europe, Asia, and Latin America, whereas a country like Costa Rica is near the top of the HPI.

Overall, the common principle underpinning measures such as ISEW, ESI, HPI, or GPI is the belief that in the post-industrial society of the twenty-first century measuring progress solely in terms of material growth does not capture the real quality of life people sense every day. Other elements such as social equity, civic activism, and environmental conditions have proven as important as material growth in determining and gauging human welfare. As I see it, heavy reliance on indicators such as GDP perpetuates the sustainability gridlock by reflecting a fake image of human development. Indeed, interpreting GDP as a main indicator of development reflects a very positive image of exponential economic growth policies that externalize ecological and social imperatives. Hence, refuting claims of this positive image of growth is one of the first steps toward a new approach supportive of sustainability. The increasingly conspicuous defects of its fragmented approach to development and the environment are ominously foreshadowing the collapse of the current socio-economic paradigm of growth. Ironically, the more this neoliberal capitalist paradigm fuels economic growth to ensure its continuation, the more strain it puts on natural resources and exacerbates social ills.

OVERCOMING THE CURRENT CHALLENGES TO SUSTAINABILITY

The current stalemate that sustainable development has reached is primarily a product of decades of maintaining a socio-economic paradigm of development that resists radical change. Calls to re-conceptualize the notions of development and sustainability have brought forth a new holistic approach to sustainable development. Revolutionized and radical as it is, this new approach is still in an embryonic state which needs more research and activism to come of age. More important than any other step at this juncture, in my view, is defining some guidelines to reform or substitute some of the tools that perpetuate the capitalist paradigm of growth. My aim in this section is, therefore, to examine how effective the new sustainability approach can be in revolutionizing established governmental bodies, private institutions, and civic pressure groups at the political, institutional, economic, and social levels.

Overcoming the Political Challenges and Reviving Green Politics

As bureaucratic inefficiency and short-sighted developmental policies have made most of today's governments part of the problem rather than part of the solution in the implementation of sustainable development, rethinking government's role has become an essential step in overcoming the sustainability impasse worldwide. Many studies (e.g., Portney, 2015; Kemp, Parto, & Gibson, 2005; Strange & Bayley, 2008) note that the interrelatedness of ecological, social, and economic issues in sustainability strategies requires more efficient collaboration among different governmental sectors than currently occurs. According to the new sustainability approach, the concept of social and economic collaboration has to replace the concept of competition valued highly in consumer culture.

Despite the neoliberal push for a minimal governmental role in the open market economy, many views still consider the government as the main body best suited to implement sustainable development. In the words of Ann Dale, "governments are the most logical leaders for this role because, due to the electoral process, they are more generally accountable than are either the business community or the non-governmental community" (2001, p. 114). Sharing the same view, researcher Susanne Müller writes that: "good governance plays a key role in sustainable development: as governments must establish the framework conditions and mandates for sustainable production and the related incentives for sustainable consumption" (2011, p. 30). As a matter of fact, more and more views (e.g., Ashford, 2004; Carter, 2007; Strange & Bayley, 2008; Stahel, 2004) call for a fundamental paradigm-shift in today's governments' bureaucracies so as to revolutionize their structures and decision-making procedures. Thus, as products of the current socio-economic paradigm of growth, today's governments will need to undergo comprehensive redesign before they can accommodate the interconnected nature of the new ecological and social imperatives.

Above all, major governmental departments and their information systems need to be transformed in such a way that the images conveyed to decision-makers would be as close to reality as possible. Ann Dale points out, for example, that "we need to reform our information systems, especially the way scientific and technological information is provided to decision makers" (2001, p. 116). These channels for conveying the information to decision-makers also need serious revision and transformation because they play an important role in connecting these decision-makers to what is happening on the ground. According to researcher Nicholas Ashford (2004), governmental bodies today need to rethink the primacy of the growth agenda that has blinded them to the catastrophic social and ecological consequences of the current unsustainable mode of growth. Contemporary governmental institutions, for instance, need to break out of the current tedious bureaucratic procedures for policy-making and impose more open and practical ones.

The required shift in governmental role vis-à-vis sustainability cannot occur without a fundamental change in the institutional approach to ecological and development issues based on decentralization and wide public participation. This new "combination of decentralization and participatory democracy," argues Neil Carter, "will produce fulfilled, other-regarding autonomous citizens prepared to accept the material sacrifices required of low-consumption sustainable society" (2007, p. 59). More than any other factor, this step of creating an "other-regarding" and environmentally conscious community is vital, in my opinion, in establishing a solid social and civic basis for a holistic, sustainable paradigm of development. According to this view, this new approach must transcend the level of mere adaptation and undertake transformation. Thus, the governmental institutions, universities, and private companies must strive to shed the old cloak of slow incremental change and accept a new type of radical transformation.

To overcome the political and institutional gridlock that has crippled the implementation of sustainable development, politicians and researchers need to reconsider the very structure and process of decision-making. Observers note, for instance, that "when it comes to sustainable development, decision making cannot take place in isolation by any one sector or civil society, including governments. Rather, it requires new levels of integration that bring natural and social scientists together with public policy practitioners and NGOs" (Dale, 2001, p. 124). According to this view, reversing the top-down, fragmented process of making decisions on development policies is essential if the project of sustainable development is to be effectively implemented (Kemp, Parto, & Gibson, 2005). To achieve this goal, the gap between bottom-up sustainable development strategies and today's governmental top-down policies must be bridged by addressing and eliminating all institutional flaws that have crippled this project.

At the institutional level, the different sectors in today's government are required to develop a strong sense of relatedness and commitment to sustainability in order to be capable of implementing this project. This transition from a top-down to a bottom-up approach to decision-making will require fundamental redesign of the governmental bureaucracies so as to institute a new type of collective decision-making that takes into account the different participants in civil society. However, all the drastic transformations to achieve sustainability would be very difficult to achieve if the planning and decision-making procedures take place in an undemocratic system. The sustainability discourse, therefore, is highly informed by principles of democracy and social cohesion. To my way of thinking, this discourse distinguishes itself not only by aiming at achieving intra-generational and intergenerational equity, but also by conceiving of new democratic ways for wide civic participation in pursuing sustainability.

Given its holistic nature of sustainable development, an in-depth insight into the tenets of this project certainly requires a great deal of dialogue among the different participants who aim at overcoming the sustainability gridlock. Establishing a common ground between the different stakeholders such as governmental institutions, corporations, and NGOs would certainly have several benefits for the implementation of sustainable development. Hence, central to this discussion are the roles civil society can play in reducing the alienation between humans and nature and transforming the current disturbed society-environment relationship to serve sustainability purposes, and what the potential benefits of such a transformation would be.

By and large, transforming the rather blurred society-environment relationship that marks the current capitalist paradigm of development requires active, effective involvement of citizens and NGOs in planning and decision-making. Researchers (e.g., Ashford, 2004; Kemp, Parto, & Gibson, 2005) note, for instance, that different stakeholders' commitment is vital in order to revolutionize the governance system through higher degrees of interaction between the decision-makers and the civil society groups. "The effectiveness of government and, ultimately, the vibrancy of democratic systems of governance," explains Ann Dale "are dependent upon the strength of civil society, which, in turn, is dependent upon creating communities of learning and knowledge through the establishment of transdisciplinary networks of collaboration" (2001, p. 160). In the holistic paradigm of sustainable development, civic engagement helps harmonize ecological concerns with other social and political imperatives in society. It does so by spreading public consciousness not only of these ecological exigencies but most importantly of the interdependence of ecological, economic, and social issues.

Politically, civic engagement cannot be effective without a propitious context that encourages bottom-up participation and establishes a solid basis for interaction between decision-makers and the citizens. Plagued by an excess of bureaucracy and hierarchy, most governments, however, often fail to take on board the imminent exigencies of sustainability. Neil Carter argues, for instance, that "liberal democracy nurtures an atomised individualistic focus on the private sphere, which makes it a poor breeding ground for the ecological consciousness and responsible citizenship needed to bring about a sustainable society" (2007, p. 55). According to other views (e.g., Kütting, 2004, p. 67), this failure has resulted in many governments today turning a blind eye to the social dislocations and environmental abuse in modern society, thus adding alienation on to the already disturbed man-nature relationship. Today's social and economic inequalities indicate clearly that the current structure of liberal democratic governments offer limited opportunities for mainstream participation in public matters. Thus, for sustainable development to be effectively implemented, the cult of individualism has to be rethought in the light of the common responsibility of safeguarding the common goods and establishing a balanced type of development.

Shaping a more responsive government with more accountable institutions that offer the mainstream people bigger access to economic and social decision-making requires fundamental changes in liberal democracy as practiced today. It is clear that a new form of democracy is needed to guarantee adequate dissemination of the information at the local level and include more segments of society in decision-making. "Replacing the self-contained individual of liberal democracy whose identity is only occasionally expressed in the public sphere (notably by voting)," contends Carter, "the individual in a participatory democracy is more likely to be a public-spirited citizen keen to promote collective activities and community identity" (2007, p. 56). Drawing on tools such social inclusion, consciousness raising, and education, this participatory democracy has a potential for effecting a positive change on the disturbed society-environment relationship. Rather than forcing the required change solely through laws and regulations, the new form of government can, therefore, progressively change these citizens from "self-regarding" to "other-regarding" elements in society.

Although it does not escape definitional problems, the notion of participatory democracy has, in my view, a great potential for boosting sustainability; all the more so because it allows for more political decentralization, civic engagement, and bottom-up decision-making. A radical transformation in government and the adoption of new open ways of decision making would make a big difference in the evolution of the project of sustainable development. Under this new approach, most environmental decisions would be taken locally and would consequently be much more sensitive to the ecological exigencies of the community than decisions taken by a remote centralized government. Engaging more citizens in decision-making through participatory democratic systems would also help change the society from a "consumer" to a "conserver" society by raising public consciousness and civic activities. However, reversing the unrelenting zeal for growth is still a big challenge that proponents of sustainable development have to take up if they are to save this project from its current stalemate. To fortify their political position, environmentalists still have to win public opinion on their side and revive green politics through forging alliances with other groups and parties working toward sustainability.

One of the priorities of green politicians and activists today is to popularize the concept of sustainability politically and socially in order to reach out to the widest public ever possible. In their struggle to popularize this concept in a hostile context of neoliberal capitalism, proponents of sustainability have had no option but to forge alliances with other political and social movements. Finding a common ground among diverse political interests, however, is not that simple. Hence, I find it essential to discuss the benefits that "green alliances" with other parties and interest groups would bring to sustainable development, and examine to what degree these alliances can help this project overcome its political stalemate. At this juncture, I believe it is also essential to discuss how cautious environmentalists have to be so as not to forge these alliances at the expense of the fundamental principles of sustainable development and end up having another weak version of this project.

One of the most important alliances that environmentalists have succeeded in forging thus far is the alliance between labor unions and the environmental groups in the United States. Dubbed the "blue-green" alliance, this coalition has evolved since the late 1990s when it orchestrated strong protests against global trade policies during WTO's meetings in Seattle in November 1999, and against IMF's and World Bank's policies in 2000. In fact, this alliance was declared by the United Nations Global Impact,[3] which is a document signed in 2000 by fifty multinational corporations and twelve environmental and labour groups. It comprises a network of almost two thousand companies such as Bayer, DaimlerChrysler, Nike, and the Royal Dutch Shell in over seventy countries, all working in partnership to better address human rights, labor, and environmental issues (Edwards, 2008). Spotlighting some features of these alliances, Neil Carter notes that "as the environment has become an increasingly mainstream issue, so the centre of gravity in environmental politics has shifted from a *radical* rejection of contemporary society and relatively *narrow* concern with ecological issues, to a *reformist* acceptance of capitalist liberal democracy accompanied by a *broader* social justice agenda" (2007, p. 9).

On the whole, I believe such alliances are vital for the survival of sustainable development in years to come because they will not only provide green activists with the necessary tools, funds, and power to implement sustainable strategies locally and globally, but will also enable them to reach out to larger segments of society than before. Equally important, successful alliances such as the blue-green one can always be a model for other parties, interest groups, and NGOs to rediscover the holistic nature of sustainable development. With such solid, balanced alliances, the project of sustainable development would, in my view, be less likely to be pigeonholed as simply a limited ecological project. As part of a broader alliance, environmentalists can also more easily raise public awareness of the necessity of such an alternative paradigm for human development, hence forging such alliances is an absolute necessity at this very critical juncture in the evolution of sustainable development.

Although forging political alliances constitutes a vital step for sustainable development, establishing other types of economic, social, and cultural alliances is equally important. Paradoxically, some of these alliances could include one of the most ferocious enemies of sustainable development, namely big business. According to many scholars such as Kent E. Portney (2015), Margaret Robertson (2014), Ann Dale (2001), Stuart Hart (2009), Paul Hawken (2001), and Andreas Edwards (2008), this type of alliance is still possible if a new business approach is adopted. Stuart L. Hart asserts, for instance, that "over the next decade or so, sustainable development will constitute one of the biggest opportunities in the history of commerce" (2009, p. 32). Given this new space for alliances, I strongly believe that the deeper these alliances cut across gender, race, political, and social lines, the more robust and thorough sustainable development would be. Thus, for this new project to survive in a hostile climate saturated by a materialistic ethic, the sustainability cause must permeate through all sectors of current paradigm of growth and disseminate its non-materialistic ethics. Clearly, it is not enough for sustainable development to win the political battle through political alliances with other parties, but this project must also win the social, intellectual, and economic battles if it is to remain faithful to its holistic nature.

Given the inextricably interdependent ecological, economic, and social imperatives that constitute sustainable development's holistic essence, this project's alliances with other parties and groups need not be solely ideological. Indeed, sustainable development would do better to avoid confining itself to rigid ideological alliances that would restrict its holistic and eclectic approach to development. Balancing alliances with other parties and sustainability's comprehensive nature is, therefore, a very important issue for activists to consider. Among other equally important spheres that can boost the sustainability agenda are national and international NGOs, the private sector, and civil society groups. Working simultaneously on these multiple spheres would give a great momentum to the project of sustainable development and help it regain popularity.

Striking the right balance between political, economic, and social concerns when forging alliances would also serve as an appealing element for more activists and contribute to the consolidation of its public base. Broad social and intellectual alliances would, for instance, urge universities and academic research centers to pilot researchers and politicians to the most appropriate ways of accommodating this new paradigm in today's political, economic, and social spheres. It is only through these institutions, that the new discourse of sustainability can change the citizenry's attitude "from a single distorting-lens view of what constitutes integrity and culture to a multiple-apertures view with the flexibility to allow for co-evolving multiple perspectives" (Dale, 2001, p. 132). Thus, consolidating a mainstream consensus on sustainability will not be possible unless environmentalists extend their political alliances and include social and intellectual alliances with universities, research centers, and think-tanks, all working together to disseminate sustainability values in place of the prevailing consumer ethic.

For their part, policymakers and politicians need a better informed framework for decision-making. If thoroughly informed about today's ecological and developmental exigencies, decision-makers would be more open to discussing alternative models of development and more likely to embrace sustainability as a replacement for the growth agenda. As Carter puts it, "the success of the alternative paradigms of sustainable development and ecological modernization will depend on their capacity to win the hearts and minds of policy elites and to persuade them that their interests are compatible with a sustainable society" (2007, p. 205). Winning the battle on the political front is, therefore, essential to the survival and effective implementation of sustainable development. With neoliberal capitalist market forces and economic globalization working against it, this project needs a new type of government on its side.

To conclude, with a new holistic environment-friendly approach to development, modern government could become part of the solution rather than part of the problem in implementing sustainability. Once they overcame the bureaucratic fragmentation that plagues their policy-making processes, governments could become a catalyst in the revival of sustainable development. With more civic engagement from local communities and NGOs, governments could also become more open to bottom-up policy-making which guarantees wider public participation and social equity. A transition from liberal democracy to participatory democracy is also key in broadening the public consensus about sustainability. Widening political alliances with unions, NGOs, and interest groups is another very effective way of gaining more ground for this new paradigm of growth. However, due to sustainable development's holistic nature, forging green political alliances is just one step in its battle against the predominant socio-economic paradigm. Hence, other economic, social, and intellectual alliances are also important tools in winning this battle.

Overcoming the Economic Challenges: Greening Business

As efforts to rebuild the consensus on sustainability and the need to develop within the carrying capacity of planet Earth gather momentum in different global summits, this project is constantly challenged by a very complex globalized economic system that primarily fosters exponential growth. Not only has the current predominant socio-economic paradigm of development been successful in disseminating the growth agenda worldwide through economic globalization, but it has also succeeded thus far to tame the project of sustainable development. Against such a backdrop, opting out of the process of globalization seems to be a rather unrealistic objective for this young project to achieve. Hence, the new role that the holistic approach to sustainable development assigns to business should be thoroughly probed if market powers are to be harnessed to work for, not against, sustainability. Within this framework, I intend to spotlight and critique some approaches that have attempted to harmonize sustainability with big business and discuss whether these new business approaches are capable of overcoming the economic challenges facing sustainable development today.

Fighting the corporate economic policies that are accelerating the exhaustion of the earth's finite resources and exploiting workers has always been one of the top priorities on the sustainability summits' agendas. In fact, despite the economic growth it has engendered since WWII, the current capitalist paradigm of development is heading for its ultimate demise according to many ecological indices[4] showing that the ecosystems upholding this pace of growth will not resist for long before they collapse. With the intensification of economic globalization, however, opposing corporate hegemony has proven extremely difficult. Daunting as this task might be, harnessing today's global economic powers to work for, rather than against, sustainability may still be possible. In recent literature, many studies highlighted the urgent need for an economy that efficiently serves the collective interests of humankind as a whole rather than those of corporate elites and suggest new approaches to green business.

As with sustainability, neoliberal capitalism, in the view of many observers (e.g., McMichael, 2017; Sachs, 2015; Hart, 2009; Wallerstein, 1999; Keil et al., 1998), has also reached an impasse as it started destroying the very natural resources that ensure its continuity. As more and more economists and theorists concur that business and sustainability are not necessarily mutually exclusive, a new business ethic of achieving economic growth within the ecosystems' carrying capacity is being preached as a basis for the "next industrial revolution" (Hawken, A. Lovins, & L. Lovins, 2008). According to many studies (e.g., Portney, 2015; Ikerd, 2005; Hart, 2009; Knowles et al., 2009; Earth Charter, 2012), an acceptance by business leaders of their responsibilities in fostering sustainability and implementing its strategies is deemed crucial today. This shift will not be possible, nonetheless, without a willingness among corporate managers to adopt a new approach to making business and expanding profits. The success of this shift to green business hinges, in my view, on how efficient the paradigm of sustainable development would be in accommodating different business interests and harnessing them to serve sustainability. Hence, sustainable development is far more likely to succeed if it wins over, rather than opposes, business. Still, the challenge remains how to work with business without being overwhelmed by it.

Though imminent, the current global ecological challenges are now regarded by some thinkers and economists as "the perfect example of challenge that pushes our companies and our policymakers beyond their traditional comfort zone" (Gore, 2009, p. xxv). This view reflects a whole new approach to business among environmentalists such as Al Gore, who puts it in the following terms: "The age of sustainability has arrived, but now we must drive it fully through our economic system. To do so, markets will have to continue to evolve to take into account the full environmental and social externalities of business in order to enable the efficient allocation of capital to its highest and best use" (Gore, 2009, pp. xxv-xxvi). Over the recent years, more and more scholars[5] have started to see business as a powerful driving force that has a huge potential for advancing sustainability in conjunction with government and a vibrant civil society. Accentuating the potential of TNCs, Stuart Hart writes:

> Business—more than either government or civil society—is uniquely equipped at this point in history to lead us toward a sustainable world in the years ahead. I argue that corporations are the only entities in the world today with the technology, resources, capacity, and global reach required. Properly focused, the profit motive can *accelerate* (not inhibit) the transformation toward global sustainability, with nonprofits, governments, and multilateral agencies all playing crucial roles as collaborators and watchdogs. (Hart 2009, p. 3)

Being the most prominent actors in today's free market economy, TNCs have a big potential in marrying sustainability to a new form of environment-friendly capitalism. Given the omnipresence of corporate power worldwide, these TNCs can uphold the sustainability agenda[6] and ensure much of its success locally, regionally, and globally. "By creating a new, more inclusive brand of capitalism, one that incorporates previously excluded voices, concerns, and interests, the corporate sector could become the catalyst for a truly sustainable form of global development—and prosper in the process," maintains Stuart Hart (2009, p. xl). Dubbed the "sustainable global enterprise," this new project is meant to be a private sector-based approach to development that enhances the quality of life for the different tiers of society, respects cultural diversity, and at the same time conserves the environment.

Despite the prevalence of the growth agenda, some relatively new laws and regulations still, in my opinion, have great potential to harness the power of business to serve and protect the environment and work toward sustainability. These laws which were enacted, primarily in Europe, from the 1980s onwards and imposed the principle of "Extended Producer Responsibility" can serve as a model to be followed in the rest of the world. Gendron et al. define this principle as "an environmental policy tool that extends producer responsibility to the post-consumption stage of the life cycles of their products" (2008, p. 1). Whereas manufacturers were only previously responsible for their products and their manufacturing processes, they became, as a result of this legislation, responsible for environment-friendly recycling.

First enacted to control packaging waste in Germany in the late 1980s, some environmental regulations have later been extended to several other industrial sectors. More importantly, these regulations now require the manufacturers to take back their products after they reach the end of their lives, thus setting a new precedent for other manufacturers to assume responsibilities even after making and selling the product. Also referred to as "Product Stewardship," the Extended Producer Responsibility principle has encouraged many other manufacturers around the world to assume responsibility for their products. According to the United States Environmental Protection Agency, this principle helped establish "a product-centered approach to environmental protection" as "it calls on those in the product lifecycle—manufacturers, retailers, users, and disposers—to share responsibility for reducing the environmental impacts of product" (as cited in Mumba & Ketola, 2009, p. 3).

For the most part, the principle of Product Stewardship represents a salient feature of the new environment-friendly holistic approach to business that gives more importance to growth within the carrying capacity of ecosystems rather than prioritizing growth at any cost. Rather than focusing solely on cheap production and more profits, TNCs are now required, for example, to take into account the entire life cycle of their products, "from the sourcing of raw materials and energy from the Earth to the reuse, remanufacture, or return of the materials to the Earth" (Hart, 2009, p. 12). Above all, such a revolutionary principle sets a very important precedent for other business initiatives. By offering some tangible solutions to unsustainable patterns of production and consumption, the principle of Product Stewardship helps significantly in articulating a blueprint for the implementation of the project of sustainable development.

The shift from unsustainable to environment-friendly business can also be facilitated by a business creed that employing green technologies does not mean less profit in different industries. More and more companies, for instance, realized that employing environment-friendly proactive strategies that reduce waste and do not abuse nature can be a good way to reduce costs of reversing environmental damage and clean up pollution. Generally, these proactive strategies try to prevent environment abuse before it occurs and thereby avoid both the environmental damage and expenses involved in reversing it. According to Stuart Hart (2009) companies can improve their competitive positions by following this new proactive approach in manufacturing goods and embracing the principle of product stewardship. Companies could, for instance, lower costs and internalize rather than externalize expenses of pollution prevention.

Notwithstanding the recent promising steps toward sustainability, the majority of companies still adhere to the classical reactive approach in accordance with which they only take action after the environmental damage is done. Ambitious and promising as they are, the different green economy initiatives have been met by strong corporate resistance, which has dramatically limited their success and effectiveness in curbing the rates of environmental degradation. On the contrary, most of today's TNCs have continued to serve the needs of the wealthy, ignore underprivileged people especially in developing countries, and look for places with lax environmental regulations to perpetrate their environmental abuses. As a consequence, incorporating sustainability in TNCs' priorities is still a far-fetched goal that signals more imminent battles between sustainable development and the current paradigm of growth. Marrying industry to ecology is still one of the major challenges to overcome if sustainability is to get out of its current gridlock. Looking at the big picture, however, sustainability involves more than a few green technology and energy-efficiency initiatives in industry. In fact, the radical transformation that this project proposes goes much further than efficiency issues and constitutes a whole new approach to industry that aims at making the processes of production and consumption operate in total harmony with nature.

As a relatively new concept, "industrial ecology" is evolving fast beyond mere efficiency objectives. Defining this new concept, Ann Dale points out that "new processes and new product is what industrial ecology is all about: it merges ecological principles with industrial practices by taking the basic principles of nature and incorporating them into the front end of industrial production processes" (2001, p. 88). Accordingly, the ecological and economic imperatives will inevitably converge in the future leading to competitive advantage, as it eliminates high costs of waste treatment and pollution clean-ups through using less energy. What marks a sea change in the sustainability discourse, in my view, is this new conviction that redesign and restructuring has a crucial role to play in the incorporation of these industrial ecology practices into businesses as a first step of this paradigm-shift in the economy. The shift from fighting business from the outside to serious attempts to transform it from the inside can significantly help sustainable development out of its current gridlock.

Embracing a sound "efficiency-substitution-redesign" process would also enable the industrial sector, according to some views, to evolve from making simple efficiency changes in the production processes to substituting manufactured products with more environment-friendly ones, and ultimately to achieving a total redesign of these production patterns (Dale, 2001). The objective of the efficiency stage is obviously to reduce waste and increase the efficiency of energy uses whereas the objective of the second phase is to replace any environment-unfriendly product, practice, or process with a more environment-friendly one such as using solar energy instead of fossil fuel or using biotechnology to change waste into a new type of energy that does not harm the environment. The last and most important phase is the redesign phase which is "holistic in its approach" which aims at "prevent[ing] environmental problems through the design and management of healthy systems based on ecological principles" (Dale, 2001, p. 89). The ultimate goal, therefore, is to move beyond waste management to the elimination of waste altogether.

Over recent years, many "ecological economists" (e.g., Hawken, A. Lovins, & L. Lovins, 2008) have argued that this paradigm-shift has to be extended beyond just changing patterns of production and consumption to conceiving of wholly new development policies. Other views (e.g., Portney, 2015; Carter, 2007; Dale, 2001) argue that governments could provide incentives for the propagation of "industrial ecology" to all sectors of the industry. According to this view, governments can also encourage this shift through policies that "redirect market forces towards sustainable development in the immediate term," and "withdrawal of ecologically damaging and economically perverse subsidies, green taxes, and a basic income scheme" (Dale, 2001, p. 91). Still, other scholars point out that "to create a policy that supports resource productivity will require a shift away from taxing the social 'good' of labor, toward taxing the social 'bads' of resource exploitation, pollution, fossil fuels, and waste" (Hawken, 1997, p. 59). Clearly, the main objective behind the green taxes is to discourage unsustainable patterns of production and consumption and redirect the industry away from these practices. Once again, the problem with these kinds of initiatives is that most of them are still in a rather embryonic phase and have not practically proven their effectiveness and reliability as a full-fledged alternative to the current economic system yet.

Over the last few years, some new initiatives have been launched to establish a revolutionary business approach that preserves the environment while making profits, not making profits at the expense of the environment. Within this context, I would like to focus on two important principles, namely the "Precautionary Principle" and the "Houston Principles," and examine how effective they can be in easing the transition from unsustainable to sustainable economy. I want also to examine whether or not these measures as well as the emerging new concepts of "eco-magination" and "green creative destruction" can become a benchmark which future development policies can be based upon. Some studies (e.g., Hawken, A. Lovins, & L. Lovins, 2008) claim that one of the causes of the current sustainability gridlock is that most industrial products and manufacturing processes usually fail to meet the criteria of sustainability. Others (e.g., WWF, 2012; Hart, 2009) warn that if the unsustainable model of growth in North America were to be replicated worldwide, this would take more than "three Earths" to satisfy this growth. Other scholars such as Robert Herman, Siamak Ardekani, and Jesse Ausubel (1990) argue that there is an urgent need for a "dematerialization" of the economy. Most of these views agree that today's sustainability challenges cannot be overcome without radical changes in the landscapes of the industrial and financial sectors. Information and service-oriented industries, for example, are now regarded as a good substitute for energy-intensive industries, which can be a promising step toward sustainability.

Dealing with the complexity and uncertainty that surround ecological crises has been a real challenge that scientists face today. To lessen the possible damage to the environment caused by industrialization, the Precautionary Principle has been set forth in *Agenda 21* in 1992 UNCED as follows: "In order to protect the environment, the precautionary approach shall be widely applied by states according to their capabilities. Where there are threats of serious or irreversible damage, lack of full scientific certainty shall not be used as a reason for postponing cost-effective measures to prevent environmental degradation" (1992, Principle 15). The ultimate goal of this important principle is to give the environment more space in national and international economic policies. In fact, this principle can be very useful in boosting sustainable development because it is "consistent with the notion of ecological sustainability in that it is about relieving pressure on the environment and giving it more 'space'" (Carter, 2007, p. 222).

The origin of the precautionary principle dates back to one of the basic environmental laws promulgated in Germany in the mid-1970s. Two decades later, this principle was mentioned in *The Rio Declaration on the Environment* in 1992 and further refined by a group of activists, lawyers, and environmentalists. Meeting at Wingspread in Racine, Wisconsin, in 1998, these participants expanded the precautionary principle in *The Wingspread Statement* as follows: "when an activity raises threats of harm to human health or the environment, precautionary measures should be taken even if some cause and effect relationships are not fully established scientifically. In this context, the proponent of an activity, rather than the public, should bear the burden of proof" (Ashford et al., 1998). The precautionary principle represents both a huge challenge to, and a valuable opportunity for, big business, for it urges this sector to rethink its responsibility to society and the environment. In defiance of the entrenched corporate profit-seeking creed, this principle simply "asks businesses to use their foresight in the development of new products and processes and, if these are deemed potentially dangerous to society, to refrain from further action" (Edwards, 2008, p. 55). The precautionary principle particularly stresses the company's responsibility and answerability not only to its owners, but more significantly to the larger community that may be affected by its actions. Guided by principles such as the precautionary principle, this new vision of doing business constitutes, in my opinion, an important step in bridging the gap between sustainability and business.

Applying the precautionary principle, in my view, necessitates a great sense of responsibility on the part of companies that have to take preemptive actions to prevent potential harm to the environment. According to this principle, companies are required to consider the full range of potential harms before taking any decision to market any new product. Andres R. Edwards asserts, for instance, that "millions of lives might have been saved had this principle been applied when cigarettes were first manufactured instead of waiting until years after the introduction of cigarettes for the US government to prove that smoking causes cancer" (2008, p. 57). Basically, this principle challenges many tenets of the capitalist model of growth as it requires a thorough evaluation of the potential harms of any new products before its production. Adherence to this principle would certainly prevent much of the economic, social, and ecological damages caused as a by-product of business activities which only take maximization of profit into account.

Globally, the precautionary principle has been denounced by many organizations and companies as an obstacle to technological innovation. Many TNCs,[7] for instance, regard this principle as a direct threat to their investments and innovative attempts to reach new heights in patterns of production and consumption. The WTO, in turn, still considers any refusal to accept a product from another country for safety reasons as an illegal barrier to free trade even if the aim of the refusal is safeguarding human health or the environment against a potential harm. Examples are numerous, one of which is the WTO rule against a European Union's ban on U.S. beef injected with growth hormones, which was rejected as lacking solid proof (Mander, 2003). Such rejections of the precautionary principle significantly indicate that these global organizations and TNCs need radical transformation from within if they are to fit in the new sustainable paradigm of development.[8]

As with the precautionary principle, the Houston Principles represent one of the hallmarks of the new holistic approach to development in the sustainability discourse. These principles were drafted in 1999 by the

Alliance for Sustainable Jobs and the Environment, which is a coalition of environmental and labor groups committed to defending labor's rights and the environment against TNCs. In their document, *Houston Principles of the Alliance for Sustainable Jobs and the Environment*, these activists assert that "recognizing the tremendous stakes, labor unions and environmental advocates are beginning to recognize our common grounds . . . [and] challenge illegitimate corporate authority over our country's and communities' governing decisions" (2005, Preamble). Reflecting a new revolutionary approach to sustainability, the interdependence of the ecological, economic, and social issues are highly echoed in the formulation of the Houston Principles. In the words of Andres R. Edwards, "the Houston Principles bring to the forefront a new holistic perspective that calls for corporate accountability to employees, the environment and the livelihoods of the communities where business is done" (2008, p. 64). For the most part, the Houston Principles hold TNCs accountable for reducing jobs and abusing the environment in their pursuit of profits, and expose much of the disruption that international agencies such as the WTO or IMF inflict on national economies. Thus, these principles have strengthened the new approach to sustainability not only because they defend local economies against powerful TNCs, but also because they have provided a successful example of the alliances that the paradigm sustainable development can entail.

Developing new technology that would go beyond the simple greening of the existing technologies would have to be driven by "ecomagination," which aims at "solving some of the world's most pressing environmental problems through the aggressive commercialization of new technologies such as wind power, solar energy, fuel cells, high-efficiency gas turbines, hybrid locomotives, lower-emissions aircraft engines, energy-efficient lighting, and water purification technologies" (Hart, 2009, p. 95). Essentially, this desired shift will require big business to go far beyond the conventional cost-benefit analysis and adopt a whole new approach that values and encourages innovation not only in the phase of production, but also in consumption and recycling. "Given their small scale and disturbed nature," maintains Hart, "such 'sustainable' technologies hold the potential to creatively destroy existing hierarchies, bypass corrupt governments and regimes, and usher in an entirely new age of capitalism that brings widely distributed benefits to the entire human community" (2009, p. 107).

On the whole, the new sustainability principles such as the precautionary principle and the Houston Principles constitute illuminating guidelines for a new business approach which strives to strike the right balance between maintaining economic growth, protecting the environment, and effectively addressing social issues. Nonetheless, this approach still needs a great deal of innovation and creation to catch the attention of entrepreneurs and tempt them to invest in environment-friendly enterprises. Applying new concepts such as ecomagination and green creative destruction also requires a broad public consensus on the need for change. To be appealing to the mainstream, sustainable development will also have to focus on serving the disadvantaged segments of society, for including people at the base of the social pyramid would then constitute a prerequisite for the fulfillment of social justice tenets this project is based upon.

Overcoming the Social Challenges: Reviving Ethics of the "Sustainability Revolution" and "Environmental Justice"

Because of the numerous social ills the current paradigm of development has brought about, the social challenges facing sustainability are no less complicated than the economic and political ones. While it distinguishes this project from other growth-oriented paradigms of development, the social imperative adds more complexity to the struggle of sustainable development in a context of neoliberal capitalism. My primary aim in this section is to examine the chances that this project has now to effect the desired social change from a consumer society to a conserver society in the light of new calls for regaining the "sustainability ethics." In particular, my aim will be focused on the potential that green business has in order to remedy some of the social ills brought about by decades of its application of the neoliberal capitalist model of growth. Ultimately, my aim is also to bring to light a recently developed aspect of the sustainability discourse that combines both the social and environmental issues under the banner of the "environmental justice movement" and highlight its potential for rebuilding a worldwide consensus on sustainability.

The late decades of the twentieth century witness a proliferation of groups known as "the New Social Movements" (NSMs), whose supporters consist of students, young professionals, and activists that belong to different social classes. By and large, this segment of society advocates a set of post-materialist values upholding equal civil rights, ecological concerns, and alternative lifestyles that challenge the conventional socio-economic paradigm of growth. As environmental groups themselves are widely regarded as an important manifestation of the NSMs (Pichardo, 1997), proponents of the project of sustainable development still have a good chance to consolidate these post-material beliefs and harness them to work for sustainability. Given their special modes of activism, the NSMs have the potential to act as an important channel of support for the sustainability cause precisely on account of the ways they differ from old social movements such as trade unions. Firstly, while old social movements like trade unions operate mainly within the traditional political system dominated by the state, NSMs "bypass the state by operating outside the established parties, trying to mobilise civil society rather than win power" (Carter, 2007, p. 91). As I see it, this feature endows the

NSMs with the required flexibility to bypass fragmented government structures and boost the sustainability agenda in society through different forms of activism. Secondly, while the overall aims of trade unions revolve around influencing established political parties and achieving legislative reforms that benefit the workers, the NSMs aim at altering the prevalent values and lifestyles by defending civil society against a whole socio-economic paradigm of growth (Pichardo, 1997). The novelty and effectiveness of NSMs' activism could also play an important role in changing the materialistic ethics of the growth agenda associated with the current socio-economic paradigm of growth.

The emergence of the NSMs and the new set of values they preach is based on some fundamental changes in the social and economic structures in the contemporary postindustrial societies (Johnston, Larana, & Gusfield, 1994; Pichardo, 1997). Accordingly, the decline in blue-collar working class that resulted from the big occupational shift from traditional manufacturing industry to a fast-growing service sector was accompanied by a rapid expansion of the white-collar class. This social shift, coupled with a considerable improvement in standards of living, a massive expansion of higher education, and the fascinating breakthroughs in telecommunication technology, "have also contributed to the blurring of traditional class division and loyalties in the 'postindustrial society'" (Carter, 2007, p. 92). Carter further explains that the outcome of this social change has been "a new class [that] is in some respects more alienated from the political system than the traditional working class and, crucially, more able and willing to criticise the established parties, the bureaucracy and the dominant materialist agenda" (2007, p. 92). Hank Johnston, Enrique Larana, and Joseph R. Gusfield (1994) also affirm that other groups such as students, housewives, pensioners, and the unemployed together with members of the "old" middle class of self-employed people represent a significant proportion of these NSMs. Empowered by "all these groups [that] fall outside the two traditional classes of capital and labour" (Carter, 2007, p. 93), the project of sustainable development has also a valuable chance to get rid of the political lethargy that undermines its potential especially in the industrialized nations where there is currently little political willingness to question the prevalent lifestyles.

The recent shift from growth ethics to post-materialist ethics is also a manifestation of a "silent revolution" that celebrates new values of belonging, self-expression, and the quality of life rather than values of material growth and well-being (Inglehart, 2000). In fact, this shift in values has signaled a new wave of change dubbed "the sustainability revolution" that is affecting the social, economic, ecological, and even political aspects of societies. It essentially aims at effecting an irreversible shift in consciousness, lifestyles, and patterns of production and consumption in contemporary societies (Edwards, 2008). As such, the sustainability revolution is not based on a single ideology but rather entails an array of values drawing upon healthy ecosystems, environment-friendly economic patterns, and social justice. The goals of the sustainability revolution encompass a wide array of issues including conservation, social and environmental justice, economic reform, population growth, human rights, women's rights, biodiversity, trade reforms, and related matters. This revolution is also characterized by a highly decentralized leadership made up of think-tanks and hundreds of thousands of activists from around the world (Edwards, 2008). Paul Hawken points out, for instance, that "no one started this worldview, no one is in charge of it, no orthodoxy is restraining it. . . . [It is] unrecognizable to the American media because it is not centralized, based on power, or led by charismatic white males" (2001, p. 10). This decentralized, nonhierarchical pattern constitutes, in my opinion, one of the main strengths of this sustainability revolution, especially because it encourages pluralistic alternative approaches to the current ecological, economic, and social exigencies.

For more than half a century, TNCs have chosen to focus all their attention on the privileged segments of society mainly because of their disposable wealth. This category comprises people of different ages who live in affluent post-industrial societies in North America, Western Europe, North-east Asia, and a few wealthy elites in the developing countries. More focus, however, has been shifted to some emerging markets in China, India, Latin America, Russia, and other Eastern Europe, which offer great business opportunities for these TNCs today (Hart, 2009). Observers (e.g., Harmon et al., 2009) contend that extending this focus to the disadvantaged people can bridge the gap between sustainability and business and boost a more sustainable way of growth based on the new concept of corporate sustainability.

Mounting criticism of the neoliberal growth strategies and the resultant developmental challenges in developing countries has increased the appeal of the sustainable development paradigm of growth. Successive financial crises, mounting developing countries' debt, environmental degradation, and increasing social inequity have raised the question of whether the neoliberal capitalist model of growth has created more problems than solutions in the developing world. However, this massive change in viewing development cannot materialize without profound structural modifications within the industrial sector and TNCs. According to some views (e.g., in Strange & Bayley, 2008; Axelrod et al., 2009), the disadvantaged segments of society constitute today a big market for any green advanced technologies that would help create a new "pro-poor growth" model. Stuart Hart concurs that "concealed below the surface of the purchasing power parity numbers is an immense and fast-growing economic system that includes a thriving community of small enterprises, barter exchanges, sustainable livelihood activities, and subsistence farming" (2009, p. 117). One reason for this choice is that these markets are usually marginalized by big business, which leaves the door wide open for this type of new technology and business to thrive. These "Great Leaps Downward," concludes Hart, "hold the potential to generate enormous growth and to address the root causes of antiglobalization sentiments, facilitating sustainable development" (2009, p. 127).

The new initiatives focusing on "the bottom of the pyramid" market have faced resistance on the part of the profit-seeking corporate system. After all, developing environmentally sustainable products and services cannot happen without investing heavily in green scientific research, which is not the priority of many TNCs today. In essence, reaching out to the base of the pyramid requires a totally different approach to business and to development than the existing approach today. Researchers such as Kent E. Portney (2015) and Harris Gleckman (1995) note, for example, that changes in patterns of production, distribution, consumption, and recycling are important prerequisites to the new sustainable approach. In addition, reaching out to the underprivileged segment of society is not as easy as it seems, especially as most of these people still adhere to their traditional lifestyles and local cultures that are usually not very welcoming to change from the outside. Therefore, global TNCs face now the challenge of correctly understanding the indigenous features of the base of the pyramid and producing for them.

Quite unlike the current model of development which steadily pushes economies to become an integral part of the global market, the new sustainability approach aims at urging nations to retain control over their national economies, preserve their indigenous cultures, and promote local crafts especially in the developing countries. Accordingly, the global corporate strategies that indiscriminately mass produce "one-size-fits-all" products for the global market clearly do not fit in this new approach because they are unresponsive to communities' local needs. Getting the TNCs to work for sustainability, however, necessitates more than just using green technologies and caring about the environment. The whole corporate creed of maximizing profits at great social and ecological costs must give way to a strong pervasive sense of responsibility of the people and the planet (Hart & Milstein, 1999). It is also important that these TNCs reconsider many of those conventional corporate strategies that focus on the mass-production of one-size-fits-all products for all consumers, ignoring cultural diversity, different needs, and lifestyles. Hart asserts that the predominant Western approach to development "has systematically failed to recognize the wealth of *indigenous* resources and alternatives," pointing out that "we have projected on the rest of the world our own Western post-war fixation with industrial production as the only path to prosperity" (2009, p. 175). Becoming indigenous is, therefore, a great challenge facing TNCs if they are to follow the sustainability path.

This new approach to address the base of the pyramid has, in my opinion, a great potential for boosting sustainability a step further. In fact, this approach presents TNCs with a unique opportunity to rethink their corporate creed in order to better serve the needs of the disadvantaged and identify with their cultural norms. Elaborating on the social aspect of this shift, James Speth maintains that "more and more people are sensing the shallowness of constantly shifting identities manufactured out of advertising pitches. People are searching for something more real and lasting and authentic [. . .] they are tired of the rat race and trying to keep up with the Joneses" (2008, p.161). To rise to this challenge of identifying with indigenous cultures, TNCs would have to adopt a whole new re-conceptualization of development and growth that is not simply reduced to GDP and material growth.

To serve the poor more effectively, TNCs need also to hear the voices of the disadvantaged segments in the current socio-economic paradigm of development. By doing so, TNCs can gradually change their image from an "alien" to a "native" element in the livelihoods of those local communities. Corporations are ultimately required to work for, not against, the project of sustainable development which provides them with the appropriate framework to develop their strategies from top-down to bottom-up strategies. Some views (e.g., Carter, 2007; Shiva, 2003, 2008) point out that for TNCs to fit in local economies of developing countries, they have to not only offer their products to the poor at reasonable prices, but also help them become an important producing force in the economy and link the formal and informal economies together in the process of sustainability. Hence, to come closer to communities, TNCs are required to build a partnership that "presume[s] active citizen participation in governance in institutions such as political parties, local government, neighborhood assemblies, voluntary associations and the workplace . . . where widespread participatory democracy means citizens are fully, freely and actively involved in the decisions that shape their lives" (Carter, 2007, p. 55).

On the whole, the sought-after business approach stresses the necessity to implement tailor-made development strategies specific to each community, each nation, and each region to make sure that the ethnic and cultural diversity of these local communities is respected in this process. A broad partnership between TNCs, IGOs, NGOs, and other civil society organizations would definitely consolidate the sense of belonging among the disadvantaged and ease their social inclusion. This interrelatedness between sound economic growth and social cohesion would, in turn, have a positive bearing on the society-environment relationship and lessen ecological degradation. The new business ethic of responsibility toward society and nature is, therefore, key in any transformation from "business is business" attitude to "business is sustainable" view. Ultimately, this shift would help the economy to get rid of the omnipresent growth agenda that has led to the ecological, social, and developmental challenges today.

As the project of sustainable development evolved, advancing the issue of social equity and the alleviation of poverty, especially in the developing countries, has become part and parcel of the sustainability agenda. In recent years, however, the popular Brundtland formulation of sustainable development has increasingly been criticized by many scholars (e.g., Lee, 2000; McNeill, 2000; Leff, 2000) for focusing more on the environmental aspect of sustainability than on highlighting the connections between the environmental, economic, and social issues and subsuming them under one major cause. Other critics (e.g., Dobson, 2003) deplore the lack of critical attention to the relationship between policies of social justice and environmental sustainability. By the turn of the century, many of these criticisms had developed into a new array of principles that focused mainly on the equity issue in the sustainability discourse and paved the way for the inception of what is referred to today as the Environmental Justice movement. It is, therefore, essential to examine how beneficial such a movement can be in rekindling the zeal for the project of sustainable development in society and easing its implementation.

As with the environmental movement, the Environmental Justice Movement has derived a lot of inspiration from social and intellectual movements of the 1960s and 1970s in America. According to some studies (e.g., Taylor, 2000), this movement was launched to effectively address the great variability of the effects of environmental degradation among places and peoples and to achieve more environmental as well as social and economic equity. Researchers Luke Cole and Sheila Foster describe this movement as "a movement based on environmental issues but situated within the history of movements for social justice" (2001, p. 31). Sharing a similar view, Susan L. Cutter notes that "environmental justice [. . .] moves beyond racism to include others (regardless of race and ethnicity) who are deprived of their environmental rights, such as women, children and the poor" (as cited in Agyeman, 2005, p. 17).

Over the last few decades, it has become evident that if deprived members of society are to be won over to sustainability, activists must stress the centrality of social issues to this new paradigm. In their landmark book, *Justice, Society and Nature: An Exploration of Political Ecology,* Nicholas Low and Brendan Gleeson, for instance, succinctly point out that "sustainable development without environmental justice is an empty formula" (1998, p. 14). Other views (e.g., Adamson, Evans, & Stein, 2002) argue that, influenced by grassroots activism in the civil rights movement, women's movement, and other movements, Environmental Justice groups have gradually expanded the dominant traditional environmental discourse. As with most contemporary concepts, that of environmental justice is a disputable concept which is open to many definitions and interpretations. In article 97, the constitution of the state of Massachusetts, USA defines environmental justice as follows: "Environmental Justice is the equal protection and meaningful involvement of all the people with respect to the development, implementation and enforcement of environmental laws, regulations and policies and the equitable distribution of environmental benefits" (as cited in Agyeman, 2005, p. 26). In the words of researchers Joni Adamson, Mei M. Evans, and Rachel Stein, environmental justice is also defined as "the right of all people to share equally in the benefits bestowed by a healthy environment" (2002, p. 4).

Although some critics (e.g., Agyeman, Bullard, & Evans, 2003; Kütting, 2003) contend that environmental justice is still a peripheral concern in global political and economic policies, the Environmental Justice movement has a great potential, in my view, to help in the implementation of sustainable development. Holding fast to the principle of intragenerational and intergenerational equity, this movement can play an essential role in ensuring the integrity of sustainable development now and in the future. By calling for an equitable distribution of ecological costs and benefits, this movement can, for instance, appeal to broad segments of society, especially those alienated by the excesses of neoliberal capitalism and today's materialistic ethics. For Dorceta Taylor, Environmental Justice offers "the first paradigm to link environment and race, class, gender, and social justice concerns in an explicit framework" (2000, p. 542).

Closely related to intergenerational and intragenerational equity is the broad issue of social justice in the sustainability discourse. Many researchers (e.g., Adamson, Evans, & Stein, 2002) question the way the issues of justice and equity have been dealt with in international economic agreements and trade regulations within today's model of development. In a similar vein, Andres R. Edwards maintains that "globally, inequalities such as famine and homelessness are seen as problems of distribution rather than lack of resources," asserting that "just and equitable resource allocation is not simply ethical but essential for the well-being of the larger community—in this case, the entire world" (2008, p. 23). Facing the social ills that the current socio-economic paradigm of development has brought about over decades of unsustainable growth, sustainability implies a commitment to maintaining ecological justice over time. Healing these social ills, however, would definitely necessitate a vital change from a consumer to a conserver society. With the deep-seated materialistic ethics prevalent in today's societies, effecting the required changes is a very challenging task for activists.

Working toward more social equity has proven all the more complicated as this issue is closely related to a number of other economic and political factors such as uneven distribution of wealth, corruption, and undemocratic political systems. Against such a complicated backdrop, the project of sustainable development still faces big challenges without recourse to the Environmental Justice movement that can effectively consolidate its popularity with new unconventional methods of activism. In essence, such movements have the potential to play a very useful role in rebuilding the integrity of the project of sustainable development that has been undermined by the proliferation of different versions of sustainability. Cementing the environmental and social equity issues together would certainly redeem many of the weaknesses of this project and enable it to overcome the gridlock it has reached in the recent years.

CONCLUSION

As a new paradigm that challenges the current neoliberal capitalist model of growth, sustainable development has faced huge challenges and obstacles erected by political, economic, and social forces that maintain the status quo. Referred to in the literature as "sustainability gridlock," this stalemate is the product of an array of principles, values, and mechanisms that perpetuate this dominant socio-economic paradigm of growth and cripple the implementation of sustainable development. An in-depth analysis of this sustainability gridlock reveals that it has many inextricable economic, political, institutional, and social features. One contributing factor in the sustainability impasse, for instance, is the lethargy governments have shown with regard to implementing development strategies that respect the ecological capacity of planet Earth. Plagued by bureaucratic fragmentation and institutional incapacity, the contemporary governmental system has become an obstacle to, rather than a channel for, achieving sustainability. This pervasive bureaucratic fragmentation has often resulted in some conflicting economic, social, and environmental policies that further shattered the consensus on sustainability. Within this outmoded governmental and political system, politicians, bound by their short-term electoral campaigns and alliances with big business, usually find it hard to endorse the sustainability agenda. As a consequence, they usually opt for less radical views that can be compatible with the predominant paradigm of development.

On the whole, the institutional incapacity and political inertia of most governments today significantly reflect a set of prevalent ethics of the current socio-economic paradigm of development. In essence, these values reflect much of the growth agenda that has deeply permeated contemporary governments, organizations, companies, and even universities and research centers, which all, to varying degrees, continue to inform and be informed by this predominant paradigm of growth and its values and ideologies. This incompatibility between sustainability, on the one hand, and the current governmental system, institutional functionality, and academic and research institutions, on the other, is an alarming sign, in my view, of how unresponsive to the current developmental and ecological exigencies these institutions and systems are. Some of the economic and social aspects of the sustainability gridlock can also be seen in the surge of the consumer culture especially in wealthy post-industrial societies. The corporate policies of maximizing profits at all costs also work toward the perpetuation of the current socio-economic paradigm of growth and tarnish the appeal of the project of sustainable development that calls for a reduction in mass consumption.

Given such an inauspicious context, it has become clear that, for sustainable development to get out of its current gridlock, political, economic, and cultural institutions and organizations will have to stop working for the growth agenda and relate more closely to sustainability. The classical public-private polarization is clearly out of place due to the increasing global developmental and ecological challenges, which demand instead the forging of a comprehensive partnership that merges the personal and the political as well as the public and the private in one holistic approach. In the light of the contemporary re-conceptualization of the concept of growth within the post-materialist discourse of some NSMs, the project of sustainable development can still be implemented if the potential of the new social change and business redesign is carried further. Stressing the high degree of interconnectedness among the economic, the social, and the ecological imperatives, a new holistic approach, under various names, has certainly offered the appropriate framework for a new vision of sustainability. More importantly, this new holistic approach has enabled the project of sustainable development to broaden its public support by offering a much wider context in which the interests of different parties in economy, politics, and civil society can be reconciled and harnessed to serve sustainability.

Politically, the principle of participatory democracy offers valuable potential for boosting sustainability through its emphasis on more political decentralization and civic engagement within a bottom-up approach to decision-making. Widening political alliances with other groups, NGOs, and labor unions constitutes also another important tool for environmentalists and activists to broaden the consensus on sustainability. Unlike conventional political coalitions, the coalition for sustainable development would be more robust if it were extended beyond ideological alliances, cutting across gender, race, and social classes' boundaries. With more civil engagement from local communities and NGOs, the coalition for sustainability would be in a better position to replace the top-down governmental mechanism of decision-making with a more responsive bottom-up process that guarantees wider participation and social equity. Hence, popularizing the notion of participatory democracy would not only reinforce the new type of government that working for sustainability requires, but also further broaden the consensus on sustainability.

On the economic level, sustainability faces the challenge of reconciling continuous economic growth and environmental protection. To my way of thinking, these two objectives are irreconcilable within the current neoliberal capitalist model of growth. New initiatives to marry business to sustainability are required to be taken a step further, for sustainability impasse will not be overcome simply by improving fuel efficiency or using less material in manufacturing. Indeed, a whole entrepreneurial mentality geared to profit maximization and exponential growth will have to be called into question. This paradigm-shift, however, requires a new revolutionized approach to the economy based on new ethics and structures that work for, rather than against, sustainability. Before making the transition from an unsustainable economy to a sustainable economy, it is imperative that sustainability ethic permeates all industrial and financial sectors so that their power is harnessed to serve this paradigm. New sustainability principles and strategies such as the precautionary principle, the Houston principles, the principle of Product Stewardship, and ecomagination constitute, in my view, illuminating guidelines for a new business approach that strikes a balance between maintaining a thriving economy, protecting the environment, and addressing the social issues. Nevertheless, putting these principles and strategies into practice remains one of the most challenging tasks facing economists and decision-makers today.

On the social level, overcoming the current sustainability gridlock hinges on two main steps: first, it is now a vital necessity to revive and consolidate the public consensus about sustainability as a comprehensive framework that balances the economic, social, and ecological imperatives in one holistic approach to human development. Second, this public consensus can also be extended to include a recognition of the current socioeconomic paradigm's incapability to accommodate today's developmental and ecological exigencies. Thus, with the help of the unconventional methods of activism that the NSMs have brought about, a new rationale for growth can be popularized through the mass media, think-tanks, research centers, and civil society if they all share and uphold the same sustainability ethics. Through their linking of the environmental and social equity issues, some of the new environmental justice movements also have exceptional potential for overcoming past weaknesses through highlighting the social aspect of sustainability.

NOTES

1. For good examples of educational institutions with curricula and research methodologies geared to sustainable development, see Lozano, Huisingh, and Delgado F., 2006, pp. 37–40; and Barth et al., 2011, pp. 313–323.

2. See Portney, 2015; Kemp et al., 2005; Hart, 2009; Ikerd, 2005; Dale, 2001; Strange & Bayley, 2008; Edwards, 2008.

3. UN Secretary-General Ban Ki-Moon explains that this document "asks companies to embrace universal principles and to partner with the United Nations. It has grown to become a critical platform for the UN to engage effectively with enlightened global business" (as cited in the United Nations Global Impact website http://www.unglobalcompact.org/).

4. See statistics about high consumption of non-renewable natural resources in developed countries in Goldemberg, 2003, pp. 57–58; Venetoulis & Talberth, 2009, pp. 18–19; and Radermacher, 2004, pp. 98–99.

5. See Portney, 2015; Hart, 2009; Dale, 2001; Edwards, 2008; Möller, 2004; Hawken, A. Lovins, & L. Lovins, 2008.

6. For a thorough analysis and specific cases of TNCs' endorsement of the sustainability agenda (such as the case with Interface Inc., Unilever, Philips Electronics, General Electric, and Wal-Mart), see Harmon et al., 2009, pp. 101–105.

7. According to some observers, opposition to the precautionary principle comes mainly from TNCs investing in new products such as the "genetically modified organisms" (GMO) whose effects on human health and the environment are still not clear (Carter, 2007, pp. 177–93).

8. For an in-depth analysis of the WTO's opposition to the precautionary principle, see Wagner, 2012, pp. 739–49.

Conclusion

The seeds of the present sustainability impasse can be traced back to the very theoretical formulation of this project itself, for its conceptualization is laden with controversies over definitions and interpretations of this new concept. Despite its wide popularity, the concept of sustainable development is excessively open to various, sometimes conflicting, interpretations. As a result, the very essence of this concept itself contributes significantly to the contested status that has become one of its prominent characteristic features. Even the Brundtland formulation of sustainability, which has achieved such an authoritative status through UN global summits dealing with development and the environment, can be criticized for certain weaknesses and ambiguities. For the most part, these weaknesses range from the very ambiguous wording of the definition of sustainable development in the WCED to the grotesque mismatch between what this definition conveys and what is really happening in the predominant model of growth nowadays. The unmistakable priority given to economic growth over protection of the environment, coupled with the unabashedly instrumental approach to nature, undermines the basis of this emerging project as a new alternative paradigm for sound human development.

Theoretically, the seeds of the incompatibility between the current socio-economic paradigm of growth and sustainable development can be better fathomed in the light of a brief overview of major development theories. It has become quite evident that the classical theories of development that have guided human growth for centuries are now incapable of accommodating the global ecological challenges of the twenty-first century. This incompatibility also reflects a deeper conflict between the theories of development underpinning these two paradigms. Accordingly, early modernization theory's definition and perception of development, especially as expressed in Rostow's theory, stand in stark contradiction with the project of sustainable development as this theory sidelines the environmental issue in the process of "linear" model of development it advocates. At the theoretical level, the sustainability discourse exhibits some affinity with a theory popularized as a critique of modernization theory, namely "dependency theory." This affinity can be seen in both discourses' focus on the need for an independent, bottom-up process of development responsive to the local economic, social, and cultural needs of the community, especially in the countries of the South. Hence, this affinity opens the door for more alliances between activists from both parts to work toward more effective implementation of sustainable development.

On the global scale, the emerging role of globalization has not only affected the evolution of sustainable development, but also proven detrimental to this project in its early years. A brief conceptualization of globalization reveals that some characteristic features of this phenomenon are highly indicative of its conspicuous mismatch with sustainability. The process of globalization in general, and economic globalization in particular, constitutes, therefore, a great challenge to the emerging project of sustainable development. Not only does economic globalization today weaken many of the developing countries' economies, threaten their local cultures, and precipitate social ills, but it also jeopardizes the entire basis of sustainable development as an alternative paradigm of growth. It does so mainly by rendering the economic, social, and intellectual climate increasingly unpropitious for achieving sustainability through the popularization of the growth agenda. Although pulling in opposite directions, globalization and sustainable development, on account of their structural affinities, do share a number of features that may constitute a seed for potential harmonization between them. This structural affinity, however, pales beside the deep ideological contradiction between the two projects. As they stand today, the ideological differences between these two projects have made them almost mutually exclusive.

For the most part, obstacles to the implementation of sustainable development can be subsumed into two big categories: extrinsic obstacles that are related to the context in which this project was initiated, and intrinsic obstacles that relate mainly to its theoretical conceptualization. The extrinsic obstacles are essentially related to the predominance of the growth agenda, which has resulted in uneven distribution of wealth in the current socio-economic paradigm of growth at dire social and ecological costs. Upholding market efficiency as the predominant gauge for development, the current socio-paradigm of development fails to take on board other equally important issues such as social equity, sustainable consumption, and equal distribution of wealth. The extrinsic impediments are also related to many corporate policies which are generally too profit-oriented for long-term sustainable development strategies to be implemented. This hindrance usually results in further alienation of the consumer from production and consumption processes and in the marginalization of environmental concerns.

Another extrinsic obstacle to sustainable development comes from what is referred to as the global governance system, which has proved rather unfavorable to a sound implementation of the sustainability agenda. Some of the major players in this system such as the WTO, the IMF, and TNCs, for instance, turned out to be rather incapable of accommodating and working toward sustainability's basic tenets such as growing within the limits of ecosystems, fostering a bottom-up model of development, and encouraging sustainable local economies in developing countries. Overall, much of the incompatibility between sustainable development and the global governance system is due to the fact that the major actors in this system were established when the environment was not a high profile issue. Within the context of the North-South divide, sustainable development has also faced rising suspicions that significantly undermined its popularity, especially in developing countries. With different approaches to the environmental issues, the North and the South hold rather divergent views of the implementation of the sustainability agenda, which constitutes another extrinsic obstacle to this project.

Unlike the extrinsic obstacles, the intrinsic impediments to the evolution and implementation of sustainable development are mainly related to the proliferation of different versions and interpretations of this project, which has resulted in an increasing controversy over its overall integrity as an alternative paradigm of growth. In the absence of a precise and exhaustive definition of sustainable development, conflicting views have been set forth as part of this project, which has almost emptied it of any coherent essence. In addition, the project of ecological modernization, which is widely celebrated as a panacea for today's developmental impasse, has been more of liability than a help to the project of sustainable development. Even the attempt to marry sustainability to the neoliberal capitalist paradigm of development under the banner of ecological modernization has, therefore, proven contentious; all the more so because this project disavows many of sustainable development's political and social aims.

Despite the daunting sustainability challenges, new initiatives to revive the project of sustainable development have shown an awareness of the weaknesses of the previous versions of this project. Attempts to expose the misconception about today's human affluence and well-being in the current socio-economic paradigm of growth have come under different names such as the "reconciliation framework" and "sustainability revolution." At the political level, the overall drastic transformations that sustainable development requires would be very difficult to achieve under an undemocratic system. With its focus on political decentralization, civil engagement, and bottom-up decision-making processes, the notion of participatory democracy has a great potential for boosting sustainable development and broadening the public consensus about sustainability. Widening political alliances with labor unions, NGOs, and interest groups is also a vital step if sustainable development is to overcome its current stalemate. Given the holistic nature of this emerging project, activists and environmentalists are required to go beyond political alliances and establish other forms of economic, social, and intellectual partnerships that cut across race, gender, and social classes. All these forms of partnership would ultimately ease the transition from a consumer to a conserver society through raising public consciousness and civil activities. To reach this goal, governments are also required to become a party to the implementation of sustainable development rather than remaining an obstacle to it.

At the economic level, new measures such as the precautionary principle and the Houston Principles constitute helpful guidelines for the establishment of a green economy. Some new initiatives to strike the right balance between maintaining economic growth, protecting the environment, and effectively addressing social issues can also play an important role in the transition from an unsustainable to a sustainable economy. "Industrial ecology" that aims at marrying economic growth and the protection of the environment stresses the leading role that TNCs have to play in making this transition happen. On the other hand, making sustainable development appealing to investors hinges on how practical these green strategies for development are. So far, incorporating sustainability in the corporate agenda has been rather inconsistent given TNCs' priority to only seek profit maximization.

Taken together, these different aspects of sustainability gridlock today make vital the forging of a partnership among governments, the private sector, and NGOs in promoting a new type of sustainability ethics that would not only ease the transition from unsustainable to sustainable paradigm of development, but also guarantee its continuity. The dissemination of the sustainability ethic is essentially the job of civil society groups and educational institutions, which need to play a crucial role in replacing the prevalent materialistic ethics with a new set of ethics. A prerequisite to the dissemination of the sustainability ethics, therefore, is the establishment of new research, teaching, and learning strategies and tools that make sustainability an integral part of planning for the future. In addition to focusing mainly on the consequences of unsustainable development, the efforts of environmentalists will be more fruitful if they focus on ways to disseminate a sustainability ethic that will gradually change the current paradigm of growth from within.

Bibliography

Adam, B. (1998). *Timescapes of Modernity: The Environment and Invisible Hazards*. London: Routledge.

Adam, B., & Kütting, G. (1995). Time to Reconceptualise 'Green Technology' in the Context of Globalisation and International Relations. *Innovation – The European Journal of Social Sciences 8*(3), 243–59.

Adams, W. M. (1990). *Green Development: Environment and Sustainability in the Third World*. London: Routledge.

Adamson, J., Evans, M., & Stein, R. (2002). Introduction: Environmental Justice Politics, Poetics, and Pedagogy. In E. Adamson, M. Evans, & R. Stein (Eds.), *The Environmental Justice Reader: Politics, Poetics, and Pedagogy* (pp. 3–14). Arizona: The University of Arizona Press.

Agarwal, B. (1998). The Gender and Environment Debate. In R. Keil, D. Bell, P. Penz, & L. Fawcett (Eds.), *Political Ecology: Global and Local* (pp. 193–219). London: Routledge.

Aghion, P., & Bolton P. (1997). A Theory of Trickle-Down Growth and Development. *The Review of Economic Studies 64*(2), 151–172.

Agyeman, J. (2005). *Sustainable Communities and the Challenge of Environmental Justice*. New York: New York University Press.

Agyeman, J., Bullard, R. D., & Evans, B. (2003). Introduction: Joined-up Thinking: Bringing Together Sustainability, Environmental Justice and Equity. In J. Agyeman, R.D. Bullard, & B. Evans (Eds.), *Just Sustainabilities: Development in an Unequal World* (pp. 1–16). Cambridge, Massachusetts: The MIT Press.

Alliance for Sustainable Jobs and the Environment. (2005). *Houston Principles of the Alliance for Sustainable Jobs and the Environment. Alliance for Sustainable Jobs and the Environment*. Retrieved December 12, 2010 from http://asje.info/principles.html

Altvater, E. (1998). Global Order and Nature. In R. Keil, D. Bell, P. Penz, & L. Fawcett (Eds.), *Political Ecology: Global and Local* (pp.19–45). London: Routledge.

Antweiler, W., Copeland, B. R., & Taylor, M. S. (2001). Is Free Trade Good for the Environment? *The American Economic Review 91*(4), 877–908.

Armer, J. M, & Katsillis, J. (2001). Modernization Theory. In E. F. Borgatta & R.J.V. Montgomery (Eds.), *Encyclopedia of Sociology* (pp. 1883–1888). 2nd ed. Vol. 3. New York: Macmillan Reference USA. Retrieved June 15, 2011 from http://find.galegroup.com/gic/infomark.do?contentSet=EBKS&docType=EBKS.Article&idigest=fb720fd31d9036c1ed2d1f3a0500fcc2&type=retrieve&tabID=T001&prodId=GIC&docId=CX3404400243&userGroupName=itsbtrial&version=1.0&searchType=BasicSearchForm&source=gale.

Ashford, N. (2004). Sustainable Development and Globalization: New Challenges and Opportunities for Work Organization. In C. Nova-Kaltsouni & M. Kassotakis (Eds.), *Promoting New Forms of Work Organization and Other Cooperative Arrangements for Competitiveness and Employability* (pp. 204–234). Athens: University of Athens.

Ashford, N., et al. (1998). The Wingspread Consensus Statement on the Precautionary Principle. *Proceedings of the Wingspread Conference on the Precautionary Principle, January 26, 1998. Science and Environmental Health Network*. Retrieved November 20, 2010 from http://www.sehn.org/wing.html.

Assadourian, E. (2005). The Evolving Corporation: When Good Corporations Go Bad. *World Watch 18*(3), 16–19.

Axelrod, V., Harmon, J., Russell, W., & Wirtenberg, J. (2009). Sustainable Globalization: The Challenge and the Opportunity. In J. Wirtenberg, et al. (Eds.), *The Sustainable Enterprise Fieldbook* (pp. 204–234). New York: Amacom Books.

Bakan, J. (2004). *The Corporation: The Pathological Pursuit of Profit and Power*. New York: Free Press.

Bakari, M. E. K. (2017). Mapping the "Anthropocentric-Ecocentric" Dualism in the History of American Presidency: The Good, the Bad, and the Ambivalent. *Consilience: The Journal of Sustainable Development* 17(1), 1–32.

Baker, S. (2006). *Sustainable Development*. London: Routledge.

Baldwin, R. (2016). *The Great Convergence: Information Technology and the New Globalization*. Cambridge, Massachusetts: Harvard University Press.

Barnett, J. (2008). The Worst of Friends: OPEC and G-77 in the Climate Regime. *Global Environmental Politics (8)*4, 1–8.

Barth, M., et al. (2011). Towards a "Sustainable University": Scenarios for Sustainable University Development. *International Journal of Innovation and Sustainable Development* 5(4), 313–332.

Baumol, W. J., & Blinder, A. S. (2009). *Macroeconomics: Principles and Policy*. 11th ed. New York: South-Western College Pub.

Baxter, B. (1999). *Ecologism: An Introduction*. Edinburgh: Edinburgh University Press.

Beck, U. (1992). *The Risk Society: Towards a New Modernity*. London: Sage.

Becker, E., & Jahn, T. (1998). Growth or Development? In R. Keil, D. Bell, P. Penz, & L. Fawcett (Eds.), *Political Ecology: Global and Local* (pp. 68–83). London: Routledge.

Bhagwati, J. (2007). *In Defense of Globalization*. Oxford: OUP.

Blair, T. (November 21, 1999). The Westminster Hour – Interview with Tony Blair at "Third Way" Summit in Florence. BBC. Retrieved June 5, 2008 from http://news.bbc.co.uk/hi/english/static/audio_video/programmes/westminster_hour/transcripts/blair_211199.txt.

Blewitt, J. (2008). *Understanding Sustainable Development*. London: Earthscan.

Bosso, C. J. (2005). *Environment, Inc.: From Grassroots to Beltway*. Lawrence, Kansas: University Press of Kansas.

Boster, J. S., Kempton, W., & Hartley, J. (1996). *Environmental Values in American Culture*. Massachusetts: The MIT Press.

Brower, M. (1992). *Cool Energy: Renewable Solutions to Environmental Problems*. Massachusetts: MIT Press.

Brown, D. (2002). *Insatiable is Not Sustainable*. Westport: Praeger Publishers.

Buechler, S. M. (1995). New Social Movement Theories. *The Sociological Quarterly 36*(3), 441–464.

Buttel, F. M. (1995). Rethinking International Environmental Policy in the Late Twentieth Century. In B. Bryant (Ed.), *Environmental Justice: Issues, Policies, and Solutions* (pp. 187–207). Washington, D.C.: Island Press.

Byrne, J., & Glover, L. (2002). A Common Future or Towards a Future Commons: Globalization and Sustainable Development since UNCED. *International Review for Environmental Strategies* 3(1) (2002), 5–25.

Campbell, C. (1987). *The Romantic Ethic and the Spirit of Modern Consumerism*. London: Blackwell Publishers.

Caradonna, J. L. (2016). *Sustainability: A History*. Oxford: Oxford University Press.

Cardoso, F. H. (2007). Dependency and Development in Latin America (1972). In J. T. Roberts & A. B. Hite (Eds.), *The Globalization and Development Reader: Perspectives on Development and Global Change* (pp. 85–94). MA: Blackwell Publishing. (Reprinted from (1972, July-August). *New Left Review* 74, 83–95).

Carter, N. (2007). *The Politics of the Environment: Ideas, Activism, Policy*. 2nd ed. Cambridge: Cambridge University Press.

Cavanagh, J., & Mander, J. (Eds.). (2002). *Alternatives to Economic Globalization: A Better World Is Possible*. San Francisco: Berrett-Koehler Publishers.

Chasek, P., Downie, D., & Brown, J. (2010). *Global Environmental Politics: Dilemmas in World Politics* (5th ed.). Colorado: Westview Press.

Choudhary, K. (2004). *Global Civil Society, Globalization and Nation-State*. Paper presented at the International Society for Third-Sector Research Conference, Toronto, Ontario, Canada. Retrieved October 9, 2012 from http://www.istr.org/?WP_Toronto.

Christoff, P. (1996). Ecological Modernization, Ecological Modernities. *Environmental Politics, 5*(3), 476–500.

Chronicles of America. (2014). Reclamation and Conservation. *Chronicles of America*. Retrieved August 11, 2015 from http://www.chroniclesofamerica.com/theodore-roosevelt/reclamation_and_conservation.htm.

Clinton, B. (2000). A Global Challenge for the New Century. *Time 155*(16A), 25.

Clinton, B. (April 1993). Reaffirming the US Commitment to Protect Global Environment. *Dispatch Magazine* 4(17). Retrieved December 23, 2010 from http://dosfan.lib.uic.edu/ERC/briefing/dispatch/1993/html/Dispatchv4no17.html

Cohen, M. J. (2006). Ecological Modernization and Its Discontents: The American Environmental Movement's Resistance to an Innovation-driven Future. *Futures, 38*(5), 528–47.

Cole, L., & Foster, S. (2001). *From the Ground up: Environmental Racism and the Rise of the Environmental Justice Movement*. New York: NYU Press.

Connelly, J., & Smith, G. (1999). *Politics and the Environment: From Theory to Practice*. London: Routledge.

Dale, A. (2001). *At the Edge: Sustainable Development in the 21st Century*. Vancouver: UBC Press.

Dam-Mieras, R. V. (2006). Learning for Sustainable Development: Is It Possible within the Established Higher Education Structures? In J. Holmberg & B. E. Samuelsson (Eds.), *Drivers and Barriers for Implementing Sustainable Development in Higher Education* (pp. 13–18). Paris: UNESCO Education Sector.

Dauvergne, P. (2005). Research in Global Environmental Politics: History and Trends. In P. Dauvergne (Ed.), *Handbook of Global Environmental Politics* (pp. 2–32). Massachusetts: Edward Elgar Publishing.

Devall, B., & Sessions, G. (2001). *Deep Ecology: Living as if Nature Mattered*. Utah: Gibbs Smith.

Dobson, A. (2016). *Environmental Politics: A Very Short Introduction*. Oxford: Oxford University Press.

Dobson, A. (1995). *Green Political Thought: An Introduction*. 2nd ed. London: Routledge.

Dobson, A. (2000). Sustainable Development and the Defence of the Natural World. In K. Lee, A. Holland, & D. McNeill (Eds.), *Global Sustainable Development in the 21st Century* (pp. 49–60). Edinburgh: Edinburgh University Press.

Dobson, A. (2003). Social Justice and Environmental Sustainability: Ne'er the Twain Shall Meet? In J. Agyeman, R. D., Bullard, & B. Evans (Eds.), *Just Sustainabilities: Development in an Unequal World* (pp. 83–95). Cambridge, Massachusetts: The MIT Press.

Dodds, F., Donoghue, A. D., & Roesch, J. L. (2016). *Negotiating the Sustainable Development Goals: A Transformational Agenda for an Insecure World*. London: Routledge.

Domhoff, G. W. (2006). *Who Rules America?* Boston: McGraw-Hill Publisher.

Dresner, S. (2002). *The Principles of Sustainability*. London: Earthscan.

Earth Charter Commission. (2012). *The Earth Charter*. Retrieved October 15, 2012 from http://www.earthcharterinaction.org/content/pages/Read-the-Charter.html.

Earth Day Network. (2011). *Earth Day: The History of a Movement*. Retrieved July 22, 2011 from http://www.earthday.org/earth-day-history-movement.

Eckersley, R. (1998). Environment Rights and Democracy. In R. Keil, et al. (Eds.), *Political Ecology: Global and Local* (pp. 353–376). London: Routledge.

Edwards, A. (2008). *The Sustainability Revolution: Portrait of a Paradigm Shift*. BC, Canada: New Society Publishers.

Ehrlich, P. R. (1986). *The Population Bomb*. New York: Buccaneer Books.

Ehrlich, P. R., & Ehrlich, A. H. (1997). *Population, Resources, Environment: Issues in Human Ecology*. San Francisco: W. H. Freeman.

Ellen, R. (2000). Local Knowledge and Sustainable Development in Developing Countries. In K. Lee, A. Holland, & D. McNeill (Eds.), *Global Sustainable Development in the 21st Century* (pp. 162–86). Edinburgh: Edinburgh University Press.

Elliott, L. (1996). Women, Gender, Feminism, and the Environment. In J. Turpin & L. A. Lorentzen (Eds.), *The Gendered New World Order: Militarism, Development, and the Environment* (pp. 13–34). New York: Routledge.

Elliott, J. (2000). *An Introduction to Sustainable Development.* 2nd ed. London: Routledge.

Ellis, E. (1996). Bordering on Disaster: A New Attempt to Control the Trans-boundary Effects of Maquiladora Pollution. *Valparaiso University Law Review 30*(2), 621–699.

Esty, D., et al. (2005). *2005 Environmental Sustainability Index: Benchmarking National Environmental Stewardship.* New Haven: Yale Center for Environmental Law and Policy.

Finkelstein, L. S. (1995). What Is Global Governance? *Global Governance 1*(3) (1995), 367–372.

Fisher, J. (1996). Sustainable Development and Women: The Role of NGOs. In J. Turpin & L. A. Lorentzen (Eds.), *The Gendered New World Order: Militarism, Development, and the Environment.* (pp. 95–111). New York: Routledge.

Forcey, L. R. (1996). The Indian Women's Movement, Ecofeminism, and the Politics of Peace. In J. Turpin & L. A. Lorentzen (Eds.), *The Gendered New World Order: Militarism, Development, and the Environment* (pp. 71–82). New York: Routledge.

Fotopoulos, T. (1997). *Towards an Inclusive Democracy: The Crisis of the Growth Economy and the Need for a New Libratory Project*. London: Cassell.

Frank, A. G. (2007). The Development of Underdevelopment (1969). In J. T. Roberts & A. B. Hite (Eds.), *The Globalization and Development Reader: Perspectives on Development and Global Change* (pp. 85–94). MA: Blackwell Publishing. (Reprinted from 1969) *Monthly Review 18*(4), 17–31).

French, H. F. (1999). *Costly Trade-offs: Reconciling Trade and the Environment.* New York: Worldwatch Institute.

French, H. F. (1993). The GATT: Menace or Ally? *Special Feature 122*, 1–21.

French, H. F. (2000). *Vanishing Borders: Protecting the Planet in the Age of Globalization.* New York: Worldwatch Institute.

Friedman, T. (1999). *The Lexus and the Olive Tree: Understanding Globalization.* 1st ed. New York: Farrar, Straus, and Giroux.

Friedman, T. (2005). *The World is Flat: A Brief History of the Twenty-first Century.* New York: Farrar, Straus, and Giroux.

Gendron, A., et al. (2008). *Extended Producer Responsibility (EPR); Current Status, Challenges and Perspectives.* Montreal: Bibliothèque et Archives Nationales du Québec.

Giddens, A. (1998). *The Third Way: The Renewal of Social Democracy*. Cambridge: Polity.

Gleckman, H. (1995). Transnational Corporations' Strategic Responses to "Sustainable Development." In H. O. Bergenses, G. Parmann, & B. Thommessen (Eds.), *Green Globe Yearbook of International Co-operation on Environment and Development* (pp. 93–106). Oxford: OUP.

Goldemberg, J. (2003). Energy and Sustainable Development. In J. G. Speth (Ed.), *Worlds Apart: Globalization and the Environment* (pp. 53–65). Washington: Island Press.

Golden, F. (2000). A Century of Heroes. *Time* 155(16), 54–58.

Gore, A. (2009). Foreword. In S. L. Hart (Ed.), *Capitalism at the Crossroads: Aligning Business, Earth, and Humanity* (pp. xxiv-xxvii). 2nd ed. New Jersey: Pearson Education.

Gupta, J. (2006). The Global Environmental Facility in its North-South Context. In P.H. Stephens, J. Barry, & A. Dobson (Eds.), *Contemporary Environmental Politics: From Margins to Mainstream* (pp. 231–253). London: Routledge.

Gruber, P. (2004). Good Global Governance: On the Necessity for Sustainable Development Awareness and Global Governance in an Interdependent World. In F. Feiler (Ed.), *Sustainability Creates New Responsibility: Basis for a New World Order, New Economics and Environmental Protection* (pp. 111–121). Frankfurt: Peter Lang.

Hajer, M. A. (1996). Ecological Modernization as Cultural Politics. In S. M. Lash, et al. (Eds.), *Risk, Environment and Modernity: Towards a New Ecology* (pp. 246–268). London: Sage.

Hajer, M. A. (1995). *The Politics of Environmental Discourse: Ecological Modernization and the Policy Process.* Oxford: Clarendon Press.

Harmon, J., et al. (2009). Developing a Sustainability Strategy. In J. Wirtenberg, W. Russel, & D. Lipsky (Eds.), *The Sustainable Enterprise Fieldbook* (pp. 89–116). New York: Amacom Books, 2009.

Harrison, N. E. (2000). *Constructing Sustainable Development.* New York: State University of New York Press.

Hart, S. L. (2009). *Capitalism at the Crossroads: Aligning Business, Earth, and Humanity.* 2nd ed. New Jersey: Pearson Education, Inc.

Hart, S. L., & Milstein, M. B. (1999). Global Sustainability and the Creative Destruction of Industries. *Sloan Management Review* 41(1), 23–33.

Hartmann, F. (1998). Towards a Social Ecological Politics of Sustainability. In R. Keil, et al. (Eds.), *Political Ecology: Global and Local* (pp. 336–352). London: Routledge.

Hawken, P. (1997, March/April). Natural Capitalism. *Mother Jones,* 40–62.

Hawken, P. (2001, Winter). The Resurgence of Citizens' Movements. *Earth Light* 11(3), 10.

Hawken, P., Lovins, A., & Lovins, L. (2008). *Natural Capitalism: Creating the Next Industrial Revolution.* Boston: Back Bay Books.

Hayden, A. (2014). *When Green Growth Is Not Enough: Climate Change, Ecological Modernization, and Sufficiency.* Montreal, Quebec: McGill-Queen's University Press.

Held, D, & McGrew, A. (2007). Reconstructing World Order: Towards Cosmopolitan Social Democracy. In J. T. Roberts & A. B. Hite (Eds.), *The Globalization and Development Reader: Perspectives on Development and Global Change* (pp. 360–369.). MA: Blackwell Publishing.

Held, D, & McGrew, A. (1994). Globalization and the Liberal Democratic State. In Y. Sakamoto (Ed.), *Global Transformation: Challenges to the State System* (pp. 57–84), New York: United Nations Press.

Hemmer, I. (1992). The State of the Art: A Critical Review of the Literature. In J. W. Arntzen, I. Hemmer, & O. Kuik (Eds.), *International Trade and Sustainable Development* (pp. 17–55). Amsterdam: VU Press.

Henning, D. H., & Mangun, W. R. (1989). *Managing the Environmental Crisis.* Durham: Duke University Press.

Herman, R., Ardekani, S. A., & Ausubel, J. H. (1990). Dematerialization. *Technological Forecasting and Social Change* 38(4), 333–347.

Hettne, B. (2008). Development, Security and Culture. In B. Hettne (Ed.), *Sustainable Development in a Globalized World: Studies in Development, Security and Culture.* (Vol. 1, pp. ix-xxv) New York: Palgrave Macmillan.

Hettne, B. (1994). Development Discourses in History. In Y. Sakamoto (Ed.), *Global Transformation: Challenges to the State System* (pp. 6–30). New York: United Nations Press.

Hettne, B. (1994). The Regional Factor in the Formation of a New World Order. In Y. Sakamoto (Ed.), *Global Transformation: Challenges to the State System* (pp. 134–166). New York: United Nations Press.

Hines, C. (2000). *Localization—A Global Manifesto.* London: Earthscan.

Holland, A. (2000). Sustainable Development: The Contested Vision. In K. Lee, A. Holland, & D. McNeill (Eds.), *Global Sustainable Development in the 21st Century* (pp.1–8). Edinburgh: Edinburgh University Press.

Holmberg, J. & Samuelsson, B. E. (2006). Executive Summary. In J. Holmberg & B. E. Samuelsson (Eds.), *Drivers and Barriers for Implementing Sustainable Development in Higher Education* (pp. 7–13). Paris: UNESCO Education Sector.

Hulse, J. H. (2007). *Sustainable Development at Risk: Ignoring the Past.* Delhi: Cambridge University Press India.

Huntington, S. P. (2007). The Change to Change: Modernization, Development, and Politics. In Ed J. T. Roberts & A. B. Hite (Eds.), *The Globalization and Development Reader: Perspectives on Development and Global Change* (pp. 56–59). MA: Blackwell Publishing. (Reprinted from *Comparative Politics* 3(3), (1971), 283–322).

Huntington, S. P. (March/April 1999). The Lonely Superpower. *Foreign Affairs* 78(2), 35–49.

Ikeme, J. (2000). Sustainable Development, Globalisation and Africa: Plugging the Holes. *Africa Economic Analysis*. Retrieved December 13, 2010 from http://www.afbis.com/analysis/Jekwu.html.

Ikerd, J. (2005). *Sustainable Capitalism: A Matter of Common Sense*. Connecticut: Kumarian Press, Inc.

Inglehart, R. (2000). Globalization and Postmodern Values. *The Washington Quarterly* 23(1), 215–228.

Isaacman, A. F., & Roberts, R. (1995). *Cotton, Colonialism, and Social History in Sub-Saharan Africa*. London: Heinemann.

IUCN. (1980). World Conservation Strategy. Retrieved October 7, 2011 from https://portals.iucn.org/library/efiles/documents/wcs-004.pdf

Jacobs, M. (1991). *The Green Economy*. London: Pluto.

Jahiel, A. (2009). China, the WTO, and Implications for the Environment. In G. Kroll & R. Robbins (Eds.), *World in Motion: The Globalization and the Environment Reader* (pp. 225–245). Lanham: Alta-Mira Press.

Jegede, F. (2001). Globalization—The New Order or Disorder? Consequences for Individuals, Nation-States and Society." *Proceedings of the 1st International Conference of the Global Studies Association, Networks and Transformations, 2–4 July 2001*. Manchester Metropolitian University, Manchester. Retrieved July 7, 2008 from http://www2.derby.ac.uk/gees/jollyfranc/page_editor.htm

Johnston, H., Larana, E., & Gusfield, J. R. (1994). Identities, Grievances, and New Social Movements. In Johnston, Larana, & Gusfield (Eds.), *New Social Movements: From Ideology to Identity* (pp. 3–35). Philadelphia: Temple University Press.

Kahler, M. (2003, November). *Global Governance Redefined*. Paper presented at the Conference on Globalization, the State, and Society, Washington, D.C.

Kates, R. W. (2003). The Nexus and the Neem Tree: Globalization and a Transition toward Sustainability. In J. G. Speth (Ed.), *Worlds Apart: Globalization and the Environment* (pp. 85–107). Washington: Island Press.

Keil, R., et al. (Eds). (1998). *Political Ecology: Global and Local*. London: Routledge.

Kelbessa, W. (2001). Globalization and Indigenous Environmental Knowledge in Ethiopia. In T. Assefa, S. Rugumamu, & A. Ahmed (Eds.), *Globalization, Democracy, and Development in Africa: Challenges and Prospects* (pp. 275–306). Addis Ababa: Organization for Social Science Research in Eastern and Southern Africa.

Kemp, R., Parto, S., & Gibson, R. (2005). Governance for Sustainable Development: Moving from Theory to Practice. *International Journal of Sustainable Development*, 8(1/2), 12–30.

Kerbo, H. R. (2006). *World Poverty: Global Inequality and the Modern World System*. New York: McGraw-Hill.

Khor, M. (1995). Development, Trade and the Environment: A Third World Perspective. In E. Goldsmith, et al. (Eds.), *The Future of Progress: Reflections on Environment and Development* (pp. 33–49). Bristol: International Society for Ecology and Culture.

Khor, M. (2001a). *Globalization and the Crisis of Sustainable Development*. Penang, Malaysia: Third World Network.

Khor, M. (2001b). Globalization and Sustainable Development: The Choices before Rio+10. *International Review for Environmental Strategies: Towards the Earth Summit 2002* 2(2), 209–217.

Khor, M. (2012). *Reaffirming the Environment-Development Nexus of UNCED 1992*. Penang: Third World Network Publications.

Kjellén, B. (2008). *A New Diplomacy for Sustainable Development: The Challenge of Global Change*. New York: Routledge.

Knowles, R., Twomey, D., Davis, K., & Abdul-Ali, S. (2009). Leadership for Sustainable Surprise. In J. Wirtenberg et al. (Eds.), *The Sustainable Enterprise Fieldbook* (pp. 26–56). New York: Amacom Books.

Korten, D. (2006). The Great Turning: From Empire to Earth Community. *YES! A Journal of Positive Futures* 38, 12–18.

Krasner, S. D. (ed.). (1983). *International Regimes*. Ithaca, NY: Cornell University Press.

Krauthammer, C. (Winter 2002/2003). The Unipolar Movement Revisited. *The National Interest*, 5–17.

Kroll, G. M., & Robbins, R. H. (Eds.). (2009). *World in Motion: The Globalization and the Environment Reader*. Lanham: AltaMira Press.

Krugman, P, & Venables, A. (1995). Globalization and the Inequality of Nations. *The Quarterly Journal of Economics 11*(4), 857–80.

Kütting, G. (2004). *Globalization and the Environment: Greening Global Political Economy*. New York: State University of New York Press.

Kütting, G. (2003). Globalization, Poverty and the Environment in West Africa: Too Poor to Pollute? *Global Environmental Politics, 3*(4), 42–60.

Lamy, P. (2005). Foreword. In G. Sampson, *The WTO and Sustainable Development* (pp. vii-xi). New York: United Nations Press.

Leach, M., Mehta, L., & Prabhakaran, P. (2016). Sustainable Development: A Gendered Pathways Approach. In M. Leach (Ed.), *Gender Equality and Sustainable Development* (pp.1–33). New York: Routledge.

Lee, K. (2000). Global Sustainable Development: Its Intellectual and Historical Roots. In K. Lee, A. Holland, & D. McNeill (Eds.), *Global Sustainable Development in the 21st Century* (pp. 31–47). Edinburgh: Edinburgh University Press.

Lee, K., Holland, A., & McNeill, D. (eds). (2000). *Global Sustainable Development in the 21st Century*. Edinburgh: Edinburgh University Press.

Leichenko, R. M., & O'Brien, K. L. (2008). *Environmental Change and Globalization: Double Exposures*. Oxford: OUP.

Leff, E. (2000). From Global Agenda to Differentiated Visions of Sustainable Development. In K. Lee, A. Holland, & D. McNeill (Eds.), *Global Sustainable Development in the 21st Century* (pp. 62–75). Edinburgh: Edinburgh University Press.

Ling, C. Y. (2012). *The Rio Declaration on Environment and Development: An Assessment*. Penang, Malaysia: Third World Network. Retrieved June 9, 2013 from http://www.twnside.org.sg/publications_end.htm.

List, F. (1885/1996). *The National System of Political Economy*. New York: Augustus Kelly.

López-de-Silanes, F., Shleifer, A., & Vishny, R. (1997, Autumn). Privatization in the United States. *RAND Journal of Economics* 28(3), 447–471.

Low, N., & Gleeson, B. (1998). *Justice, Society and Nature: An Exploration of Political Ecology*. London: Routledge.

Lozano, F. J., Huisingh, D., & Delgado, M. F. (2006). An Integrated, Interconnected, Multi-disciplinary Approach for Fostering Sustainable Development at the Monterrey Institute of Technology, Monterrey Campus. In J. Holmberg & B. E. Samuelsson (Eds.), *Drivers and Barriers for Implementing Sustainable Development in Higher Education* (pp. 37–47). Paris: UNESCO Education Sector.

Lubchenco, J. (2003). Waves of the Future: Sea Changes for a Sustainable World. In J. G. Speth (Ed.), *Worlds Apart: Globalization and the Environment* (pp. 21–31). Washington: Island Press.

Mander, J. (2003). Intrinsic Negative Effects of Economic Globalization on the Environment. In J. Speth (Ed.), *Worlds Apart: Globalization and the Environment* (pp. 109–129). Washington: Island Press.

Marinelli, J. (1991). Ecology Goes Mainstream: The Growth of American Environmentalism. *Brochure Articles for Environmental Action Program Package*, 1–7.

Martens, K. (September 2002). Mission Impossible? Defining Nongovernmental Organizations. *Voluntas: International Journal of Voluntary and Nonprofit Organisations* 13(3), 271–285.

Martin, A., & Huckle, J. (2001). *Environments in a Changing World.* Essex: Pearson Education.

Martin, H., & Schumann, H. (1997). *The Global Trap: Globalization and the Assault on Property and Democracy.* London: Zed Books Ltd.

Marx, K, & Engels, F. (1844/2007). Alienated Labor. In J. Roberts & A. Hite (Eds.), *The Globalization and Development Reader: Perspectives on Development and Global Change* (pp. 33–34). MA: Blackwell Publishing.

Marx, K, & Engels, F. (1848/2007). Manifesto of the Communist Party. In J. Roberts & A. Hite (Eds.), *The Globalization and Development Reader: Perspectives on Development and Global Change* (pp. 25–32). MA: Blackwell Publishing.

Maxwell, S, & Fernando, A. (1989). Cash Crops in Developing Countries: The Issues, the Facts, the Policies. *World Development* 17 (11), 1677–1708.

McAdams, C. (1996). Gender, Class, and Race in Environmental Activism: Local Responses to Multinational Corporation's Land Development Plans. In J. Turpin & L. Lorentzen (Eds.), *The Gendered New World Order: Militarism, Development, and the Environment* (pp. 51–69). New York: Routledge.

McLaren, D. (2003). Environmental Space, Equity and the Ecological Debt. In Agyeman, Bullard, and Evans (Eds.), *Just Sustainabilities: Development in an Unequal World* (pp. 19–37). Cambridge, Massachusetts: The MIT Press.

McMichael, P. (2017). *Development and Social Change: A Global Perspective.* 6th ed. London: SAGE Publications.

McMichael, P. (2007). Globalization: Myths and Realities. In J. Roberts & A. Hite (Eds.), *The Globalization and Development Reader: Perspectives on Development and Global Change* (pp. 216–232). MA: Blackwell Publishing.

McNeill, D. (2000). The Concept of Sustainable Development. In K. Lee, A. Holland, & D. McNeill (Eds.), *Global Sustainable Development in the 21st Century* (pp. 10–29). Edinburgh: Edinburgh University Press.

McNeill, J. R. (2001). *Something New Under the Sun: An Environmental History of the Twentieth-Century World.* London: The Penguin Press.

Meadows, D. H., Meadows, D.L., Randers, J., & Behrens, W. W. (1974). *The Limits to Growth.* 2nd ed. New York: Universe Books.

Mellor, M. (2000). Women, Development and Environmental Sustainability. In K. Lee, A. Holland, & D. McNeill (Eds.), *Global Sustainable Development in the 21st Century* (pp. 145–161). Edinburgh: Edinburgh University Press.

Milanovic, B. (2016). *Global Inequality: A New Approach for the Age of Globalization.* Cambridge, Massachusetts: Harvard University Press.

Mitchell, R. B. (2003). International Environmental Agreements: A Survey of Their Features, Formation, and Effects. *Annual Review of Environment and Resources 28*(1), 429–461.

Mittelman, J. H. (2000). *The Globalization Syndrome: Transformation and Resistance.* Princeton University Press.

Mlambo, A. S., & Pangeti, E. S. (2001). Globalization, Structural Adjustment and the Social Dimensions Dilemma in Zimbabwe, 1990–1999. In T. Assefa, M. Rugumamu, & M. Ahmed (Eds.), *Globalization, Democracy, and Development in Africa: Challenges and Prospects* (pp. 163–177). Addis Ababa: Organization for Social Science Research in Eastern and Southern Africa.

Moghadam, V. M. (2007). Gender and the Global Economy. In J. Roberts & A. Hite (Eds.), *The Globalization and Development Reader: Perspectives on Development and Global Change* (pp. 135–151). MA: Blackwell Publishing.

Mol, A. P. (2002). Ecological Modernization and the Global Economy. *Global Environmental Politics 2*(2), 92–115.

Mol, A. P. (2003). *Globalization and Environmental Reform: The Ecological Modernization of the Global Economy.* Cambridge, Massachusetts: The MIT Press.

Möller, U. (2004). Sustainability: Expectations and Reality. In K. Feiler (Ed.), *Sustainability Creates New Responsibility: Basis for a New World Order, New Economics and Environmental Protection* (pp. 19–25). Frankfurt: Peter Lang.

Mooij, M. K. D. (2011). *Consumer Behavior and Culture: Consequences for Global Marketing and Advertising*. (2nd ed.). London: Sage Publications.

Mulinge, M., & Munyae, M. (2001). Globalization and Sustainable Development in Africa: Putting Old Wine in a New Wineskin? In T. Assefa, M. Rugumamu, & M. Ahmed (Eds.), *Globalization, Democracy, and Development in Africa: Challenges and Prospects* (pp. 101–119). Addis Ababa: Organization for Social Science Research in Eastern and Southern Africa.

Müller, S. (July/August 2011). Green Governance: The Role of Governments on the Way to Sustainability in Asia-Pacific. *Pacific News* 36, 29–33.

Mumba, A., & Ketola, T. (Eds.). (2009). *Responsible Leadership: Proceedings of the Corporate Responsibility Research (CRR) Conference, December 2009, the University of Vaasa, Finland*. Vasaa: Vaasan Yliopisto.

Nadeau, R. (2006). *The Environmental Endgame: Mainstream Economics, Ecological Disaster, and Human Survival*. NJ: Rutgers University Press.

Næss, A. (1995). The Deep Ecology Movement: Some Philosophical Aspects. In G. Sessions (Ed.), *Deep Ecology for the 21st Century* (64–84). Boston: Shambhala Publications.

Norberg, J. (2003/2007). In Defense of Global Capitalism (2003). In J. Roberts & A. Hite (Eds.), *The Globalization and Development Reader: Perspectives on Development and Global Change* (pp. 263–276). MA: Blackwell Publishing.

Orton, D. (1994). Ecologism, Environmentalism and the Green Party. [Review of the book *Green Political Thought: An Introduction*] *Canadian Dimension 28*(3). Retrieved August 11, 2015 from http://home.ca.inter.net/~greenweb/Ecologism.html.

Parkins, C. (1996). North-South Relations and Globalization after the Cold War. In C. Bretherton & G. Ponton (Eds.), *Global Politics: An Introduction* (pp. 49–73). Oxford: Blackwell Publishers.

Payne, R. A. (1998). Can the GEF Prevent Environmental Conflict? *Journal of Peace Research 35*(3), 365–78.

Peet, R., & Hartwick, E. (1999). *Theories of Development*. New York: The Guilford Press.

Peffer, R. G. (1998). World Justice, Carbon Credit Schemes and Planetary Management Authorities. In Roger Keil, et al. (Eds.), *Political Ecology: Global and Local* (pp. 141–156). London: Routledge.

Pepper, D. (1996). *Modern Environmentalism: An Introduction*. New York: Routledge.

Peterson, R. (Winter 2002). Government, the Private Sector, and NGO Roles in the Next Generation of U.S. Environmental Policy. *Colorado Journal of International Environmental Law and Policy* 13(1), 87–97.

Petesh, P. (1992). *North-South Environmental Strategies, Costs and Bargains*. Washington, D.C.: The Overseas Development Council.

Pichardo, N. A. (1997). New Social Movements: A Critical Review. *Annual Review of Sociology* 23(1), 411–430.

Pizzigati, S. (2010). The Difference More Global Equality Could Make. *Too Much: A Commentary on Excess and Inequality*. The Institute for Policy Studies, Washington, DC. Retrieved October 14, 2011 from http://toomuchonline.org/the-difference-more-equality-could-make.

Porter, G., & Brown, J. W. (1996). *Global Environmental Politics*. 2nd ed. Colorado: Westview Press.

Portney, K. E. (2015). *Sustainability*. Cambridge, Massachusetts: MIT Press.

Radermacher, F. (2004). Neoliberalism against Sustainable Development. In K. Feiler (Ed.), *Sustainability Creates New Responsibility: Basis for a New World Order, New Economics and Environmental Protection* (pp. 83–102). Frankfurt: Peter Lang.

Raman, M. (2012, April). North-South Divide over Rio+20 Outcome Document. TWN Third World Network. Retrieved October 17, 2013 from http://www.twnside.org.sg/title2/sdc2012/sdc2012.120402.htm.

Raustiala, K. (1997). States, NGOs, and International Environmental Institutions. *International Studies Quarterly* 41, 719–740.

Redclift, M. (2000). Global Equity: The Environment and Development. In K. Lee, A. Holland, & D. McNeill (Eds.), *Global Sustainable Development in the 21st Century* (pp. 98–113). Edinburgh: Edinburgh University Press.

Redclift, M. (1993). Sustainable Development: Needs, Values, Rights. *Environmental Values 2*(1), 3–20.

Rena, R. (2008). Globalization Still Hurting Poor Nations. *Africa Economic Analysis*. Retrieved January 27, 2011 from http://www.africaeconomicanalysis.org/articles/gen/globalisation_0507.html.

Renner, M. (1989). *National Security: The Economic and the Environmental Dimensions*. Washington, D.C.: Worldwatch Institute.

Repetto, R, et al. (1989). *Wasting Assets: Natural Resources in the National Accounts*. Washington, D.C.: World Resources Institute.

Richardson, D. (1997). The Politics of Sustainable Development. In S. Baker et al. (Eds.), *The Politics of Sustainable Development: Theory, Policy and Practice within the European Union* (41–58). London: Routledge.

Robbins, R. H. (2009). Introduction: Globalization and the Environment: A Primer. In G. M. Kroll & R. H. Robbins (Eds.), *World in Motion: The Globalization and the Environment Reader* (1–15). Lanham: AltaMira Press.

Roberts, J. T, & Hite, A. B. (2007a). Development and Globalization: Recurring Themes. In J. T. Roberts & A. B. Hite (Eds.), *The Globalization and Development Reader: Perspectives on Development and Global Change* (pp. 1–16). MA: Blackwell Publishing.

Roberts, J., & Hite, A. (Eds.). (2007b). *The Globalization and Development Reader: Perspectives on Development and Global Change*. MA: Blackwell Publishing.

Roberts, J. T., & Parks, B. C. (2007). *A Climate of Injustice: Global Inequality, North-South Politics, and Climate Policy*. Massachusetts : The MIT Press.

Robertson, M. (2014). *Sustainability: Principles and Practice*. New York: Routledge.

Robertson, R. (1992). *Globalization: Social Theory and Global Culture*. London: SAGE Publications.

Robinson, J. (2004). Squaring the Circle? Some Thoughts on the Idea of Sustainable Development. *Ecological Economics 48*(4), 369–384.

Rodrik, D. (2007A). Has Globalization Gone Too Far? In J. T. Roberts & A. B. Hite (Eds.), *The Globalization and Development Reader: Perspectives on Development and Global Change* (pp. 312–319). MA: Blackwell Publishing. (Reprinted from, *Has Globalization Gone Too Far? By D. Rodrik*, 1997, Whashington, D.C.: Institute for International Economics).

Rodrik, D. (2007B). The New Global Economy and Developing Countries: Making Openness Work. In J. T. Roberts & A. B. Hite (Eds.), *The Globalization and Development Reader: Perspectives on Development and Global Change* (pp. 305–312). MA: Blackwell Publishing.(Reprinted from *The New Global Economy and Developing Countries: Making Openness Work*, by D. Rodrik, 1998, Baltimore: Johns Hopkins University Press).

Rollin, B. E. (1988). Environmental Ethics and International Justice. In S. Luper-Foy (Ed.), *Problems of International Justice* (pp. 131–178). Boulder, CO: Westview Press.

Rootes, C. (2004). Environmental Movements. In D. A. Snow, S. A. Soule, & H. Kriesi (Eds.), *The Blackwell Companion to Social Movements* (pp. 608–640). Massachusetts: Blackwell Publishing.

Rosenbaum, W. A. (2017). *Environmental Politics and Policy*. 10th ed. *London*: SAGE Publications Ltd.

Rostow, W. W. (1991). *The Stages of Economic Growth: A Non-Communist Manifesto*. 3rd ed. Cambridge: Cambridge University Press.

Rudra, N. (2002, Spring). Globalization and the Decline of the Welfare State in Less-Developed Countries. *International Organization* 56(2), 411–445.

Rushkoff, D. (2011). *Life Inc: How Corporatism Conquered the World, and How We Can Take It Back*. New York: Random House Trade Paperbacks.

Sachs, J. D. (2015). *The Age of Sustainable Development*. New York: Columbia University Press.

Sachs, W. (1997). Sustainable Development. In M. R. Redclift & G. Woodgate (Eds.), *The International Handbook of Environmental Sociology* (pp. 71–82). Cheltenham: Edward Elgar.

Sagoff, M. (2000). Can Technology Make the World Safer for Development? The Environment in the Age of Information. In K. Lee, A. Holland, & D. McNeill (Eds.) *Global Sustainable Development in the 21st Century* (pp. 115–143). Edinburgh: Edinburgh University Press.

Salih, M. A. (2001). Globalization and Human Insecurity in Africa. In T. Assefa, S. Rugumamu, & A. Ahmed (Eds.), *Globalization, Democracy, and Development in Africa: Challenges and Prospects* (pp. 61–81). Addis Ababa: Organization for Social Science Research in Eastern and Southern Africa.

Sakamoto, Y. (Ed.). (1994). *Global Transformation: Challenges to the State System.* Tokyo: United Nations Press.

Salamon, L. M., et al. (1999). *Global Civil Society—Dimensions of the Non-profit Sector.* Baltimore, MD: The Johns Hopkins Center for Civil Society Studies.

Sampson, G. P. (2005). *The WTO and Sustainable Development.* New York: United Nations Press, 2005.

Sandilands, C. (1998). The Good-natured Feminist: Ecofeminism and Democracy. In R. Keil, et al. (Eds.), *Political Ecology: Global and Local* (pp. 240–255). London: Routledge.

Scheffer, V. B. (1991). *The Shaping of Environmentalism in America.* Seattle: University of Washington Press, 1991.

Schrijver, N. (2008). *The Evolution of Sustainable Development in International Law: Inception, Meaning and Status.* Leiden: Martinus Nijhoff Publishers.

Sheffield, J. (2010). Theodore Roosevelt, "Conservation as a National Duty" (13 May 1908). *Voices of Democracy* 5, 89–108.

Sen, A. (1999). *Development as Freedom.* Oxford: OUP.

Shiva, V. (2005). *Earth Democracy: Justice, Sustainability, and Peace.* Massachusetts: South End Press.

Shiva, V. (2003). The Myths of Globalization Exposed: Advancing toward Living Democracy. In J. G. Speth (Ed.), *Worlds Apart: Globalization and the Environment* (pp. 141–154). Washington: Island Press.

Shiva, V. (2009). Pepsico for Peace? The Ecological and Political Risks of the Biotechnology Revolution. In G. M. Kroll & R. H. Robbins (Eds.), *World in Motion: The Globalization and the Environment Reader* (pp. 132–154). Lanham: AltaMira Press.

Shiva, V. (2008). *Soil Not Oil: Environmental Justice in a Time of Climate Crisis.* New York: South End Press.

Shiva, V. (1992). Recovering the Real Meaning of Sustainability. In D. E. Cooper & J. A. Palmer (Eds.), *The Environment in Question: Ethics and Global Issues* (pp. 187–193). London: Routledge.

Silverstein, Michael. (1993). *The Environmental Economic Revolution.* New Delhi: Universal Book Traders.

Sklair, L. (2007). Competing Connections of Globalization (1999). In R. J. Timmons & A. B. Hite (Eds.), *The Globalization and Development Reader: Perspectives on Development and Global Change* (pp. 233–346). MA: Blackwell Publishing. (Reprinted from *Journal of World Systems Research* 5(2), (1999), 144–163).

Smith, A. (1976). *An Inquiry into the Nature and Causes of the Wealth of Nations.* Ed. Edwin Cannan. Chicago: University Of Chicago Press.

Speth, J. G. (2005). *Red Sky at Morning: America and the Crisis of the Global Environment.* New Haven: Yale University Press.

Speth, J. G. (2008). *The Bridge at the Edge of the World: Capitalism, the Environment, and Crossing from Crisis to Sustainability.* New Haven: Yale University Press.

Speth, J. G. (2003). Preface. In J.G. Speth (Ed.), *Worlds Apart: Globalization and the Environment* (pp. xi-xii). Washington: Island Press.

Speth, J. G. (2003). Two Perspectives on Globalization and the Environment. In J. G. Speth (Ed.), *Worlds Apart: Globalization and the Environment* (pp. 1–18). Washington: Island Press.

Stahel, W. R. (2004). Risk and Sustainability. In K. Feiler (Ed.), *Sustainability Creates New Prosperity: Basis for a New World Order, New Economics and Environmental Protection* (pp. 159–183). Frankfurt: Peter Lang.

Stiglitz, J. E. (2002/2007). Globalism's Discontents. In R. J. Timmons & A. B. Hite (Eds.), *The Globalization and Development Reader: Perspectives on Development and Global Change* (pp. 295–304). MA: Blackwell Publishing. (Reprinted from The *American Prospect*, (2002, winter), 16–21).

Strange, T., & Bayley, A. (2008). *Sustainable Development: Linking Economy, Society, Environment*. New York: OECD Publishing.

Strong, M. (2003). Stockholm Plus 30, Rio Plus 10: Creating a New Paradigm of Global Governance. In J.G. Speth (Ed.), *Worlds Apart: Globalization and the Environment* (pp. 33–50). Washington: Island Press.

Sydee, J., & Beder, S. (2009). Ecofeminism and Globalization: A Critical Appraisal. In G. Kroll & R. Robbins (Eds.), *World in Motion: The Globalization and the Environment Reader* (pp. 248–270). Lanham: AltaMira Press.

Tanner, M. (2012). The American Welfare State: How We Spend Nearly $1 Trillion a Year Fighting Poverty—and Fail. *Policy Analysis* 694, 1–22.

Tarnoff, C. (1992). The Environment as a Foreign Policy Issue. *CRS Brief Issue*, 1–13.

Taylor, D. E. (2000). The Rise of the Environmental Justice Paradigm. *American Behavioral Scientist* 43(4), 508–80.

Taylor, R. (December 2002). Interpreting Global Civil Society. *Voluntas: International Journal of Voluntary and Nonprofit Organizations* 13(4), 339–347.

Thomas, C. (1992). *The Environment in International Relations*. London: The Royal Institute of International Affairs.

Thompson, M. (1993, April). The Meaning of Sustainable Development. *Proceeding of the Conference on Global Governability, London School of Economic and Political Science*. London: The Centre for the Study of Global Governance.

United Nations. (2011). *United Nations Global Impact*. Retrieved May 5, 2011 from http://www.unglobalcompact.org/.

United Nations Conference on Environmental Development (UNCED). (1992). *Agenda 21: A Programme for Action for Sustainable Development*. New York: The United Nations.

United Nations Conference on Environmental Development (UNCED). (1992). *The Rio Declaration on Environment and Development*. New York: The United Nations. Retrieved May 12, 2014 from http://www.unesco.org/education/pdf/RIO_E.PDF.

UN Office of the High Representative for Least Developed Countries, Landlocked Developing Countries and Small Island Developing States. (2010). *World Statistics Pocketbook 2010*. New York: the United Nations. Retrieved March 23, 2013 from http://www.unohrlls.org/.

U.S. Environmental Protection Agency. (2011). *History of Sustainability*. Retrieved April 23, 2011 from http://yosemite.epa.gov/r10/oi.nsf/8bb15fe43a5fb81788256b58005ff079/398761d6c3c7184988256fc40078499b!OpenDocument

Venetoulis, J., & Talberth, J. (2009). Ecological Footprints of Nations, 2005 Update. In G. M. Kroll & R. H. Robbins (Eds.), *World in Motion: The Globalization and the Environment Reader* (pp. 18–28). Lanham: AltaMira Press.

Vidal, J. (June 2012). Rio+20: Earth Summit Dawns with Stormier Clouds than in 1992. *The Guardian*. Retrieved September 12, 2012 from http://www.guardian.co.uk/environment/2012/jun/19/rio-20-earth-summit-1992–2012

Vig, N. J., & Kraft, M. E. (Eds.). (1990). *Environmental Policy in the 1990s: Toward a New Agenda*. Washington, D.C.: Congressional Quarterly Press.

Vig, N. J., & Kraft, M. E. (1990). Toward a New Environmental Agenda. In Vig & Kraft (Eds.), *Environmental Policy in the 1990s: Toward a New Agenda* (pp. 369–382). Washington, D.C.: Congressional Quarterly Press.

Volgy, T. J., et al. (2008). Identifying Formal Intergovernmental Organizations. *Journal of Peace Research* 45(6), 849–862.

Wade, R. H. (2007). What Strategies Are Available for Developing Countries Today? The World Trade Organization and the Shrinking of "Development Space." In J. T. Roberts & A. B. Hite (Eds.), *The Globalization and Development Reader: Perspectives on Development and Global Change* (pp. 277–294.). MA: Blackwell Publishing. (Reprinted from *Crisis States Programme: Working Paper 31* (2003). London School of Economics and Development Studies Institute).

Wagner, M. (2012). Taking Interdependence Seriously: The Need for a Reassessment of the Precautionary Principle in International Trade Law. *Cardozo Journal of International and Comparative Law* 20 (713), 713–770.

Wallerstein, I. (1999). *The End of the World as We Know It.* Minneapolis: University of Minneapolis Press.

Wallerstein, I. (2007). The Rise and Future Demise of the World Capitalist System: Concepts for Comparative Analysis . In R. J. Timmons & A. B. Hite (Eds.), *The Globalization and Development Reader: Perspectives on Development and Global Change* (pp. 96–113.). MA: Blackwell Publishing. (Reprinted from *The Capitalist World Economy*, by I. Wallerstein, (1979), London: Cambridge UP).

Weber, M. (2007). The Protestant Ethic and the Spirit of Capitalism. In R. J. Timmons & A. B. Hite (Eds.), *The Globalization and Development Reader: Perspectives on Development and Global Change* (pp. 36–46). MA: Blackwell Publishing. (Reprinted from *The Protestant Ethic and the Spirit of Capitalism, by M. Weber, (1958),* New York: Charles Scribner's Sons).

Wilk, R. (2009). Preface. In G. M. Kroll & R. H. Robbins (Eds.), *World in Motion: The Globalization and the Environment Reader.* (vii-ix). Lanham: AltaMira Press.

Wright, S. (2000). The Risks of Globalization and a Call for Sustainable Development. *The Brown Journal of World Affairs* 7(2), 147–158.

World Commission on Environment and Development (WCED). (1987). *Our Common Future.* Oxford: OUP.

World Council of Churches. (2012). *World Council of Churches*. Retrieved August 10, 2012 from http://www.oikoumene.org/.

World Trade Organization. (2001). *Doha Declarations: The Doha Development Agenda.* Geneva: WTO Secretariat.

World Wide Fund for Nature (WWF). (2012). *Living Planet Report 2012: Biodiversity, Biocapacity and Better Choices.* WWF Global. Retrieved July 22, 2013 from http://wwf.panda.org/about_our_earth/all_publications/living_planet_report/.

Yeh, S. H. (1989). *Understanding Development: Modernization and Cultural Values in Asia and the Pacific Region.* Paris: UNESCO.

Yilmaz, M. E. (Winter 2008). "The New World Order": An Outline of the Post-Cold War Era. *Alternatives: Turkish Journal of International Relations* 7(4), 44–58.

York, R., & Rosa, E. (2003). Key Challenges to Ecological Modernization Theory. *Organization and Environment 16*(3), 273–88.

Zurn, M. (1998). The Rise of International Environmental Politics: A Review of Current Research. *World Politics* 50, 617–649.

Index

About the Author

Mohamed El-Kamel Bakari holds a PhD in American Studies from the University of Manouba, Tunis, Tunisia, and is now seconded to King Abdul-Aziz University, Jeddah, Saudi Arabia. He is a published author and an active researcher in American culture studies, environmentalism, sustainability, and globalization studies. He taught at different universities in Tunisia, the UK, and the Middle East.